# 25

# EMINENT

# INDIANS

# 1947-2005

25 Eminent Indians : 1947-2005
©Copyright 2006 : H.N. Verma
D-49, Press Enclave, New Delhi-110017

*Cover* : Alias Abraham
*Typeset* : Alias Abraham
(Verma Print-O-Graphics)

ISBN 81-901814-1-6

Dedicated to Our Friend

# JAGANNATH PRASAD GUPTA

# CONTENTS

# INTRODUCTION

*25 Eminent Indians : 1947-2005* is a sequel to authors' *100 Great Indians Through The Ages'*.

The 100 Great Indians represent pluralist and multidimensional India from ancient to modern times. So do the 25 Eminent Indians. Both categories- Great and Eminent - come from country's different parts, walks of life and faiths and have pronouncedly contributed to diverse spheres-politics, literature, art, music, film, science, engineering and technology, medicine, law and justice, and business and industry-that affect peoples' lives. They made their own destiny without assuming that their destinies were predetermined. In fact the 25 have contributed to the making of history of recent India.

Everyone reads history but very few write history and those who make history are rare. While addressing an audience, Jawaharlal Nehru made a factual error to which Prof. Ishwari Prasad drew his attention. Nehru jovially told him, "Ishwari Prasad, you write history, I make history."Light heartedness aside, historians' job is really difficult, especially where assessment of facts, events and personalities is involved. The concept of history as narration of events in terms of rulers and leaders is no longer acceptable. Politicians, scientists, businessmen, industrialists, professioals, creative people and others are changing the course of events and their contributions claim attention. Rightly so.

Of the 25 Eminent Indians who figure in this book, eight are politicians. A politician's niche is settled by multidimensional forces like caste, creed, class, race, dialect, and people's will etc.

He (she included) uses these factors to his (her) advantage as and when an opportunity arises or comes his way. A politician, places on his chaste the badge of patriotism and swears by secularism. He boasts of his lineage- to influence his polity. Frankly speaking, he is out to make his leadership felt.

The quality of a politician's leadership distinguishes him from others. Leadership ignites the circuit between the leader and the led. The leader sets the pattern and pace of thoughts and actions for his followers. A shrewd leader translates his thought into action and converts it into deed. He conducts public transactions and affirms his capacity to bring and move people together. His success or failure depends on his goal, needs and followers for without followers a leader is worthless. A leader must act in response to the rhythm of time and adapt himself to the moment's responsiveness. He should seize the opportunity provided by time, hopes, fears, frustrations, crises and potentialities, which may turn people's inchoate emotions to his advantage. He succeeds in his efforts to the extent events have prepared the way for him. The community awaits their leader's arrival. The rest will depend on his capacity to clarify and organize his ideas, though sycophants may announce that their leader is infalliable or is an avatar. A politician's ego is uncotrollable. He is ever ready to prove that like a filmy hero he is imbued with qualities of omnipotence, omniscience, and omnipresence. He may or may not leave his mark on history , or circumstances may conspire to make him a pawn of history. To an extent his success depends on his priorities and on how he acquits himself. Those politicians who are not far sighted and accord priority to self interests over the public good rarely achieve success.

The eight politicians in the section 'Politics' played prominent roles in the war of independence. Most of them occupied high positions and those who kept themselves aloof helped Indian democracy to function smoothly.

The 'Science' section covers scientists who are 'visionary, dynamic and devoted'. Scientists, engineers, technologists and medicine men have contributed to the progress and well-being of humanity. C.V.Raman, Dr. V.N.Shirodkar, Homi J.Bhabha and S. Chandrashekhar (NRI) who are world class personalities figure in the section.The authors have, because of limits on space, denied themselves the honor of writing about Vikram Sarabhai and Har Govind Khurana. M.S. Swaminathan, Kurien Verghese, Baba Amte, and Bindheswar Pathak improved the quality of common man's life. Green Revolution, White Revolution, leprosy care and Sulabha Shauchalaya etc are because of them.

There is no doubt that the industries in the country are

making progress. Even so, technical personnel in large numbers remain unemployed because of limited job opportunities. Lack of job satisfaction, stagnancy also force some to emigrate. On the other hand the young people from rural areas find technical education beyond their means. The financial formula for admission in technical institutes has almost barred them from technical education.

The 'Humanity' section includes Dr. S. Radhakrishnan, Paramahansa Yogananda, Mother Teresa, and Amartya Sen (NRI). Meghnad Desai, Jagdish Bhagavati, and Vinod Agarwal, all PIOs, are noted economists known for their original researches.

In India, 'Literature, Music, and Arts' command high respect for enriching people's life. A Sanskrit *Shloka* says 'A man devoid of knowledge of Sahitya (literature), Sangeet (music) and Kalaa (arts) is like a cattle without tail and horns'. Poet Nirala and fiction writer R.K.Narayan, film maker Satyajit Ray and Sitar player Ravi Shankar, and artists Nandalal Bose and M.F.Hussain add to emotional richness. They are authors' choice. Mr.Sachchidanandan, Secretary of the Sahitya Akademi helped in making up authors' mind on Nirala on considerations of quality and output of his literay works. Art Teacher Elizabeth Bresnan of the De Anza College, Cupertino (California) helped authors with material on the two artists, one of whom is classical and the other 'progressive'.

For the Law and Justice Section, the selection of Senior Advocates M.C.Setalvad and Nani Palkhiwala is that of the authors, themselves members of the Bar, and of their colleagues at the Bar. M. Santhanam, a former Judge of the Madras High Court, and K.L. Verma have provided prefatory notes to law and Business sections.

The selection of business tycoon Dhirubhai Ambani was made in consultation with lawyer, businessman and journalist friends. The business world is clustered with big names like Tata, Birla, Premji, Narayan Murthi, Bajaj, Godrej, besides NRIs Vinod Khosla, Lakshmi Mittal, Lord Swaraj Paul and others. Considering pros and cons we have abided by the expert advice that Dhirubhai Ambani was a self made and the wealthiest man.

After the terrible incident of 9/11, the world's attention is focused on 'terrorism'. How can this scourge be eliminated? In the opinion of our friend B.K.Rao, Hindu mythology provides an effective solution to the problem. This is the treatment of Raktabeej by Kali. When Kali saw a blood drop of the demon was producing another demon , she scutlled the source and finally killed it. Humanity has faced such terrible eleements in the past. For instance Thuggee and Sati made people's life miserable. The former one was treated with a firm hand and it has disappeared. The Sati was treated as a criminal problem and was almost extinct when it received support from religious minded and superstitious people. Take out this support, inconsiderate of victory or defeat in elections, and Sati will disappear.

On the international plane, responding to people's sentiments governments joined to eliminate inhuman and horrible activities which slavery and witch craft. Caught in the battles, the slaves were treated worse than chattle. Read Cervantes's and G.K.Chesterton's descriptions of events at Lepanto in which thousands of innocent people were slaughtered by the Turks, the commander's body was impaled, skin was filled with straw and hung outside exposed to the public view and to frighten the enemy. Christians returned the compliment with equal vehemence. It took centuries to end slavery. (Even now in the Middle East the attitudes have not changed.) The other problem was dealing of the so-called witches; they were hunted and burnt. Even some scientists met the same or similar fates. Fortunately change came in and eventually witches became synonymous with a barbarian past. The monolithic certainties started diminishing and faded over generations.

Dr Radhakrishnan advised Indians to refrain from becoming Indinist that is to think that India provides cure for every ailment and deficiency. Indian Constitution provides for equality for all Indians. Will India produce another great man who will guide his people to work with courage and remove the man-made distinctions between man and man among indians first and then take the message to others to realize the goal of universal brotherhood.

# 1
# RAJAGOPALACHARI
(1878-1972)

Rajaji joined the band-wagon of Gandhiji and as his Southern General waged non-violent non-cooperation war against the British rule over India. When in power, Rajaji fought against two demons whom he called sins: people's sin-liqor- and God's sin-untouchability. He fought, also, for temple entry of Harijans. Both successfully. On the negative side, Rajaji suggested that the Muslim League might join the Congress demand for independence in exchange of a promise that after independence the Muslim majority areas would be allowed to vote on the issue of Pakistan. None agreed. Had his suggestion been agreed to, the story of South Asia, according to some historians, would have been one of progress and without any civilizational conflict or rancor.

Chakravarti Rajagopalachari, popularly known as Rajaji or simply CR, was one of the 'We Five', referred to by Jawaharlal Nehru in the context of their closeness to Mahatma Gandhi. Those apostle-like five, also close to each other- Rajaji, Jawaharlal, Vallabhbhai, Rajendra Prasad and Maulana Azad-were bound by their intense patriotism to a common goal – freedom of the Motherland. In the struggle for freedom, Gandhi was experimenting with non-violence and non-cooperation. So intense was the faith of the Congress members in Gandhi's leadership that without any hesitation they whole heartedly abided by his wish. Each one of them in the prime of youth sacrificed his ego and closed his future to the unknown that lay before him.

By the time Rajaji met Gandhiji, he was established as a lawyer and had a thriving practice. He had raised a family and the responsibility of supporting it rested on him and he knew that any diversion of energy at this stage could lead to misery. But his self confidence and devotion to the noble cause of freedom of his country emboldened him to risk the present for a bright future. It was a gamble and it ended well. When India became independent, he was made the Governor General of India, the apex office and status an Indian could have aspired for.

India won freedom from the British rule after a long struggle on August 15, 1947. History remembers Rajaji as the last Governor General of India and the first Indian Governor General of India (from June 21, 1948 to January 26, 1950). With this came to closure the travesty of an alien rule and the dominion chapter of India. The adoption of a new Constitution by 'We, the people' changed the colonial character of the country to a democratic form of republicanism.

Rajaji had fought the British on principles under Gandhi and his fighting spirit did not cease even after his mentor's exit from the scene. When the bond amongst the 'We Five' loosened, Rajaji remained ever ready to fight for other causes which he felt were just. From late 1950s up to 1972 (when he breathed his last) he battled against the 'undemocratic practices' of free India's governments.

Rajagopalachari was born on December 10, 1878, the third son of Sringaramma and Chakravarty Venkataraya Iyengar, a revenue official of Thorapalli village in the Salem District. The family had moved to Thorapalli from Panchampalli in the Hosur sub-taluka of Mysore State. In 1887, Venkataraya became the Munsif of Hosur , an important post to hold. He was well versed in local language but suffered from the complex that he could not converse in English with his British friends. Rajagopalachari would obviate this deficiency soon.

In his young age, Rajagopalachari was a brilliant but not studious student. Determined to improve his son's prospects and brighten his future, father sent him for studies at the age of 11 to Bangalore. He matriculated in 1891.The father bought him spectacles to correct his vision. In fact Rajaji's eye sight was defective from an early age but father had resisted buying spectacles for him all the while thinking that the boy wanted spectacles to look smart; he wanted them more for looks than for studies! In the façade-like black spectacles that Rajaji donned, his detractors later found in him a Machiavelli who hid behind his spectacles hidden courage, conviction and wisdom.to move alone, if and when a need arose.

During his student days, Rajaji was good at making friends, and his friendship with some proved life-long. He kept up contacts with his teachers, particularly with John Gutherie Tait, who had taken interest in his studies. At the same time, he did not remain unaffected by the events that were taking place around him. The arrest of Lokamanya Tilak for sedition made him a hero in people's eyes and the seeds of patriotism sprouted in many a young people, including Rajagopalachari.His mother's death in 1898, left a void in his life which the family tried to fill it by marrying him off to 11-year old Mangalamma.

In 1900 Rajaji passed his LL.B.examination. He was enrolled as a pleader and he began his legal practice at Salem. His success as a defense lawyer in the very first criminal case brought him overnight fame. The court was presided over by an English judge and he was opposed by a well known prosecutor. Now onward, more and more cases came to him than he could cope with.

Rajaji's advocacy made a mark on his clients and colleagues as also on the court. The court 'would come to life' as he rose to speak. Biographer Raj Mohan Gandhi wrote about Rajaji's qualities as a lawyer : his voice was mellow, thoughts were clear, arguments precise, delivery deliberate and forceful. He was brief and terse. His cross examination was sober but not intimidating, yet deadly. In murder and serious cases, he would pose only a few questions, some of which appeared innocent or pointless, but were sufficient to demolish the prosecution case. His language was polished and his court room manners enviable. His strong memory helped him in arguments. He had an intuitive power to attack the weakest points of his opponent's case. Not greedy, his observation about the client was telling. Once, he said: A client comes to a lawyer because he is in some trouble. It is immoral for the lawyer to take advantage of his client's condition and extract money from him. He often urged his clients to reach an out of court settlement in civil suits.

Rajagopalachari's interests were not confined to legal matters. He was interested in politics. He was thrilled by the news of Japan's victory over Russia, the triumph of an Asian power over a European power. The division of Bengal on communal lines by Viceroy Curzon surged in him patriotic feelings. In 1906, he journeyed to Calcutta to attend a session of the Indian National Congress. He was impressed by the Congress's decision to launch a program to boycott foreign cloth and President Dadabhoy Nauroji's call for swaraj. But he found the Congress itself was a house divided into moderates and extremists. The moderates cooperated with the Raj and expressed their profound devotion to the throne; they aired resolve to stand by the Empire in all hazards and at all costs. Rajaji was with the extremists who were ever ready to stake everything for the cause. The Surat session of the Congress in December 1907, presided over by Ferozeshah Mehta, saw a clash between the two groups, and it had to be postponed.CR felt heart-broken.(The moderates continued to contro! the Congress up to 1915).

Rajagopalachari had applied and was enrolled as an advocate in 1906 at the High Court of Madras. However, he did not shift from Salem.He would go to Madras, if he had to appear before the High Court. That very year, he became familiar with M.K. Gandhi's civil disobedience movement and became an ardent follower of his ideology.

In 1915, Manga (Mangalamma) died at a very young age of 26, leaving behind five children. Now Rajaji's responsibilities increased as he had to look after the children also. His increasing interests in social activities also took more of his time. In 1916, Rajaji joined the Home Rule League whose object was to urge the government to confer self government on India. The Government responded :'the demand was beyond practical policies'. In 1917, he was selected chairman of municipality of Salem. He selected two demons to oppose – drink and untouchability. He got two scheduled caste boys admitted in the municipal school. The opposition raised a hue and cry. Orthodoxy raised the bogey of impurity of religion. Rajaji paid no heed and stuck by his decision. This settled Rajaji as a social reformer. Besides this, he opened a Swadeshi store which, he thought, would help South Indians feel at ease in Northern India, and encourage people to learn Hindustani and befriend Muslims.

# C. RAJAGOPALACHARI

Rajaji was a crusader for freedom. He was a good administrator and was respected even when his adversary did not see eye to eye with him.Rajaji took up causes of Backward Castes and Muslims, Zamindari Abolition and Prohibition, in spite of his opposition by Europeans and non-Congress Muslims. (After the Lucknow Pact in 1916, some change in the outlook of the Muslims was perceptible.) Well known by now, Rajaji was recognized as Gandhiji's Southern General.

In the First World War that was being fiercely fought against Germany, England was experiencing several difficulties. To add to these was unrst in India.To suppress it, Britain promulgated Defense of India  The British wanted to recruit Indian youth for their army. Tilak and Anne Besant sought to bargain the British recruitment of Indians in the war effort against a promise of Home Rule. Congress was conscious of the indignities heaped on Indians and wanted the foreign rulers to be thrown out of India. But they could not ignore the prevailing social evils of Indian society such as child marriage, child mothers, girl widows, polyandry, inequalities of caste, prostitution in the name of religion, animal sacrifice et al. These maladies needed to be removed to improve the conditions in India. The freedom struggle was not merely political The socio-economic conditions also deserved attention.

The Indian response for Home Rule came from Punjab.The authorities accused Home Rule champions of indulging in revolutionary and subversives activities. On February 6, 1919 in the Imperial Legislative Council at Delhi two Rowlatt Bills were introduced. Congress requested for postponement of their consideration. On March 20, 1919 Gandhiji urged the Viceroy to withhold assent to the bills. The request was ignored and the bills were passed. In response, Gandhiji asked his countrymen to observe general *Hartal* (strike), suspend their business and observe the day as one of fasting and prayer. The Government met the Congress demand by passing the Rowlatt Bill which gave government powers to intern, gag, arrest and imprison any one ,without trial or public inquiry.On April 6, the whole country responded to Gandhi's call. When Gandhiji was on his way to Amritsar, he was compelled to return to Bombay under escort, as per orders of Sir Michael O' Dwyer. Also, in Punjab under his orders  Satyapal and Kitchlew, two prominent Congressmen, were arrested. The arrests created a stir. Protesters took out a procession which was fired at. The crowd retaliated and killed 5 to 6 Englishmen and assaulted one Miss Sherwood, a school teacher. Next day, April 13 was a festival day and about ten thousand people assembled to celebrate the occasion in the Jallianwalla Bagh. They were peaceful but a British officer named Reginald O Dyer precipitated a tragedy. He ordered firing on the peaceful people. The soldiers opened fire on an unarmed gathering and 379 men and women were killed and 1100 wounded. O' Dyer imposed martial law and declared that anyone who passed the road on which Miss Sherwood was killed would have to crawl. Many men were flogged and women tortured. This drew country-wide protests. Even in the distant Madras Presidency, CR organized a protest. The Punjab Government termed Gandhiji a conspirator and set up an inquiry commission. Congress responded by setting up another inquiry manned by Gandhi, Motilal Nehru and C.R. Das.The repercussions were serious and it became obvious that Rowlatt had struck at the roots of the Empire. It united Indians of all shades. The people who were honored by the authorities with medals returned them to the authorities.The entire country except the Muslim League stood behind Gandhi.

In 1921, Rajaji was made the General Secretary of AICC. (From 1922 to 1942, he was a member of the Congress Working Committee.)

On November 17, 1921, when the Prince of Wales arrived at Bombay there was general Hartal. Protesters including CR were arrested, tried and sentenced to three months rigorous imprisonment.This was followed by the Chauri Chaura incident in U.P. C.R. was again arrested. In jail CR kept himself busy with translation work. In his jail diary, he wrote,"We all ought to know that Swaraj will not come at once. Or, it may not come far a long time, nor (will) there be better government or greater happiness for the people. Elections and corruption, injustice and power, and tyranny of wealth and inefficiency of administration will make life a hell as soon as freedom is given to us. Men will look regretfully back to the old regime as one of comparative justice and efficient, peaceful, more or less honest administration. The only thing gained will be that as a race we will be saved from dishonor and subordination." What a prophetic statement !

In 1926, Viceroy Hardinge wrote Sir Harcourt Butler, governor of U.P. that Hindu-Muslim riots served a very useful purpose for the British Raj. Willingdon, Governor of Madras, wrote Viceroy expressing surprise why Gandhi in his scanty dress had not died of pneumonia and that his death might have saved them of all trouble.(How broadminded and benevolent these English officers were !)

In 1927, Gandhi said, "He (Rajaji) is my only possible successor." But after 1942, he changed his mind : "Not Rajaji but Jawaharlal will be my successor."

In December 1929, the Congress adopted complete independence as its goal.

Rajaji was at Wardha when he decided to attack two great sins: one, the government sin- the sale of liquor which he thought made man a beast, and two, the people's sin- untouchability which treated some people worse than beasts. CR pleaded : Do nothing wrong in the eyes of God and resist injustice. Rajaji's pleadings would go over the heads of Hindu orthodoxy.This was a Christian thought which Christian officers also would not understand.

In 1930 , Gandhiji announced his program of Salt Satyagrah.People mocked at him. They said that all along Gandhi used to advise, 'Wear Khadi. and it will get you Swaraj. `Now he says we must make salt. Buying salt means accepting government orders and owing it allegiance, while making salt is refusing to owe allegiance to government. The two measures are contradictory'.

The Viceroy accused Gandhiji of inciting danger to the public peace. Gandhi responded: "On bent knees I asked for bread and I have received stone instead." Rajaji marched to Vedaranyam to make salt and addressed people who had gathered there. The Governor questioned his minions why and how they had permitted 'a notorious agitator' to address meetings. Obviously, the government had lost control over its nerves and temper. But Gandhi was cool and retained his poise..The Viceroy and Gandhiji reached an understanding . The political prisoners were released.

In July 1937, in accordance with the policy enunciated in the government of India Act, 1935, Rajaji was made the premier of Madras Presidency. Prior to this, he had suffered five spells in prison and according to his critics he had earned a bad name for taking unpredictable actions and having a high strung temperament. Some of his statements had attracted countrywide attention, including the attention of the white administrators. But at the same time, several of Rajaji's actions had won him people's acclaim. His popularity increased when he expressed his idea of reducing public expenditure and effecting maximum savings. One, he reduced salaries – his own and that of other ministers – from Rupees 50000 to Rupees 9000 per annum. He fixed lower salaries for new entrants and introduced sales tax. Second, he released political prisoners much to the annoyance of administration. Third, he created amicable relations between the politicians and the Services. In a letter he wrote, "I shall be unworthy of the culture of the land and false to principles I have professed if I give room to rancor or prejudice against any group or class or individuals for anything done or suffered in the past. I want the entire service, including the police, to look upon me as a friend."

Rajaji did not interfere in the way of life of English officials.In summer they used to go to Ooty. He left it to their discretion. He was very cautious to make appointments to posts. He tried to accommodate people's susceptibilities. Some Muslim members criticized singing of the Vandemataram before the proceedings of the legislature began. He found a way out:the Vandemataram should be recited before the proceedings began so that those who did not want to join could enter the Assembly before the beginning of the proceedings.

Rajaji's government introduced prohibition which reduced the revenue but served a good social purpose. As the consumption came down, domestic brawls ceased, more food became available to families, and the grip of money lenders relaxed. Those toddy tapers who lost jobs were absorbed in jaggery- making. The legislature passed a Debt Relief Act which lightened the load of the peasantry, provided for a modest subsidy to spinners, and saved thermal power for better use. When some people shouted against administration, Rajaji responded,"Every act of administration cannot be disposed off by a crowd." He took up the cause of temple entry by untouchables, and despite opposition by Brahmins and high castes, he succeeded in his effort. He popularized Khadi also. Rajaji broke the narrow caste rules when he agreed to the marriage of his daughter Rajalakshmi with Gandhiji's son Devadas.

The Muslim League heightened fear among Muslims and articulated demand for a separate homeland. They derided the administration as Hindu Raj. Some people wrongly criticized Rajaji for foxing and opportunism which impression they had formed because Rajaji's approach was pragmatic and political. He liked idealism to the extent it did not harm a cause. Some even lauded him. The chief of All India Radio ,Lionel Fielding wrote , "Rajaji is the nearest human being to a saint that I have known."

In 1939, following the Congress Party's decision to withdraw from government and to practice non-cooperation with respect to the British war policy, Rajaji favored a united front of nationalist leaders. In 1942, he asked the National Congress to reach an understanding with the Muslim League about the country's political division on the basis of religion. (The Congress members of the Madras Legislature passed a resolution asking the National Congress to consider the claim of the Muslim League for a separate state. He pronounced that if the Muslims really wanted to go and take their belongings, let them go.) The Congress Party was unhappy at Rajaji's action and repudiated the idea of a separate Muslim State.

On August 9, 1942 the Congress launched a 'Do or Die' agitation. The government reacted strongly and arrested Congress leaders. Jinnah exploited the absence of Congress leaders and consolidated his hold on Muslims between 1942 and 1946. In 1943-44, Rajaji suggested that the Muslim League join the Congress demand for independence in exchange of a promise that after Independence the Muslim majority areas would be allowed to vote on the issue of retaining that part of India. No one agreed with this. After this Rajaji was inactive for sometime. It appears that Rajaji had not fully realized the implications of the unreasonable and irrational approach of Jinnah and his Muslim League who were not willing to cooperate in any way. Their call to observe Deliverance Day had spread so much poison that some Muslims went to the extent of reminding the Muslim masses that the Hindu Somanath temple had been destroyed a thousand years ago by their forefathers, implying they too take recourse to similar acts. At a Muslim League conference in 1941 at Mymensingh an Urdu poem was recited. ( It

was published in the newspaper Azad.) Its translation is as follows:
*The oppressed remain silent by seeing the hypocrisy*
*of the idolatrous Hindus -Oh Death like eddy*
*Where are the Muslim youth ? We shall attain*
*desire of their hearts by tying down the wild tiger*
*Come quickly -break down Somanath.*

On August 15, 1947, India became independent. Mountbatten agreed to continue as the Governor General of India. When in June 1948, he left for England, Rajaji took over as the Governor General of India. He laid down his charge on January 26, 1950, when Dr. Rajendra Prasad became the President of India

After laying down the office of Governor General , for sometime Rajaji was the Governor of Madras. He could at times be mischievous and impish. There is a story about Vasan, the owner of the famous Gemini Studio of Madras. In August 1953, Vasan announced that the production of Avvaiyar , under production for eight years, would be completed and be ready for release by Independence Day,  August 15, 1953. He worked on it like a possessed man. He thought of its promotion and after discussing with critics felt that the film would get a good boost if Rajaji attended the preview of the film. But Rajaji's coming was like, wrote an art critic, "Morarji Desai's  presiding over a  made for each other smoking couple contest." It was a miracle. Rajaji came to the preview and sat throughout. A committee of the citizens of Madras under the chairmanship of Sir C.P. Ramaswamy publicly honored Vasan for Avvaiyar.  Rajaji, however, gave a taste of his view of the film. One evening he silently entered the hall with a ticket for the film bought by his driver. But someone had seen Rajaji enter the hall and the word spread that Rajaji was so impressed by the film that he was seeing it for the second time, this time by paying for the ticket. Rajaji frowned behind the dark glasses. His diary of the day noted, " The picture was poor. After so much expenditure how can one condemn it. The music is execrable. The well known critic Ashokmitran wrote: "I was relieved that Vasan was spared the knowledge of diary jotting."A similar incident took place in 1954 when Ramsay McDonald, the British Consul General sent to Rajaji Aubrey Menen's *Ramayana*.Rajaji returned it with comments "pure nonsense."

It so transpired that despite thorough calculations and preparations, the next chief minister of Madras lost his seat in the general elections. The Congress Party asked Rajaji to take over as the chief minister. Rajaji accepted the offer. His first action was to decontrol the ration. This ended the long queues. A few ordinances that were issued brought considerable relief to the poor.

Rajaji recommended the creation of Andhradesh out of Madras Presidency but this was not accepted. However, later on the Government created Andhra Pradesh. Sri Prakasam was its first chief minister.

Rajaji introduced an employment- oriented education scheme. But some people did not like it and it became controversial. Rajaji resigned on the ground of ill health. In 1954, the scheme was dropped. Governor V.K. John wrote, "Although I strongly criticize your government's measures, but the fact remains that your government is the most incorruptible" Rajaji never interfered in the work of judiciary.

Rajaji was presented with the Bharat Ratna award on January 26,1955 by President Dr. Rajendra Prasad.

In 1961, when the Soviet Union broke an implicit understanding regarding nuclear pause , America planned to retaliate by scheduling blasts in the Pacific Ocean. In New Delhi the Gandhi Peace Foundation took a lead and organized a meeting to discuss disarmament. The meeting decided that a four-member delegation led by Rajaji should meet President Kennedy. The meeting was fixed for September 28 after consultation with U.S. government. The U.S. Ambassador Chester Bowels wrote Rajaji that disarmament had received wide attention in U.S. which was in no small measure due to Rajaji's eloquent plea. A little while afterwards, Rajaji learned with great regret the sad news of passing away of President Kennedy.

In March 1967, Rajaji advised Prime Minister Indira Gandhi to form a national government with Morarji Desai in her government as Dy.P.M. and Finance Minister. Acting on his advice, she included Morarji in the cabinet as Finance Minister but not as the Deputy. P.M. Nor did she form a national government.

Rajaji next pleaded for the release of Sheikh Mohammed

Abdullah and to give him back the power. But he did not hear from her. Therefore after sometime, he sent a letter to the President, Dr. Zakir Hussain . Abdullah was released but he would have to wait another seven years to become the Chief Minister of Jammu and Kashmir.

In May 1967, Ram Manohar Lohia met Rajaji and asked for advice on how mass of people could be moved to act. Rajaji replied: "We just do not know how to make our people work whether it was for bread or for revolution or for effecting any changes ; the question of quality or unreality did not arise and an unreal carrot would not do the trick." Lohia detested people's passivity but he himself would not work for them, observed an onlooker.

At the end of 1969, Rajaji tried to make a grand coalition to oust Indira but he did not succeed. Instead Indira Gandhi's slogan Garibi Hatao did the trick for her. She won the elections on the strength of that slogan.

By the end of 1971, Rajaji had ten grand children. As age advanced, at 93, Rajaji was not that jovial. Even so when a friend asked him whether he had lost the will to live.'No', Rajaji replied, 'but there has to be some purpose for which one may continue to live'. As his friends were leaving the world, he added, the God of Death was working overtime. He refrained from saying that he too was in the queue.

In 1972, Rajaji's health deteriorated and he grew weak. One day he fell down. Someone jokingly said that Rajaji was in the habit of returning from active politics but only to return to party or government- al power. Indira Gandhi observed about Rajaji's Swantrata phase that he was a great man given to a small party but was meant for a great nation.The Rashtra Bhasha controversy Rajaji raised did good to none. In December 1972, doctors diagnosed that Rajaji was suffering from uremia and dehydration. On December 25, the Christmas Day he breathed his last.

Rajaji will be remembered for popularizing nationalist feelings and for many of his acts and qualities like prohibition, erudite scholarship, temple entry by untouchables.Rajaji was known for his wit, humor and repartee. Asked whether God helps man, Rajaji replied,: God will be by us if we don't shut our doors on him. He will sit by us and speak to us if we don't plug our ears.

# 2
# Dr. RAJENDRA PRASAD
(1884-1963)

Learned and knowledgeable, soft spoken and devoted to the cause he took up, Rajendra Prasad retained his simplicity even after he occupied the highest office.He maintained its dignity and duly weighed tradition against modernity. He stressed  the need of qualifications for legislators.

Rajendra Prasad , son of Mahadev Sahai and Kamleshwari Devi, was born in village Zeradei, in Saran District of Bihar. Mahadev Sahai's ancestors  had migrated from Amroha to Balia, both in U.P., where from they had moved on to Zeradei. Rajendra Prasad was the youngest of Mahadev and Kamaleshwari's five children – two boys and three girls. After his preliminary education in the village school, where he was an outstanding student and had secured the first position in the Entrance Examination, he joined the Presidency College, Calcutta. He topped  the Intermediate, B.A., M.A., LL.B., and LL.M. examinations.

Rajendra Prasad observed that students coming from Bihar to Calcutta experienced difficulties of sorts. To help them, he established a Bihar Students Conference. He was popular amongst his people and participated in various activities and  had not to make much of effort to secure employment. His first job was that of a lecturer in a college at Muzaffarpur. In 1909, he joined the City College in Calcutta as a Professor of Economics. In 1911, he joined the bar and had opportunity to work with eminent lawyers, like Ras Bihari Ghosh  and Sir C.P. Sinha. In 1916, when  a separate High Court was established in Patna,  he shifted over to Patna, where he developed a good  legal practice. That very time, Gandhi's call took him to Champaran where a non-violent non-cooperation agitation was going on. He proved a perfect disciple of Gandhiji. A little later, he was appointed a member of the Senate and Syndicate of the Patna University. The same year, he met Gandhiji in the Lucknow session of the Indian National Congress.

In 1920, Rajendra Prasad left his legal practice and jumped into the national struggle. Not only he, his two sons, Mrityunjay and Dhananjayay also drifted into national movement. They left English medium schools and joined the nationalist institutions- Bihar Vidyapeeth and National School, respectively. To highlight the Congress activities, Rajendra Prasad launched a Hindi weekly, titled *Desi*. He became one of the Directors of the bi-weekly *Searchlight,* which in course of time became a daily and an important medium of public opinion in Bihar.

In 1927, Rajendra Prasad addressed a Congress session at Madras (Chennai) and was nominated to the Congress Committee. He visited Ceylon (Sri Lanka) and next year went to Britain to appear in the famous Burma Case. In 1930, he organized the Salt Satyagraha in Bihar and was made the President of the Bihar Provincial Congress Committee. Now onward, he was in the forefront of every political activity. He was prosecuted in a political case in Chapra and was sentenced to six months' imprisonment and later was sent to the Hazaribagh Jail.

In 1934, Bihar was struck by a severe earthquake which was followed by floods. These calamities played havoc with the lives of hundreds of thousands of people and their properties were destroyed. Rajendra Prasad organized relief for the affected people. The same year at the Congress's Bombay session, he was elected Congress President.

In 1937, when the Congress formed ministries in provinces, Rajendra Prasad and Maulana Azad were nominated as members of the Parliamentary Board under the chairmanship of Sardar Patel. Later, at the request of the UP Government, he conducted an inquiry into a labor disturbance in a factory at Kanpur. He submitted a report which was highly appreciated and he was appointed to three such committees in Bihar. The Committee reports were eye openers and these brought Rajendra Prasad a lot of appreciation. In 1939, the Allahabad University conferred LL.D.

on him.The next year when Subhash Chandra Bose resigned, Rajendra Babu was made the President of the Indian National Congress.

Rajendra Prasad was known for his hard work, dedication and sacrificing nature. He suffered jail sentence several times e.g. 6 months jail in Salt Satyagraha, three years' detention (from August 1942 to 14 June 1945) in Bankipur Jail. In 1943, when a man-made famine struck Bengal which took lives of millions of people, he was in jail and felt his helplessness that he could not be of any help to his suffering compatriots. It may be recalled that he had considerable experience of relief work in earthquake that had earlier struck Bihar in 1934.

The Second World War that had begun in 1939 came to an end in 1945. The War had shattered the British economy and made it so weak that the British Government decided to transfer power to Indian hands. A Cabinet Mission was sent to India. It landed at Delhi in March 1946 and held a series of conferences with the leaders of the Congress and the League. The Congress and the League could not reach an understanding about matters connected with British quitting India. On May 16, 1946, the Mission issued broad outlines of the future government of India. It also laid down the procedure for framing a Constitution of India and recommended the establishment of an interim government by reconstituting the Viceroy's Executive Council from among the leaders of different parties.

The Muslim League accepted the Mission's proposals, reiterating that the objective of the Muslim League still remained to attain complete, sovereign Pakistan. The Congress rejected the proposal of an interim government, though they agreed to participate in the Constituent Assembly. The Cabinet Mission left India on June 29, 1946.

There now developed an acrimony between the Viceroy and the Muslim League about the reconstitution of the Viceroy's Executive Council. The Muslim League, to press its point, fixed 16 August for Direct Action. When launched, it caused communal violence in which a large number of Hindus died in Calcutta and Noakhali. Shops were looted and burnt. Hindus retaliated at places in Bihar and at Garhmukteshwar in U.P.

On September 2, 1946, Jawahar Lal Nehru and his colleagues were sworn in as members of Viceroy's Council. Dr. Rajendra Prasad was nominated as Food and Agriculture Minister in the interim government. The Council under Nehru's guidance changed the spirit and outlook of the Government of India. To counterpoise Congress influence, the Viceroy reconstituted the Executive Council by bringing League members in it. This destroyed the Council's team spirit. It repudiated the idea of collective responsibility. Mr. Jinnah's explanation was that the League had never agreed to join the Council!

The Constituent Assembly met on December 9, 1946 without the members of the League. On December 11, Rajendra Prasad was unanimously elected as the Chairman of the Assembly. Several committees were formed to draft different parts of the Constitution. The tense atmosphere continued till February 20, 1947, the day the British government announced its intention to quit India by June 1948 and appointed Lord Mountbatten as the Viceroy to arrange the transfer of authority from British to Indian hands. The League again launched direct action. Riots broke out in Punjab and NWFP. Successive communal outbreaks had an unfortunate affect on the Hindus and Sikhs. The Congress realized the impracticability of the idea of a United India and demanded partition of Punjab and Bengal.

On March 24, 1947, Lord Mountbatten assumed the office of Viceroy and broadcast the declaration of transfer of power.

Both the Congress and the League accepted the partition plan and agreed to abide by the decisions of the two commissions chaired by Cyril Radcliffe. The British Parliament passed the India Independence Act 1947, fixing August 15, 1947 as the date of transfer of power. Accordingly, on the midnight of 14-15 August 1947, a special session of the Constituent Assembly was held at Delhi. It declared the independence of India as a part of the British Commonwealth and appointed Lord Mountbatten as the first Governor General of the Dominion of India.

In the midnight of 14-15 August, Nehru, Prasad and other Congress leaders took pledge to serve India and her people. The Constituent Assembly assumed power for the governance of India. Dr. Rajendra Prasad was nominated as the first President of India.

On November 16, 1949, the Constituent Assembly under Dr. Prasad passed the Constitution of India and on January 26, 1950 the ther. Governor General of India, Shri Rajagopalachari declared the birth of the Republic of India in the Durbar Hall of the Government House (now Rastrapati Bhawan). After the declaration, Dr. Rajendra Prasad, the President-elect was to take the oath of office in the presence of the Chief Justice of India, as prescribed in the Constitution. An interesting incident is said to have occured. Nehru went to Dr. Rajendra Prasad's house and reqested him and his wife to come to the oath ceremony.Prasad's wife told Nehru that she won't join. Nehru asked Prasad to persuade her. To Prasad also , she gave the same reply.Prasad then asked Nehru to leave the room for a few minutes. Prasad went near his wife and spoke something in her ear and she agreed. Nehru later asked Prasad, "How could you persuade her? What did you tell her?" Dr.Prasad told Nehru,"I told her if she did not go for the ceremony, I would lose my *chakri* (job)".

As Dr. Prasad was sworn, the flag of the Governor General was brought down and in its place the President's Flag was hoisted and unfurled, accompanied by a salute of 31 guns. (The President is the Supreme Commander of the Armed Forces .) After the swearing-in, Dr. Rajendra Prasad declared that he would accept an allowance of Rs. 2500 per month and not the full salary of Rupees 10000. India became a sovereign democratic republic.

The Constituent Assembly continued to function as the Provisional Parliament from 1950 to 1952. In 1952, General Elections were held throughout the country. Dr. Rajendra Prasad was elected as the President of India for five years. The swearing-in ceremony was held in the Constituent Assembly Hall on 13 May 1952.

## QUALIFICATIONS OF LEGISLATORS

On May 16, 1952, President Dr. Rajendra Prasad in his address said, "There is no resting place for a nation or a people on their onward march". Another time he advised, "I would have liked to have some qualifications laid down for members of the legislatures. It is anomalous that we should insist upon high qualifications for those who make it except that they are elected." These views explicitly expressed by Dr. Rajendra Prasad made an impression on jurists.Well known lawyer, Palkhiwala appreciated the view that some minimum qualifications should be prescribed for those who seek election to Parliament. He said our people need years of training to attend to a boiler or to mend a machine, to supervise a shop floor or build a bridge, to argue a case in a court of law or operate on a human body, but it was shocking that to steer the lives and destinies of millions of their fellow men, there is no requirement of any education or equipment at all. One would agree that democracy should be for all, but democratic values cannot be preserved by an elect who is a dacoit or swindler or acts for selfish ends. (Elections of 2004 and elected representatives in India, many of whom have a criminal backgroud, subtantiate Dr. Rajendra Prasad's view. It is surprising that no change has been effected.

In 1957, after the second general elections, Dr. Rajendra Prasad was elected for a second term for five years as the President of India. In 1960, Dr. Rajendra Prasad made known his intention that he would retire after the second term. (He refused the third term.) On May 13, 1962,Dr. Rajendra Prasad retired from the presidency of the Republic of India and left with his wife, Rajbansi Devi for his former place, Sadakat Ashram in Patna. He neither asked for a residence in Delhi nor a final resting place near Jamuna. Babuji, as he was affectionately called, was a simple soul. Many mocked at his dhoti unto knees and called him an orthodox Hindu. He never vented out his feelings, leave aside disgust, at such a shallow snide. Those who saw him from near had many stories to tell about his greatness – how he carried out President's function with distinction from 1952 to 1962. There is a story about his second term. After his first term was over, though Prasad had shown his willingness to continue, Nehru had tried to nominate Dr. Radhakrishnan as President.Dr Prasad's old friends and colleagues, as Authors learnt from some of them, pressed him hard to continue as the President for the second term but Prasad showed reluctance. However, he could not just shake off Maulana Azad whose words still arouse concordant notes. "If I can be a good Muslim (following Muslim way of life), why can't Dr. Rajendra Prasad be respected as a good Hindu in his Hindu way of life.?"

When the question of third term came up, Dr. Prasad said a firm no. "No more. Two terms are sufficient", he told a colleague a friend who had long association with him. Like some of his friends, he left it for his sons to find their moorings in the world and did not interfere or give them what politicians call "a helping hand". In 1963, he breathed his last.

Dr Rajendra Prasd is author of four works – *India Divided,. At the Foot of Mahatma Gandhi, An Atmakatha. History of Champaran,* and *Since Independence.*

Dr. Prasad was soft spoken. He was a person of reserved temperament. Chester Bowles, U.S. Ambassador to India, said, "His magnificent face always seemed to be holding back a smile at the strange twist of history which took him from the British Viceroy's jail into the Viceroy's own palace with the Viceroy's own bodyguard." Babuji himself jovially said, "From a lawyer, I became a law-breaker and ultimately a law giver". He was simple in appearance, attire, thinking and living. He was a simple, good soul. Nehru had once said, " We often commit mistakes , our steps falter, our tongues falter and slip. But here is a man who never makes a mistake , whose steps do not falter, whose tongue does not falter or slip and who had no occasion to withdraw what he once said or was undone what he once said."

Although differences, it is well known, arose between Nehru and Prasad, their relations remained cordial till the end.. Two controversies relate to Dr.Prasad: President's power and Hindu Code Bill. The President raised the question of President's powers in his address at the inaugural function of the Indian Law Institute on November 28, 1960. The Code has proved a boon to some but others think that it has lowered the ethical values. The Attorney General Setalvad's view was that the President was a constitutional head and was bound to act in accordance with the "aid and advice" tendered to him by the Council of Ministers.

## PRESIDENT'S POWERS

"Our Constitution is a comparatively new constitution. It is based largely on the model of the British Constitution. As such it has a history if not an ancestry which may well go back to centuries. It is being worked, I venture to presume, successfully and to the satisfaction of all concerned, although within the short period of 10 years it has had to undergo not less than seven amendments. The Constitution is very largely founded on the British Constitution. There are certain differences which are obvious. The British Constitution is a unitary constitution in which the Parliament is supreme, having no other authority sharing its power of legislation except such as may be delegated. Our Constitution is a federal constitution in which the powers and functions of the Union Parliament and the State Legislatures are clearly defined and one has no power or right to encroach upon the right and powers reserved to the other. The Head of the State in the British Constitution is a Monarch and the Crown descends according to the rules of heredity. In India, the Head of the State is an elected President who holds office for a term and can be removed for misconduct in accordance with the procedure laid down in the Constitution. It is generally believed that like the Sovereign of Great Britain, the President of India is also a constitutional head and has to act according to the advice of his Council of Ministers. The executive power of the Union is vested in the President and shall be exercised by him either directly or through officers subordinate to him in accordance with the Constitution. The Supreme Command of the Defense forces of the Union is also vested in him and the exercise thereof shall be regulated by law.

"The powers of President (laid down in the Articles of the Constitution) have many provisions which lay down specific duties and functions of the President. The powers and functions of the President differ from those of the Sovereign of Great Britain. Furthe, it may also be considered if the procedure by which the President is elected and is liable to be removed or impeached introduces any difference, constitutionally speaking, between the President and the British Monarch. Generally what are the points in respect of which the powers and functions of the two are the same and what are the points if any and the extent to which they differ? In this connection, it may be pointed out that there is no provision in the Constitution which in so many words lays down with the advice of his Council of Ministers. The relation between the President and his Ministers is laid down in Articles 74 and 75. Articles 74 lays down that there shall be a Council of Ministers with the Prime Minister at the head to aid and advise the President in the exercise of his functions. The question whether any, and if so what advice was tendered by Ministers to the President shall not be inquired into in any court. Article 75 lays down that the Prime Minister shall be appointed by the President and the other Ministers shall be is appointed by the President on the advice of the Prime Minister.

The Ministers shall hold office during the pleasure of the President and the Council of Ministers shall be collectively responsible to the House of the People. Other provisions may be said to be subsidiary or ancillary to these provisions. The question which has to be investigated is how far these and other provisions go towards making the functions and powers of the President identical with those of the Monarch of Great Britain.

"In this connection a wider question of much import is how far we are entitled to invoke and incorporate into our written Constitution by interpretation the conventions of the British Constitution which is an unwritten constitution. All this will necessarily involve a consideration of the question how far the words and expressions used in our Constitution shall be treated as words and expressions which have a meaning attached to them which is fixed and which is not necessarily the literal meaning of those expressions. This is necessary in view of the fact that our conditions and problems are not on par with the British and it may not be desirable to treat ourselves as strictly bound by the interpretations which have been given from time to time to expressions in England. We have got used to relying on precedents of England to such an extent that it seems almost sacrilegious to have a different interpretation even if our conditions and circumstances might seem to require a different interpretation. I do not think it is necessary for me to formulate the problem precisely or in definite terms. I hope I have given an indication of the questions which I have in my mind and I leave it to the Institute to define more precisely the scope of the investigation so that more or less precise answers may be formulated. I may add that in making this suggestion I do not have any particular question in view much less any incident. I put forward this subject purely as a subject of study and investigation in a scientific manner so that we may know exactly what is the scope of the powers and functions of the president".

( The above are  excerpts from Dr. Rajendra Prasad's Address on the occasion of foundation laying ceremony of the Indian Institute of Law.)

## THE  HINDU  CODE  BILL

Before the Hindu Code Bill came up for  discussion in Parliament, the President Dr. Rajendra Prasad had made it clear to the Prime Minister, Jawaharlal Nehru, that he was not in favor of the Bill, that as the present cabinet had not been elected by the people they had no right to pass the Hindu Code Bill without the consent of the people. It is said that at one point of time, Dr. Rajendra Prasad warned that in case the government went ahead with the Bill, he would be left with no other alternative but to tender his resignation from the office of the President. He had pointed out that a Provisional Parliament had no authority to enact legislation affecting fundamental matters because it was indirectly elected and did not consist of the representatives of the people elected at a general election.

Various social organizations had in their memoranda before the three-member committee expressed themselves against the Hindu Code Bill. The President Rajendra Prasad also raised constitutional points,including powers of the Prime Minister and the President, to be answered by legal luminaries.

Dr. Rajendra Prasad told Nehru, "Personally I am as much opposed to the Bill as you are in its favor." The Prime Minister said that there was no difference of opinion on the provisions of the Bill on its Dayabhaga part. The main difference of opinion was with regard to the provisions regarding monogamy and divorce. On monogamy, there was not much difference as the custom of having more than one wife was on its way out.

(Dr. Ambedkar had played a major role in the Hindu Code Bill and Nehru had agreed with him.)

The three men Committee which prepared the draft of the Hindu Code Bill comprised of B.N. Rau, Dharamvira, and Dr. Dwarikanath Mitra. Dr. Mitra had submitted a note of dissent pointing out that majority of the organizations which submitted memoranda to the Committee or gave oral or written evidence had opposed the Bill.)

The Prime Minister told that in the opinion of the Cabinet, the President had no such powers and that he had obtained legal opinion on the subject. That means that the President should act only on the advice of the Council of Ministers and he cannot do anything on his own or contrary to that advice. "I find that the provisions of the Constitution are very clear, an occasion can arise when the President can act independently in his own discretion. No doubt, the President has to act on the advice of the Council of Ministers, but the import of the above provisions is sought to be diluted with reference to the British convention because in England the King has to assent to the Bills on the advice of the Cabinet".

The President pointed out, "In so far as I have been able to understand the British Constitution, one of its basic tenets is that no important subject is brought before the Parliament in the form of proposed legislation unless it has been placed before the people for their mandate. If that is so, we should also establish a constitutional convention to that effect. In other words, the British convention should be strictly adhered to. No important legislation should be brought before Parliament unless it has been made an issue for the elections so that the people can give their opinion on it. It would not be proper, therefore, to accept one convention and not the other. It is the contention of the Prime Minister that if President did something contrary to the advice of the Council of Ministers, there would be serious conflict between me, on the one hand, and the Council of Ministers and the Parliament, on other.I wrote back to the  Prime Minister that if the Council of Ministers and the Parliament understood in proper perspective the limits of their powers given to the President, under the Constitution are sought to be curbed, they should also include another, namely, that so long as the people have not been consulted such an important legislative measure should not be brought before Parliament."

About the Hindu Code, Mr. Ayyangar had warned Nehru that the ground on which the President was opposed to the passage of the Bill was extremely significant and a majority of the members of Parliament appeared to agree with the President and if a direct confrontation took place between the President and the Cabinet, the Prime Minister, and not the President, might have to resign.

# 3
# SARDAR VALLABHAI PATEL
## (1875-1950)

An iron fist symbolizes solid strength. An opponent fears its hit. What about the hit of Iron Man as such? Sardar Patel was known as Iron Man and his threat generaetd stir among opponents. With ingenuity and shrewdness, Sardar Patel consolidated the country into the Union of India.

India, although geographically and culturally one entity, was for a long time politically fragmented into small units that constantly waged war against each other. From time to time there emerged strong willed administrators who brought smaller units under their control and established their hegemony on most of the landmass of the country. It is however a fact that those who could achieve success in consolidating were just a few. To name them – Chandragupta Maurya, Samudra Gupta, Akbar and Vallabhbhai Patel, popularly known as Sardar Patel, who can be counted as the last in the line. As the first Home Minister of independent India,Sardar Patel integrated most of the 562 princely states with the existing or adjacent provinces and merged some to form new states and thus consolidated the country to constitute the Union of India.

The enormousness of the problems posed by the princely states before their merger could be imagined when it is kept in mind that they occupied 40 per cent of land area that had to be 'fitted well into the jigsaw of independent India'. How to organize a unitary government for the entire country, including princely states? The struggle for independence had become intensified after the

First World War which made it difficult for the British to keep their hold on India. On June 3, 1947 they announced their plan to partition the country into India and Pakistan. The next day Governor General Mountbatten in a broadcast enunciated his policy and methodology for the transfer of British power to Indian hands. The British Parliament passed the India Independence Bill providing for the transfer of power and lapse of suzerainty over British India on August 15, 1947 and the lapse of treaty obligations and sanads with princely states on that date. Sardar Patel played a crucial role in the merger and integration of princely states in India. He proved as good and shrewd as Chanakya who had by his policy of *Sam, Dam, Dand* and *Bhed* (peace, riches , advice and disguise) consolidated the country for Chandra Gupta Maurya. Not only did he stabilize the country that was  weakened by Alexander's invasion in 326 BC but he also threw out the vestiges of the foreign intrusion and merged smaller states in his empire. Sardar Patel during 1947-48 followed Chandra Gupta's model in uniting and consolidating India into a strong Republic. A little biographical sketch of Sardar Patel would help in understanding the man and his success.

Vallabhbhai was born the fourth son of Jhaberbhai and Ladoba Patidar of village Karmsad, near Anand in Gujarat, on October 31, 1875. Of his three elder brothers, Vithalbhai was Vallabh's role model and he followed in his footsteps. Vithal after matriculation took law for profession, did Bar-at-law from London ( how he reached London is an  interesting story ) and joined politics. He earned both money and fame. Vallabh followed the drill. After passing matriculation, he did a law course from the Gokhale Law Classes and, after qualifying,  got himself enrolled as a pleader and started practicing at Godhra. Vallabhbhai , not satisfied with his legal education at the Gokhale's,  aspired to go to London for bar-at-law. From his practice, he saved Rs. ten thousand and deposited the amount for passport and passage with Thomas Cook. (Till now Vithal had not thought of it.) Some time later, one day a postman brought a packet addressed to V.J. Patel. V.J. could be  Vithal or Vallabh. '.J' denoted  Jhaveribhai, father's name, and Patel, the end name indicated their caste. The postman delivered the packet to Vithal who opened it. It contained a passage ticket to England. Vithal had also aspired to be a barrister. He told Vallabh that it should be the privilege of an elder brother to go to London first.

The affectionate Vallabh did not murmur even a word of protest. Vithal left for London. Vallabhbhai would take his turn and go to London at a later date to do his bar-at-law.

Vallabhbhai went to london; did his bar-at -law and came back. He started his practice at law which developed pretty fast. He took active part in social work also .and decided to fight against social evils. Seeing the harmful results of child marriage, which were common, he sarcastically said, "The Brahmin who in the name of religion gets people to marry children of tender age is no Brahmin, he is a monster". (He himself had married at an early age and had two children – Dahyabhai and Manibehn.) It was but natural for him to shift from social work to politics. This did not take long. He happened to be at Ahmedabad and by chance attended a Congress meeting that was presided over by Mohammed Ali Jinnah and addressed by Mohandas Karamchand Gandhi. Vallabhbhai was much impressed by the speaker's personality and thought of joining the Congress Party. But to ascertain the justness of the step he was going to take , in 1916, he attended the annual conference of Congress at Lucknow and it was there that the Congress and the Muslim League entered into a pact (later known as the Lucknow Pact) to conduct together, in the larger interests of the country, struggle for independence.

Vallabhbhai next visited Champaran where Gandhiji was experimenting on his method of non-violence and non-cooperation to solve political problems. Vallabhbhai made up his mind and joined the Congress. In 1917 he joined the Gujarat Sabha and devoted himself full time to Gandhi's program when plague swept Gujarat. He organized relief and agitated the Government for speedy relief to the needy. His legal experience in municipality came handy. But instead of extending help to the needy, the collector-administrator imposed tax on the farmers who were in genuine need of help. Vallabhbhai did not sit idle and intensified the agitation. The government could no longer ignore the plight of the farmers and waived off the tax. But the obdurate administrator did not show any leniency and continued to be rigid. The Mamlatdar levied a tax of Rs. 2 to 3 per farmer. From the value and standards of those days even this amount was a burden.What hurt Vallabhbhai was the loose tongue of the Mamlatdar who sneered at the agitators by calling them beggars and dacoits, and adding that they did not want to pay even the small amount. Patel replied to that officer's heartlessness: "We are not beggars. The government wants the money after calling farmers the associates of dacoits. If the government admits that its authority has vanquished and the farmers are poor, we shall be prepared to take over the administration (and give relief to the needy)". Lest someone should raise a finger at him, Vallabhbhai said he had no selfish motive in agitating the Government to give relief to hard pressed peasants and added that today his practice was flourishing and he was doing very well but the peasant's struggle in Kheda was bigger than his practice. He may or may not have the practice tomorrow and his money may be blown up by his inheritors. He concluded by saying that he would like to leave for them a legacy of service and sacrifice rather than money

The First World War was coming to an end. Indians had cooperated with the government and helped them in their war efforts. They expected the government to reciprocate their gesture by giving them freedom or at least to take a step in that direction. But, to their shock, the British applied repressive measures. At Jalianwalla Bagh in Amritsar, the British administrator ordered shoot at sight and the action by the armed soldiery on unarmed Indians took a heavy toll of life. The Montague reforms too failed to give relief to the suffering Indians. In November, 1922, the Gaya Congress provided a forum for discussion on 'council entry.' Opinions were divided. On one side were Rajendra Prasad, Motilal and Vithalbhai, while the other side was led by Vallabhbhai and Rajagopalachari. Next April, Vallabhbhai opposed civil disobedience for he saw his countrymen were not yet ready for independence. The Chauri Chaura incident proved the correctness of the stand of Vallabhbhai. He was by this time recognized as the leader of peasants and farmers. The time was now coming when he would be known as a man of iron will.

The government raised land tax by 22%. In protest the peasants refused to pay and under Vallabhbhai's guidance a Satyagraha was launched at Bardoloi on February 12, 1928. The government retaliated. They not only took away from the peasants whatever meager possessions they had but also imprisoned them. The agitation continued for six months and despite their suffering, the peasants did not give in. At last the government released political prisoners, agreed to return the confiscated goods and reduced the raised tax to previous level. This was a great success for the peasants and their leader Vallabhbhai Patel. Earlier, Gandhiji had given him a honorific of Sardar and throughout his life he would be known as Sardar Patel.

The next Congress Session was to be held at Calcutta (now Kolkata).The Gujarat Provincial Congress Committee (PCC) proposed Vallabhabhai's name for presiding over the Calcutta Session. But things were to shape differently. There were two more aspirants. Motilal Nehru wanted his son Jawaharlal, known for his internationalism, to be installed as the Congress President during his life time. The name of Subhash Bose, known as a man of action, was also under consideration. Thus it would have been a triangular contest but for Gandhiji who tried to resolve the issue without any rancor. He asked Motilal to preside over the session. However, the session which was to consider the Nehru Report also did not have a smooth sailing. While it had whole hearted support of Dr. Ansari, Maulana Azad and Abdul Qadir Kasuri (from Punjab), Jinnah and Mohammad Ali attacked Motilal's draft alleging that it did not provide for sufficient Muslim representation. It was rather unfortunate that two brothers, Mohammad Ali and Shaukat Ali who were once very close to Gandhiji took a turn. Gandhiji had in the past stayed with them and touched by their cordiality had written, "I have never received warmer or better treatment than under Mohammad Ali's roof. A cow was purchased from a butcher and escorted to the safety of a cow home. What love has prompted the act?" It was strange that the same Mohammad Ali now went to the extent of exhorting Muslims to stay away from the Congress and called Gandhi by bad names. Jinnah castigated the Calcutta conference as 'the parting of the ways'.

Patel undoubtedly was full of reverence for Gandhiji but he did not like the Mahatma's fads. He joined the Salt Satyagraha and observed, "The Mahatma was manifesting disobedience not salt." He had an acute sense of humor and did not miss his lawyer's mode of repartee. He told Mahadev Desai, private secretary to Gandhiji, "Mahadev, if you give up the struggle, they will all write nice letters to you". Another instance: A man questioned Patel, "How can a man weighing three maunds ( about 117 kg) avoid crushing ants when he walks on the earth?" Promptly Patel replied, "Tell him he should walk on his head." May sound rustic but the prompt reply (*hazirjawabi*) showed his sense of amusement. The questioner was silenced.

Mention may here be made of a few events associated with Sardar Patel not mentioned so far.

1932: Vallabhbhai's elder brother Vithalbhai died in October 1932 in a clinic in Geneva. Vallabhbhai loved his brother and was sad. But when Vithal's will was opened and read, he felt hurt that Vithal had left more than three-fourths his estate for Subhash "for the political uplift of India preferably for public work", and not for Vallabha's Congress. (Forgetting all that, Vallabhbhai extended whole hearted support for the defeat of the government case against Subhash Bose's INA that was going on in the Red Fort. In fact he was with Jawaharlal Nehru a key negotiator on behalf of INA.)

1934 : Congress agreed to enter the central assembly.(Patel was in favor.)

1936: Congressmen wanted Patel to be the Congress President but at Faizpur, Jawaharlal made it known that since he had been president for only eight months, he would be ready to do another term as the President. Annoyed at this but without losing his balance, in a humorous way Patel wrote Mahadev Desai, "The decked up groom is ready to marry at one stroke as many girls as he can find." As expected, Gandhi asked Sardar Patel to withdraw, which he did.

1937: Eelections were held in accordance with the provision of Govt. of India Act 1935. Gandhi advised the Congress to contest the elections. Congress won by majority and Congress ministries were installed in UP, Bihar, Central Provinces, Madras and Orissa where Congress had won by absolute majority. It also formed ministries in Bombay, Bengal, Assam, and NWFP where it had won the largest number of seats. These ministries were headed by senior Congress members : Rajaji in Madras, BG Kher in Bombay, NB Khare in CP, GB Pant in UP, SK Sinha in Bihar, Dr. Khan in NWFP, Dass in Orissa, Gopinath Bardoloi in Assam. Patel, Nehru and Prasad kept out of ministries.

That year (1937) Jinnah wrote to Gandhiji about Hindu-

Muslim unity and asked that two members of Muslim League be taken as ministers in the Bombay Ministry. Patel counter offered and said that Congress would agree to Jinnah's proposal if the Muslim League members – legislators first got merged in the Congress. Jinnah's intentions were dubious; he wanted coalition of the two parties. The talks broke down. It was apprehended that Muslim League members would obstruct, defy, sabotage or blackmail. Unable to force his views, Jinnah remarked that the Congress government was nothing but Hindu Raj. At this time two rape cases allegedly involving legislators occurred in CP (Centra Provices) which affected the scenario and forced Khare, Chief Minister of CP, to resign. Patel was a disciplinarian and he refused to accommodate Khare. Khare joined the Hindu Mahasabha.

The newly installed Congress ministries in provinces did their very best. The Congress image was however besmeared because the Congressmen did not behave well.

1939: On September 3, Britain declared war on Germany. Soon thereafter Governor General Wavell announced, but without seeking consent of the Constituent Assembly, that India had joined the war. The Congress Party reacted sharply. Patel was opposed to resigning the seats. He was willing to India's joining the war efforts provided Britain promised India freedom when the war came to an end. But as the English did nothing, by November 27, 1939 all Congress ministries in provinces resigned. The British Secretary of State Zetland and Governor General Linlithgow derided the resignations and said that it was nothing but blackmail. His Majesty's Government started playing the divide and rule game, and encouraged Jinnah and the Chamber of Princes to take anti-Congress stands on matters affecting the country. The Muslim League, at Jinnah's suggestion, observed a Day of Deliverance on December 22. Violence erupted. It caused immense loss of life and property. Jinnah had the cheek to accuse the Congress of being a communal party. For the rebuttal of this insinuation, Gandhiji proposed Maulana Azad's name for the office of Congress President. In 1940 the League retaliated by passing a resolution that made demand for Pakistan. In its turn, the Congress adopted a policy of affirmation of freedom.

In Europe the war was at its zenith. The German blitzkrieg

caused the collapse of several governments. England was being heavily bombarded. The Chamberlain Government, under severe criticism, was replaced by Churchill as the Prime Minister. The Labor Party joined the Churchill Government.

In India the Congress was a divided house. The members discussed whether the Congress should help the British in their hour of peril. This ambivalence was the result of non-reciprocation of India's sentiments by the British politicians. While Subhash Chandra Bose and Jaya Prakash Narayan were opposed to giving Britain any help, Rajaji was sympathetic towards Britain. The Congress Working Committee agreed to the defense of India by non-violent means. The British apprehended Japanese attack on India and said that if they left India, the country would be in trouble, and added that it was in India's interest to help Britain without expecting any return from her. Strange logic indeed!

1940-41: Vallabhbhai participated in the individual civil disobedience movement.

December 7: Japan invaded Pearl Harbor. This forced USA to discard neutral stand and join the Allies. Roosevelt and Chiang Ki Shek urged Churchill to talk to Gandhi and the Congress Party. But Churchill remained evasive. Patel's reaction was noteworthy. He told Gandhiji, "The more you try to get closer to them, the more they flee from you." Gandhiji was disturbed by the British attitude.

1942: January 11, Gandhiji designated Jawaharlal as his heir and said, "When I am gone, he will speak my language."

March 7: Singapore fell to the Japanese forces. The Allied forces started withdrawing into India and asked India to participate in war as an ally against the Axes. Britain sent the Cripps Mission to meet political leaders of India. The Mission arrived on March 15 and announced that soon after the war, India would have full dominion status, and also a Constituent Assembly to work out a constitution with the right of cessation from the Commonwealth. However, for the present India would have a national government composed of representatives of leading political parties. This appeared prima facie a British ploy to divide Indians. It meant the provinces would have the right of cessation and the result could be devastating. The country would be Balkanized. Rajaji was in favor of giving the Muslim majority areas right to secede. Gandhi, Patel and Subhash were against the Mission's scheme. Historian Dr. S. Gopal states that Nehru was willing to help the war beleaguered Britain. The Cripps Mission was a failure and returned to England.

August 8: There was resentment against the British in India. The Congress Working Committee decided to launch Quit India movement. Gandhi gave a call "Do or Die". The authorities in India arrested Congress leaders and sent them to prison. Gandhiji was sent to Pune, and Nehru, Patel and other prominent leaders to Ahmednagar Jail. It was rumored that the British were keeping a warship ready to take Gandhi to Aden and the Congress Working Committee members to Nyasaland. Violence erupted everywhere in which a hundred thousand Indians were arrested. Some leaders managed to go underground so as to continue the movement. For sometime, the movement went on but in the absence of senior leaders, it petered out. Lull fell over the country.

1943: The Muslim League exploited the absence of Congress leaders. and formed ministries in Sind and Assam and the next year, in 1943, in Bengal and NWFP. The British proved shrewd and took measures to divert attention of Indians from the demand of independence. They resorted to rationing and commodities of common utility disappeared from the market, causing great suffering and inconvenience to people. A famine situation was created in Bengal. Grains were cornered by black - marketeers so as to sell them at exorbitant price. This led to starvation deaths of people and an artificial famine, thus created, took a heavy toll of people. Millions died. It was mismanagement of food, not scarcity, that caused this human tragedy. The British propagandist's boast of teaching Indians a lesson proved right. There was silence of the graveyard all around.

November: The Congress Working Committee members in jail discussed the country's situation. Rumors about its decisions were afloat. There was a rumor that the Congress President Maulana Azad intended to send to the Viceroy a proposal regarding the suspension of the disobedient movement. When Patel heard of this, he was furious, and said that any weakness at this stage would prove disastrous. No proposal was sent. A similar suggestion was rumored to have been mooted by GB Pant. Patel opposed these.

1944: February: Kasturba died in jail. Patel used to look up to her respectfully and the news disturbed him. If Perceval Moon's account is not incorrect , Chruchill asked Wavell in a telegram why Gandhi had not died yet. (Moon's biography of Wavell page 78) It was indeed very ignoble of Churchill to have even thought of such an evil idea.

May 6: The authorities released Gandhiji who now tried to find a way out of the stalemate.

September: Gandhi thought Jinnah could be persuaded and pressure was exerted on authorities to work towards India's freedom. He went to Jinnah House in Bombay as many as 14 times, much to the annoyance of Patel, Nehru, Maulana Azad.( Patel would keep in mind which members favored Gandhi's visit to Jinnah.) Gandhiji had under consideration Rajaji's formula that Congress and League jointly demand a national government enabling contiguous Muslim areas to recede following independence, if adult Muslim population preferred separation. Jinnah put forth demand for Pakistan. Patel felt disgusted and said it was better if a gangrenous part was cut off and thrown away rather than the whole body is let to get gangrenous. He saw the Leaguee Muslims as problematic,whether they be contained or discarded rather than becoming a problem for fellow Indians.(In the year 2005, countries of European Union are facing similar situation.)

1945: April 14: Patel was aggrieved to learn of the death of Roosevelt, U.S. President, for whom he had great respect. Roosevelt was known for his sympathies with India's demand for freedom. In a letter to the Viceroy, Patel expressed his anguish for the great statesman's death.

Now, as the war had come to an end, Wavell went to London to plead for the release of Indian leaders from jail. In stead, Churchill talked to Wavell of dividing India into Hindustan and Pakistan. After his return to Delhi, Wavell invited Indian leaders for talks at Simla (now Shimla). At Shimla the Congress okayed the proposal, Jinnah did not. The Shimla talks failed and with it, Jinnah's stock soared high.

July: The British voters defeated Churchill. The Labor replaced the Tories and formed the government.

August: Japan surrendered. Patel was sorry to recieve the news of the death of Subhash Chandra Bose. Soon thereafter, elections were held in British India. In its propaganda, the League used provocative communal slogans, such as 'Islam in Danger'. This helped the League and the election results showed that it commanded the Muslim votes everywhere except in NWFP. The League had secured all the 30 Muslim seats in Central Assembly. Congress won 56 seats in Central Assembly and 430 seats in provinces. The high Muslim votes in provinces was due to Wavell's capitulation, his encouragement to Jinnah and Muslims in general, besides Gandhi's too many knocks at Jinnah's doors. The League had been so much pampered that its members made a demand that the British restore power to the Muslims from whom they had 'snatched' it.

As was logical, following election results, Congress formed ministries in eight provinces, and shared seats with Akalis. In Punjab the Unionists formed government headed by Khizr Hayat Khan who had a balanced view and was opposed to the policies of Muslim League, according to Sr.Advocate B.S. Malik. The Muslim League controlled Bengal and Sind. In NWFP, Khan Brothers defeated the League and formed the ministry.

It is noteworthy that Patel held independent views about giving election tickets. He preferred that tickets be given to those candidates who stood for the country's unity and integrity. He clashed with Azad in the case of Asaf Ali whom Azad gave preference for leadership of a group in the Central Assembly. Patel had opposed Asaf Ali because Asaf Ali had favored Gandhiji's frequent visits to the Jinnah House. He also opposed giving ticket to Syed Mahmood because the Election Board had already rejected his case. He also remembered that Mahmood had written to Viceroy that he was dissociating himself from the Quit India movement. In either case Patel had opposed tickets as a matter of principle and not because the candidates were Muslim. Patel had disapproved also the behavior of Desai, Speaker of the Central Assembly because he had on January 15, 1945 initialed a pact with Liaqat Ali Khan regarding a Congress – League government in the Center. (Desai had informed the Viceroy and Gandhiji about the matter.) It gave His Majesty an opportunity for political interference. When Patel then in jail learned of this unscrupulous action, he was angry at the goings on. Liaqat Ali Khan denied and called it a cock and bull story. Jinnah disowned it because it did not bar Congress from including a non-League Muslims. At this juncture, some members of the Royal Indian Navy mutinied which embarrassed the authorities. Another event was the coming of the Cripps Mission sent by the British Cabinet. The Mission had announced on May 16, 1946 its plan, recommending establishment of an interim Government and grouping of provinces into ABC categories. Nehru, Azad and Rajaji were agreeable to the scheme, but Gandhiji and Patel opposed it because, they felt, it could become a stepping stone to greater Pakistan. About Cripps, Churchill mockingly, though affectionately, said, "There but for the grace of God goes God" (*Churchill* by Jenkins).

1946: July: In the first week of July Azad's term as Congress President was to be over, and Nehru was to take over from him. But, it was said, Azad wanted to continue till November 1946 so that he could be the leader of the Congress, and as such become Vice President of the Viceroy's Executive Council and thus de facto Prime Minister. Gandhiji wrote to Azad to clarify that he had no intention to be president again and that in the existing circumstances he would like Nehru to be the president. The Congress members wanted Sardar Patel to be Congress President and he was nominated by 12 out of 15 Provincial Congress Committees. But Gandhiji preferred Nehru to be the leader of India as he thought Nehru would play a greater and better role in international affairs and might be able to secure support from a section of Muslims also. One more reason was that Nehru could conduct relations with Englishmen in a better way. Nehru became the President.

The Muslim League revoked the agreement and on July 29, 1946 called for Direct Action to secure Pakistan. August 16 was chosen for Direct Action. On the chosen date (August 16, 1946), the League launched a Direct Action leading to Calcutta riots, Noakhali killings, and riots in Bihar, UP and Punjab, and it boasted of its success. Patel sarcastically remarked (about League) : "It is like a dog walking under a full loaded cart but feels it is dragging the cart". In Noakhali, 300 Hindus were killed, women were raped and temples were destroyed. Hindus felt frustrated. To instill courage in them and also to create tolerance in Muslims,

Gandhiji toured the riot-torn areas. In the meantime, there were anti Muslim riots in Bihar and Garhmukteswar in UP.

October 15: The Muslim League joined the coalition at the Center but the cabinet could not meet up to December 19, 1946. From the very first day the League tried to weaken the government from within. The coalition was a house at war. Patel saw the dirty politicking and decided to pay them in the same coin.

Britain announced its plan to leave India in June 1948. It also announced Wavell's replacement by Mountbatten as Governor General and Viceroy. On his arrival, Mountbatten met the political leaders and after hearing them concluded that Partition alone could help avoid the impasse. Tandon and Gidwani opposed partition plan and Khan Abdul Gaffar Khan expressed unhappiness. Some of the leaders were of the view that severance from Pakistan would help India to have a strong Central Government over residuary India. Also by creation of Pakistan, the League would lose its capacity of obstruction tactics as there would be no more separate Muslim electorate.( But after sometime of Partition , the Muslim League in its new avatar again started playing communal game.).

Partition involved division of territory, civil services, railways, soldiers, cash in treasuries, bank balances, records and archives, institutes, debts, and communication system etc-all by experts, partition council and arbitration tribunal.

1947: Nehru, as the Congress President, signed the Partition Plan on May 17, 1947. Mountbatten announced 15 August 1947 as the advanced date to leave India. Jinnah agreed to the partition of Bengal and Punjab. Pakistan asked for six months time for joint control over Calcutta but Patel flatly refused. He ridiculed Jinnah's demand for a 800-mile corridor to link East and West Pakistan as 'fantastic nonsense'.

At the time of Partition, there were disturbances in Punjab. Khizr Hayat Khan resigned as he found the Nawab of Mamdot, aspirant Chief Minister, had conspired to create disturbances. For peace's sake, a Punjab Boundary Force of 55000 men under Maj. Gen. T.W. Rees was placed along the borders. (Of them not one was English). Contentious territorial issues were dealt with by Radcliff Commission. His award related to the Gurdaspur District and Chittagong Hill Tracts. (The Tracts had 97% non-Muslim population and yet it was allotted to Pakistan.)

In Lahore, Hindus and Sikhs held anti-Pakistan demonstrations. Wide spread riots engulfed rural areas. At places entire population was wiped out. Revenge and retaliation followed. These atrocities left behind a legacy of mistrust and hatred. Partition of Bengal and advance transfer date also aggravated communal massacres. Even the Police turned communal. Paramilitary forces viz Muslim League's National Guards and Akalis and RSS volunteers contributed to safety as well as unrest. By mid-July thousands of Hindu and Sikh homes were burnt down. Hindus and Sikhs retaliated by throwing bombs into crowded Muslim localities. Exodus of Hindus and Sikhs began in full swing. They locked up their houses, hoping someday they would return after things settled down and peace and goodwill returned.

On August 8, as Jinnah left for Karachi to celebrate the birth of Pakistan, Patel in New Delhi said, "The poison has been removed from the body of India. As for the Muslims, they have their roots in Pakistan. (But ) it will not be long before they return to us." Patel's would remain a pious hope. H.M.Seervai, an author, commented, rightly so, on Patel's statement, (It is ) "hardly to promote goodwill and neighborliness either now or in the days to come." But Patel's remarks were justified because of the crudeness of the Leaguees.

The Radcliff Commission submitted its award on demarcation of boundary lines to the Viceroy on August 12. But its publication was differed to August 16 so that in the meantime Independence Day could be celebrated undisturbed.

The British termed India's freedom as the Transfer of Power; the Indians would call it Towards Freedom. To "Towards Freedom," Sardar Patel's contribution was immense and unique in the Freedom Struggle. In the new government , he was the Dy Prime minister and he handled the post- partition problems with thoroughness and ruthless efficiency for which he was admired both as statesman and politician.

The British India could be partitioned. The partition of princely states, however, posed difficulties. Their consolidation also

posed serious problems. To resolve these the Government of India·
had set up a Department of State under Sardar Patel, with VP
Menon as its Secretary. The states would either enter into federal
relationship or make some political arrangement. These were like
islands surrounded by India. Each of the princely states, numbering
562, had its own history. Before the advent of the British, India was
fragmented into states – large, small and very small – which were
ruled by dynasties. The British had defeated them in battles or on
negotiating table. The State Department guaranteed them
independent and autonomous status with an hierarchical protocol.
Most of them were feudal and over the years had become
anachronistic.

Now that the British were to quit, the princes had two
options: either they could revert to their previous status or work out
equation with India or Pakistan. The princely states could not be
partitioned. Their status depended on their geographical contiguity
to India/Pakistan and the wishes of its people. The decision,
however, rested with the ruler who hardly bothered about the wishes
of people. Law Minister Dr. Ambedkar clarified that states that did
not sign the Instrument of Accession by August 15, 1947 would be
deemed under Indian suzerainty, because India would be the
successor state. The perceptions of India and Pakistan in this
respect differed. The Congress hoped that after the integration of
states, India would be secular and strong. The Muslim League
projected itself as the sole voice and arbiter of Muslims and envisaged
a strategically vital and strong Islamic state. At the same time,
Jinnah and the Muslim League hoped for the balkanization of India
into independent units.

To facilitate the integration of states into the Indian Union,
India offered the princes liberal terms – large tax free emoluments,
retention of lands and palaces, honors and fortunes for the princes.

Jinnah hoped that Junagarh, Bariawar, Bhopal and
Hyderabad ruled by Muslim Nawabs, even though located inside
Indian territory and having majority of Hindu population, would
accede to Pakistan. He also hoped that Kashmir, a Muslim majority
state, though ruled by a Hindu Maharaja would also join Pakistan.
States like Kutch, Bikaner, Jodhpur, Jaisalmer and Bahawalpur
contiguous to both India and Pakistan could join one or the other.

Excepting Bahawalpur which acceded to Pakistan, the rest joined India. To be fair, most princes inside India, like Bikaner, Patiala, Baroda, Cochin, Jaipur, Rewa showed patriotic fervor and signed the instrument of accession. Bhopal, Udaipur, Indore, Jodhpur initially pretended to ignore call for merger. Travancore announced its intention to set up an independent state and planned to appoint a Trade Agent in Pakistan. Menon persuaded the rulers to join India.

In the end by 14 August 1947, only Hyderabad, Jammu and Kashmir, and Junagarh remained undecided. Junagarh tried to accede to Pakistan on September 13, 1947 despite people's protests. Then a leader Samaldas Gandhi established a provisional government and as Arzi government entered Junagarh, the Nawab flew to Karachi. To avoid further disorder in November 1947, India took over the state and after poll results were found in favor of India, they joined India.

The Nawab of Hyderabad vacillated. In early 1947 the Nizam delcared his intention to remain independent with dominion status, and in league with Viceroy's Adviser, Conrad Corefield tried to play mischief with Bastar's natural resources. The Nizam created a militia and signed a standstill agreement with India. He bided away a year in making up his mind about accession. Meantime, the Nizam gave Pakistan a loan of $62 million and allowed the state's military to terrorize the 80% state's Hindu population. The violence by Razakars also increased. On September 13, 1948 India took action to restore law and order in the state. According to historian Walpole, Nizam hired Pakistani fighter planes to attack India and achieve nationhood for Hyderabad. But Patel tamed the Nizam. He dispatched two divisions of Army and on September 18, after minor skirmishes , the Nizam's forces capitulated. Hyderabad acceded to India. The Razakars and their chief Kasim Rizvi who had boasted to unfurl their flag on Red Fort in Delhi were properly treated.

Kashmir : Kashmir signed an agreement of accession to India on October 26, 1947. The state comprised of three natural parts - Jammu, Kashmir Valley, and Ladakh. Of these Kashmir Valley had the largest population, 77% of whom were Muslims. The ruler a Hindu, Maharaga Hari Singh initially tried to retain his independence and signed a Standstill Agreement with Pakistan.

But after tribal and Pakistani army men disguised as tribal invaded Kashmir, the Maharaja signed the instrument of accession to India. The Authors' effort to trace Patel's role in the matter of Kashmir brought two interesting facts: One, how the Kashmir matter was shifted from the State Department to Nehru's Ministry. (See next paragraph). Recently, there came up another interesting reference whose veracity the Authors have not been able to confirm. Owen Bennet Jones in his book Pakistan ( publication of 2002 page 69) refers to a meeting of Liaqat Ali Kahn (sic) in November 1947 at which Sardar Patel was also present. When Kahn (sic) compared Junagarh with Kashmir, Patel protested why not talk of Hyderabad and Kashmir and "we could reach an agreement". Jones's source for this information is Hasan Zaheer's The *Rawalpindi Conspiracy* 1951 (Oxford University Press Karachi 1998 Pp55,56). It is not clear how this reference, without relevance, has been manipulated.

The accession of states was a subject dealt with by Home Ministry under Sardar Patel. But Nehru singled out Kashmir and decided to handle it himself with the assistance of Gopalaswami Aiyangar, Minister Without Portfolio. Patel was against this change and said the step proposed by Nehru would create complications. Patel's correspondence in regard to Kashmir and Tibet shows his understanding of the problems and astuteness. Many an expert thinks that had Patel been allowed to handle the Kashmir problem, it would have not become so complicated and would have been solved long back. The accession of Kalat, a Muslim State to Pakistan involved invasion on that state by Pakistan which shows Pakistan's credentials are not above board. Pakistan by threat and coercion annexed princely states adjacent to or inside NWFP and Baluchistan. The Gilgit region and Northern Areas were similarly occupied by Pakistan with the connaivance of Gilgit Scouts. Patel was a matter of fact man. He could not be taken over by deceit. When he heard that Pakistan had accepted Junagarh's accession to Pakistan, Patel could not ignore that Pakistan had sent tribal mobs to capture Kashmir by force.( see Authors' Decisive Battles of India Through The Ages Vol II)

Finally it may be said that Sardar Patel was a pragmatic man. He was popular among peasants because he realized their problems and even looked like one of them. He was popular among princes because he talked to them politely and assuaged their hurt feelings. He gave them tempting terms for merger and kept his word. He was popular among businessmen because he did not twist their arms. He kept even the religious minded people happy though he was secular. Gujarat's Hindus were satisfied that Patel cared for Somanath – silently. Muslims also trusted him. Novelists like KM Munshi had prepared necessary background that for centuries, Hindus had been maltreated by Muslim rulers and that Muslims should not get agitated if some small favor was done by them.In the matter of Tibet also, Patel had asked Nehru to be cautious. In the film titled 'Sardar', Patel says that Nehru might repent his concessions to China.

# 4
# MAULANA AZAD
(1888-1958)

Determined not to lose their hold on India,the British rulers tried all tactics, including divide and rule, to retain their hold on tne Jewel in their Crown. They propped up feudalists among Muslims to form the Muslim League which later under the leadership of M.A. Jinnah pressed its demand for a separate state for the Muslims of India. But the nationalist Muslims, amongst whom Maulana Azad was the most prominent, fought for a Unified India. An erudite scholar, Azad opposed orthodox Muslims.He had the courage to stand up to Jinnah's separatism. When the plan for partition of India was accepted, he asked his co-religionists not to leave the land of their birth. Azad was a true nationalist.

If quizzed about the real name of Maulana Azad, most Indians would fumble; they would be puzzled as the name Maulana Azad comes to mouth quite naturally. One may assert that the question itself is absurd. No, it is not. His family had named him 'Ahmad.' Another question : Where was Maulana Azad born? Kolkata, most people would say because of his parent's long association with that city. No, sorry, the reply is wide off the mark. Ahmad was born far west in Mecca, in Saudi Arabia, on November 11, 1888.

Both of Ahmad's parents came from scholarly families. His mother was daughter of a scholar of Medina , named Sheikh Mohammad Zaher, and his father Pir Khairuddin, was known for his scholarship of Arabic. When Ahmad was 2, Khairuddin and his family returned from Mecca to his former residence in Calcutta. Khairuddin taught  Arabic and Persian to his children at home.

They received instructions in other subjects from private tutors. While young, Ahmad developed revulsion against Pir-worship. By 16, his Islamic education was over and he got interested in and was impressed by the writings of Sir Syed Ahmad, more by his rationalism than scholarship. But this had an adverse affect ; he became more skeptic about religion. His atheism lasted till he came of the age of 22 when he came in contact with a Bengali revolutionary, Shyam Sunder Chakraborty, and decided to generate political awareness for freedom amongst fellow Muslims. With the faith thus revived, Ahmad began to write in Urdu. His readers were so much impressed by his learning and depth of knowledge that they named him Maulana, meaning teacher. Ahmad adopted Maulana as his pen name and Azad as his poetic name. That is how Ahmad became known as Maulana Azad.

Maulana Azad traveled extensively in the Middle East. He was influenced by two reformers- Mustafa Kamal and Sheik Abduh-especially by their anti-imprialism as also their life styles. He started publishing a journal *Al-Hilal*, meaning Crescent. Al Hilal called on Muslims to develop revolutionary nationalism and attacked the British for planting fear of Hindu majority in their minds. The journal interpreted Islam for its readers and brought India's Muslims on to the platform of freedom movement. It aroused them out of political lethargy and inspired them to work with the Hindus. Thus Al Hilal tried to bring Hindus and Muslims closer. Maulana Azad was a harsh critic of the loyalist politics of Aligarh University. He said, "Aligarh had paralyzed the Muslims"and made them lifeless puppets dancing to the tune of the British Government. Prior to Azad, Badruddin Tyabji had suggested that the proper course for Muslims was to join the Congress and take part in its deliberations. Azad's propagation of nationalistic feelings and his anti-British writings made Al-Hilal look seditious in the eyes of the government. He was expelled from Bengal and interned in Ranchi (Bihar). Because of its revolutionary spirit, the publication of Al-Hilal was proscribed in 1914. Azad remained in jail for seven long years and was released in January 1920. Maulana Azad started a new journal *Al Bilagh*. His feature Taskariah, a new style of writing belle letters, impressed his readers. In 1920, he joined the Congress.

During his internment, Maulana Azad had busied himself with translation of the Koran and wrote a three-part commentary on it. Unfortunately, during a police raid, the manuscript of the translation was lost and he had to re-do it afresh. But so tedious did it prove that he could complete only two of its three parts. Even so, his commentary on Koran was lauded and for larger audiences, it was translated into English. Today, it is considered a unique work.

Azad moved to Delhi where he met Gandhiji and joined his non-cooperation movement. Muslims had earlier started the Khilafat movement against British action in Turkey. The Congress had adopted the Khilafat movement as one of its own programs. This encouraged many Muslims to join the freedom movement. Maulana Azad, being an active participant, was arrested but was soon released. Because of his imprisonment and conviction in Congress ideology, Azad's stature rose high and he began to be counted among its important leaders..

In 1919, the Government of India introduced an Act (of 1919) but it failed to win favor of India's political leaders. To the contrary, it spread communalism, separatism and internal conflicts. The Congress – League de-tente that had started in 1916 ended and Hindus and Muslims drifted apart. How much venom had entered people's mind can be gauged from Mohammad Ali ( Ali Brothers)'s 1924 statement : "However pure Mr. Gandhi's character may be, he must appear to me, from the point of view of religion, inferior to any Mussalman, even though (he) be without any character." Not a single non-Congress Muslim leader protested against this blatant statement. One reason was the League was autocratic and none of its members dared stand up to Jinnah. .

Maulana Azad was the only nationalist scholar-intellectual Muslim who could stand up to Mohammad Ali Jinnah, a separatist against a unified India. Between 1924-26, the Hindu – Muslim relations showed marked deterioration. In 1927, the British Government set up Simon Commission.( In 1928, as serious differences arose between Congress and League, Azad opposed Jinnah and cutoff his relations with the League.) The Simon Commission took more than a year to reach India in February 1929. Indians boycotted it because it did not have even one Indian as its member. The Commission tottered towards failure. An All-Party Conference then devised a draft constitution but Jinnah rejected it. He wanted that separate electorate should continue and weightage should be given to Muslims, in addition to other safeguards,including one-third seats in Central and provincial legislatures. Seeing the League pressing for seperatist demands, Sikhs also made demands. Jawahar Lal Nehru and Subhash Chandra Bose wanted Purna Swaraj. Gandhi started a Civil Disobedience (CD)campaign. One hundred thousand men and women were arrested and sent to prisons.In 1930, Azad was arrested and was given a 4-year long sentence. Azad was perfectly clear in his mind that India was a religious pluralist country; yet the relations between the two could improve while they could continue practicing their respective religions.

The Viceroy resorted to ordinances. But as these too did not work, the British Government organized a Round Table Conference (RTC) to formulate a constitutional structure for India and to resolve the question of safeguards for the minorities. The first RTC was adjourned sine die. The British Government concluded that it would be futile to work out a constitutional solution for India without the cooperation of Congress. The Government released Congressmen. Gandhi had several meetings with Viceroy Irwin and he called off the Civil Disobedience.

The Second RTC was held in London in 1931- from September to December. But it achieved nothing. Willingdon, the new Viceroy, passed a series of repressive ordinances. When Gandhi returned from the Conference at London, he found the country in the throes of political upheavals. In January 1932, Gandhi began a civil disobedience ( CD) movement. The Govt. arrested Gandhi and other leaders and banned the Congress. In August Ramsay McDonald, the new British leader, announced his patently communal award in favor of Muslims. He allotted them 51 per cent seats in Punjab and 48.4 per cent in Bengal, while Hindus were given 27 per cent in Punjab and 39.2 per cent in Bengal. Besides Hindus and Muslims, the Depressed Classes were given seats and separate electorates. Gandhiji felt the award was a blow to national unity. In Pune Jail he went on fast until death. Malviyaji persuaded SC leader Ambedkar not to agree to the provision for depressed classes. Ambedkar conceded and signed what came to be termed as Pune Pact .Gandhiji then broke his fast. Malviya passed a resolution forbidding Hindus to regard anyone as untouchable. (Unfortunately, precepts and practice continue at variance.)

The Third RTC was held in November 1932. Congress did not attend the Third Conference but the Conference passed several resolutions and in 1933 its report was published. In November 1934, a Joint Parliamentary Committee issued a report on constitutional reforms. In 1935, the Govt. issued a Bill which was enacted into law in August as Government Of India Act, 1935.The Act separated Burma from India, created new provinces of Orissa and Sind, made 11 autonomous provinces under governors, placed provincial subjects under ministers responsible to legislature, provided a federal government for whole of India, including princely states with Central Legislative to have the provision of two-third seats for princes (later Chamber of Princes). The ministerial authority extended to all subjects except Defense and External Affairs. (Responsibility for princely states rested with the Viceroy.) The princes were to sign the Instrument of Accession to join the Federation which could come into existence only when 50 per cent of states had joined the Union. Elections were to be held in 1935.

The Act of 1935 was favored by the Muslim League but it did not satisfy the nationalists who had expected much more from the British Government.The League pressed its demand for Pakistan.In pursuance of the Act elections were held. The Congress secured 70 percent of the votes that were cast.This gave the Congress a clear majority in 6 out of 11 provinces. In the rest of the provinces it emerged as the single largest party. The Muslim League won less than 25 percent of the Muslim reserved seats and lost in all the provinces, which meant they could not form ministry anywhere. Jinnah tried and sought to form coalition ministries with the Congress but Nehru did not agree with the proposal. Jinnah next tried a Muslim mass base to the Muslim League, alleging that the Congress worked against Muslim interests and wanted to destroy Muslims.He took the stand that the Congress ministries had introduced recitation of Vandemataram and teaching of Hindi in schools. This was Jinnah's appeal to the Muslims that only the Muslim League looked after their interests and was their friend.

The Muslim League's plea for Pakistan had already surfaced first in England and then in Lahore. Jinnah now harangued the Muslims with the cry 'Islam in danger'.This beguiled the Muslims who turned militants.Jinnah's propaganda succeeded in poisoning poorer classes of Muslims because the appeal of carving out a separate Islamic state made an immediate impact on them.However, this alerted the nationalist Muslims, especially intellectuals among whom Maulana Azad was outstanding. He stood up to the separatists. The Muslim League preached loyalty to the British Crown and asked Muslims to keep aloof from freedom movement.

The nationalist Muslims had suffered a great loss when Mohammad Iqbal joined the Muslim League. The poet -philosopher who wrote *Sare jahan se achchha Hindostan hamara* and was a protagonist of Hindu-Muslim unity joined hands with the communalists who became the cause of partition of India. Iqbal forgot that the Muslim demand had been for the economic upliftment of Muslims.He gave it a wrong twist by introducing a point about cultural differences between Muslims and Hindus.In a letter he wrote Jinnah, "It is absolutely necessary to tell the world both indside and outside India that economic problem is not the only problem in the country.From the Muslim point of view, the cultural problem is of much greater consequence to most Indian Muslims." He ignored Hindu-Muslim syncretism of hundreds of years.

Maulana Azad was elected and became the Congress President. In 1942, when the Congress launched a 'Do or Die' movement, Azad was arrested for participating in the movement and imprisoned in the Ahmadnagar Jail. He remained in the prison until June 1946 and conducted the Congress affairs from jail. He utilized the long detention period in writing Ghubar-i-Khatir, i.e.personal affairs.

Maulana Azad had played an important role as the Congress spokesman: for talks with the Cripps Mission (1942); Simla Conference with Lord Wavell (1945) and the Cabinet Mission (1946). As it was becoming difficult to rule over India, the British decided to transfer power to Indian hands. In 1946, the Viceroy formed an Executive Council with Jawaharlal Nehru as Vice Chairman. Maulana Azad was made the Education Minister.

The Congress opposed the partition of the country on the basis of religion and rejected the proposal. Had they acted otherwise, it would have been considered communal. They hoped the Muslims in India would relegate religion to a secondary place in politics. Congress stood for pluralist India. But secularism failed to triumph over obscurantism. Pacification of Muslim community was decried by others. They did not accept that Muslim prejudices were superficial, though it would not be true that majority of Muslims or Hindus were fundamentalists.

{The Muslims of Pakistan stress and maintain the cultural divide. The co-author Amrit Verma gathered this impression from her hosts in Lahore during her visit to Pakistan in 1988.She was one of the members of a group of ladies from India that visited Pakistan to participate in the 75th anniversary of her alma mater, Kinnaird College. Her hosts consisting of alumna were very gracious. One evening Mrs. Iqbal (daughter-in-law of poet-philosopher Mohammad Iqbal-his son was a judge of Pakistan's Supreme Court) invited the visiting group and selected ladies of Lahore, for a get-together at her residence. There was gaiety all around The Indian group thought of complimenting the hostess by singing Iqbal's 'Sare Jahan Se Achchha Hindostan Hamara Hum Bulbulen Hain Iski Yeh Gulistan Hamara'. When the recitaion was over, the Pakistani ladies got up and much to the surprise of the Indian ladies, started singing Pakistan's national anthem.They did not appreciate the gesture of their Indian guests.)

In pursuance of the 1935 Act, elections were held. The Congress secured 70 percent of the votes that were cast. This gave the Congress a clear majority in 6 (later 7) out of 11 provinces. In the elections held for provincial assemblies , Congress captured 711 out of 1585 seats. The Muslim League managed to secure only 104 out of 489 Muslim seats. The League won less than 5% of total Muslim vote. In the Punjab it won only 2 out of 84 seats reserved for Muslims, in Sind 3 out of 33, in Bengal 39 out of 117, and in NWFP not even one . In 1945-46 the league won 755 of the Muslim vote and emerged as the single largest party. The Muslim League won less than 25 per cent of the reserved Muslim seats and lost in all provinces which meant they could not form ministry anywhere. Jinnah proposed to Congress that they form coalition ministries. Congress did not agree and rejected Jinnah's coalition proposal because they had sad experience in the past. The League had created obstacles and did not let the government function. The Congress formed ministries in provinces and set up a supervisory three - member board to oversee their work. Maulana Azad was one of the three members of the Board, and was in- charge of Bengal, Bihar, United Provinces (UP), Punjab, Sind and NWFP.

Maulana Azad symbolized India's nationalist and secular Muslims. As Rahil Khan, rightly, observes, "Azad remains an icon of secular nationalism in modern day India". In the beginning Jinnah had been an ardent supporter of Congress. Later, he joined the League and tried to forge unity of the two - the League and the Congress- with the help of young Muslim thinkers.Later, he turned into a supporter of orthodox Islam.

1947: An apocryphal story circulating about Maulana Abul Kalam Azad was that in August 1947, Muslims from areas adjacent to Delhi envisioning a wonderful life in a land governed according to Islamic tenets, came to Delhi on way to Pakistan. In Delhi they went to Maulana Azad to bid good bye. The Maulana pleaded with them that it is for them to decide their future but they should think that they would be leaving behind an unsettled life for their Muslim brethren. Some of them changed their mind and went back to their villages and assimilated in the national stream. This would have been a pleasant end but for the secularists who did not allow communalism to die. The Pakistani leaders projected it differently. One wit wisely observed that those who left a home found solace that they were getting a country. No doubt a country of their own but in which even after half a century they would be known as Mujahids!

It was unfortunate that Muslim leaders who could have helped uplift their followers found no time, no energy to map out future of Muslims. Maualana Azad, Rafi Ahmad Kidwai and Sheikh Mohammad Abdullah were great leaders.( Now none of them is alive.) The ruling Congress always thought of immediate solution to problems and quick gains. They promoted those Muslims who could find a balance between Congress's needs for Muslim votes and the Muslim needs for help.

If we look closely we may find that a change had come in Muslim attitude after 1971 War. The new generation thought that the Muslims had asked for Pakistan and got they got it.Those who opted to live and die here in this place of their birth, India is their homeland. Muslims living in small cities (like Ahmedabad, Jabalpur, Moradabad, Aligarh, Calicut and Bhiwandi) have created employment through craft and trade. Unfortunately they became prone to religious violence and at places some got involved in undesirable activities like smuggling, terrorism under the protection of underworld dons and front-men of black money.( An interesting objective study of Hindu-Muslim relations in the six cities was conducted by Prof. Varshneya and has since been published. Authors commend it.)

It was sad that the rumor mill did not spare a gentleman like Maulana Azad and canards were spread that he possessed a romantic nature and had other interests. Which was why, they said, Azad did not welcome visitors after the sun-set. This was nonsense and utterly false. A person fond of scents does not become romantic. They forgot Maulana Azad and C. Rajagopalahari were great friends. When Azad died and the capital grieved, CR was asked by a friend, Rama Rao, whether all what was being said of Azad was true, CR replied, "He (Maulana Azad) was a good type – broadminded, scholarly and gracious. He had a kind of hold on PM (Nehru ) due to much association, a common dialect and a pro-Muslim complex in the latter. He liked me and I liked him." Another thing the Maulana and Nehru shared was rationality. Azad weighed everything rationally. Besides interest in literature, Azad was interested in science and technology also. He was also the founder-member of the Indian Council of Cultural Relations (ICCR). It was as Education Minister that Azad set up three Akademis of Sahitya, Sangieet and Kala..

Azad was a person of deep aesthetic sense. Once a year in February a flower show was organized in the lawns of his house. In February ,1958, like the previous years, a show was organized. A large number of entries were received and many flower lovers turned up. It was unfortunate that Maulana Azad passed away on that very day. He was only 70. Our historian friend Eileen David who had never missed the Flower Show in Azad Sahib Ki Kothi , as his residence was known, nostalgically remembered the event. After Azad's death the house was designated as VP House (Vice President's Residence) and the venue of the flower show shifted to the Zoological Park compounds.

A book authored by Maulana Azad titled *India Wins Freedom* was published by Orient Longman, Madras. It stipulated that the book did not carry 30 pages and that these would be published after 30 years. It was surmised that these pages contained some offensive information, perhaps not to the liking of some VIPs. It was desired that these pages should be placed in the custody of the National Archives of India. Many people thought that the 30 pages carried critical references to Mr. Nehru and a rumor was spread that the government might supplant these pages by their own doctored 30 pages. This apprehension turned out wrong. The 30 pages that were to be made public were taken out after the period was over from the vaults of the National Archives of India. These were opened before the designated authority and made public as per prescribed procedure They had not been within anybody's reach and the question of effecting change or getting rid of any matter, inconvenient or otherwise, did not arise, told us a senior officer retired from the Archives. The matter was original; no change, no protest.

Maulana Azad was honored posthumously in 1992 with the award of Bharat Ratna, the highest honor the country offers its deserving sons and daughters. More than four and half decades have passed for the death of the eminent person secular in totality.

Religion, however, continues to be exploited for votes. Those seeking votes in the name of religion incite communal passions and political expediency harms the nation. In the case of Shah Bano, the judicial decision was circumvented at the highest level by a Parliamentary Act. Besides communalism, regionalism, casteism, and disputes relating to languages, boundaries, rivers etc are also causing immense harm to the country. It is not wrong to say that everything seen from strict minority angle is also bedeviling the nation.

Conservative Muslim leaders mobilize Muslim mass on the basis of Muslim Personal Law and Muslim identity. The well-being and financial condition should be the criterion of a man or woman for uplift, irrespective of his or her religion. Not alone Muslims, Hindu, Christian, Sikh and other conservatives have similar attitude. It is amply clear that a common civil law can be of great help as is evident from the Western societies. It can remove one cause of friction. But even Muslim intelligentsia opposes change.

At the time of Partition there were both pleasant and unpleasant experiences.Good people in East Punjab and West Punjab helped those in sad plight while bad people added to their misery. The authors saw events on both sides and are of the view that Azad's rationality would have done a lot good. The attitudes had been formed by communal propaganda. An actual incident involving Azad is worth narrating. In 1940 Azad was the president of the Indian National Congress. Some extracts from his presidential address are given below:

"I am a Muslim and proud of that fact.Islamic splendid tradition of thirteen hundred years are my inheritance. In addition, I am proud of being an Indian. I am part of that indivisible unity that is Indian nationality. It was India's historic destiny that many human races and cultures and religious faiths should flow to her, and many a caravan should find rest here. One of the last of these caravans was that of followers of Islam. We brought our treasures with us and India too was full of riches of her own precious heritage.Full eleven centuries have passed by since then. Islam has as great a claim on the soil of India as Hinduism. Hinduism has been the religion of people here for thousands of years. Just as a Hindu can say with pride that he is an Indian and follows Hinduism , so also we can say with equal pride that we are Indian and follow Islam. Eleven hundred years of common history has enriched India with our common achievements, our language, our poetry, our literature, our culture, our art, our dress, our manners, and customs, the innumerable happenings of our daily life, everything bears the joint stamp of our joint endeavors. Fortunately, communal frenzy and hatred have almost extinguished. The Kashmir problem however continues to bedevil the relations between the two countries. There is no endeavour of our national life which has escaped this stamp. This joint wealth is the heritage of common nationality and we do not want to leave it and go back to the times when this joint life had not begun."

This is meaningful to all of India's Muslims They are witness to Maulana Azad's advice of 1947 that religion canot be the basis of a nation come true.Bangladesh 's creation is a proof that religion cannot be the basis of a nation. In India which is a pluralist country, people of all faiths hold highest offices. Faith is a personal thing. Azad was a true Muslim and true nationalist. He never supported movement of seperation and he should be the role model for people of all faiths.

# 5
# Dr. B. R. AMBEDKAR
## (1891-1956)

The British rulers of India had tried to divide Hindus and Muslims so that they may not make a joint effort for independence of their country. Next, they tried to create a rift between the High caste and Schedule caste Hindus, by trapping in Dr. B.R.Ambedkar with the bait of Achhutistan for Scheled Castes,on the pattern of Pakistan for Muslims. Only because of the understanding reached between Malviyaji and Ambedkar and the Pune Pact between Gandhiji and Ambedkar, the country escaped a trifurcation. Thanks to Ambedkar for not falling in Jinnah's footsteps.

A wearer alone knows the pinch of the shoe. A scheduled caste (SC) man/woman alone feels the hurt of the caste system. Dr. B.R. Ambedkar, born in a 'low' caste, experienced an intense hurt from the behavior of caste Hindus. He studied the caste system and realized his helplessness to effect any change in the system. He was born an SC, would remain SC and die SC, irrespective of his material and intellectual achievements so far or in future. For, the Hindu religion ordains birth in a particular caste to divinity. The faith also believes in rebirth depending upon the deeds,-good or bad he does in this life. Howsoever good deeds a man may do in this life, his caste will not abandon him in this life. He will have to suffer the stigma of being a low caste or enjoy the fruits of being born in a high caste until his death. Later in life, Ambedkar studied scriptures and questioned why the caste system was prevalent only amongst Hindus and not in other religions.

.The Caste System evolved as an index of people's occupation which over centuries has been twisted and shaped into the preset pernicious caste system. History shows that in the past efforts were made from time to time by enlightened souls to reform the system. Ambedkar tried to improve the lot of the SCs who were being maltreated and exploited by the upper castes. Gandhiji also took up the cause of upliftment of the Harijans, as Gandhi was to call S.Cs. Gandhi did not succeed in changing the outlook of orthodox Hindus, particularly in rural areas. One of the reasons of Gandhiji's failure was his adherence to the Varna Vyavastha, as propounded in the Bhagvadgita. Even his living amidst the Bhangis, the lowest of the low, could not bring round the high castes nor could his example soothe the bitterness of the S.Cs. as can be discerned from the correspondence of the office bearers of the Jat-Pat-Todak Mandal (an organization in Punjab that was opposed to caste system) with Ambedkar and Gandhiji. But it was undeniable Gandhiji's himaneness and sincere intentions impressed the need of ameliorating conditions of SCs..

Ambedkar's sexperience of suffering as SC was first hand. During the course of his first employment, Ambedkar observed that his colleagues maintained distance from him and some even contemptuously derided him simply because he was untouchable, having been born a low caste Hindu. Gandhi's rationalization in the *Harijan* was suspected by S.Cs.as another ruse of the Savarnas. Ambedkar could not forget that similar efforts made by Buddha's teaching had disappeared in India, whereas abroad Buddha's followers suffered from no such practice or prejudice. How come there the society was not divided on communal lines. In India, unfortunately the pendulum seems to be swinging at the other extreme as we find that whereever an S.C.has come to power, he has become clickish and orders display of statues and images of Buddha and Ambedkar. Jain and Sikh religions, both of Indian origin, also do not suffer from such practices or prejudices nor do they have castes.

Ambedkar returned the hurt to the Savarnas, who had derided him for his caste, at the time of the Round Table Conference organized by the British colonialists in London. Had the British succeeded in their effort of divide and rule, things might have been very bad for India and her freedom. Thanks to Ambedkar and Malviyaji, a 'high caste' Hindu leader, who did not let the British rulers' mischief succeed.

How did that trauma grow up in Ambedkar? Let us go back to Hindu scriptures - to Rigveda, the oldest sacred book. Its *Purushasukta* makes the division of Purush (social system, according to authors) in four parts adept in performance of different types of functions, which later, according to some, turned into Varna (that is function and also complexion) Vyasvastha (system). The four parts were Brahmin, Kshatriya, Vaishya and Shudra, each contributing to the well-being of the whole and enjoying equal status. Ambedkar analyses the development and says the Brahmin cornered the most prestigious position. The enumerative categories became distinctive and turned into status categories. The growth was automatic perhaps but it proved disadvantageous to the other three categories as their status declined. The next two, Kshatriyas and Vaishyas manoevred second and third positions. Obviously the lowest, Shudra, bore the brunt of social decline and received the most ignoble treatment from the other three. The Shudra was to serve the dwijas i.e. twice born.(Birth in one of the three castes and undergoing the ritual of thread ceremony marks one a Dwij.) Is this the reading of jaundiced eyes of Ambedkar and his ilk of the past? How strange modernization efforts have created one more division - OBC - Other Backward Castes. Is it to silence some of them?Even so,the untouchables remain untouched by modernization and measures to ameliorate their economic conditions do not show much improvement. Happily, there has been no violence and even though the democratic growth is slow, it is good that it is non-violent.

There are different versions about the birth place of Ambedkar. According to the *National Biography*, Bhimrao Ramoji (or B.R.) was born at Mhow in Madhya Pradesh, the youngest of 14 children of Subedar Major Ramoji Maloji Sakpal, and Bhimabai Murbadkar on 14 April 1891.This leaves some doubts because of two different end names of parents. Another view is that he was born in Bombay Presidency. In his student days Bhimrao faced hardships. Nothing wrong, because in India most of the students of all classes, face hardship. But unlike others, Bhimarao faced indignities and humiliations also. How about his name Ambedkar? This shows the man came from village Ambed. But nothing of the sort in case of Bhimrao. He took the surname from his teacher named Ambedkar who was kind to him. Bhimrao was educated at the Elphinstone High School, Bombay and he graduated from the

Elphinstone College. He got a job of an Assistant. Administrative Officer in an office at Bombay but found life unbearable because other employees, including clerks and office boys, treated him with contempt for his belonging to a scheduled caste. Out of disgust, he left and took up a job at Baroda. But in India caste is not rid off like that by mere moving to another place. The stigma did not leave Ambedkar. It is well said, in India rumor becomes a fact and gossip passes for history.

At Baroda, Bhimrao applied for a scholarship for study abroad. The Maharaja of Baroda granted him a scholarship and he went to the Columbia University in USA. He received a degree and returned to Baroda, to serve the state government for some time as per the condition of scholarship. He joined the State Government service. In 1918, when he secured the job of a lecturer in political economy in the Syndham College at Bombay, he left Baroda and moved on to that metropolis.

In 1920, Ambedkar went to England. Next year he obtained M.Sc. and a diploma in Law. In 1922, he was called to the bar. In 1923, he was awarded D.Sc. for his thesis 'Problems of Rupee'. It was published and widely acclaimed. After a brief stay at the University of Bonn, he returned to India and started legal practice at Bombay. Even in the professional practice at the bar, his being a Schedule Caste affected his career. He was well versed in law but his combative manner proved that he was a better jurist than lawyer and he proved a better politician than a lawyer. Oppressed by untouchability and engrossed in finding a way to end the suffering of the untouchables, he started making them politically conscious of their status. In 1924, he founded a Society for the Welfare of Outcastes. Three years later he was nominated, by the Government, a Member of the Bombay Legislative Assembly as a representative of the untouchables. He was now a public figure. Also, he joined the Government Law College, Bombay as a Professor.

In 1930, Bhimrao Ambedkar was invited to the Round Table Conference (RTC) as a representative of depressed classes. This was a milestone in the social-economic struggle of untouchables for better life. They had so far never been consulted in making the future of India. Ambedkar used this vantage point to question Gandhi's claim to represent all Hindus, including untouchables who constituted a sizeable per centage of the population. Ambedkar as the political representative of Schedule Castes asked for safeguards for the six crore untouchables and other underprivileged castes through separate electorates. However, he did not lose sight of larger national goal and saved the nation from further fragmentation. He did not press for independent reservations and accepted reservation within the general joint electorates.Thanks to Madan Mohan Malviya for passing a resolution that "henceforth, among Hindus no one shall be regarded as an untouchable for reason of his birth, and those who have been regarded hitherto will have the same right as other Hindus in regard to the use of public wells, public schools, public roads and all other public institutions. The right should have statutory recognition and shall be one of the earliest Acts of the Swaraj Parliament. It shall be the duty of all Hindu leaders to secure an early removal of all social disabilities (imposed on untouchables) and their admission to temples." This helped Ambedkar to change his stand.

This modification formed part of the recommendations of the Round Table Conference, after it was accepted by the British Government. To serve as a constant reminder of the pledge. and to propagate uplifting of Harijans, Mahatma Gandhi started publication of a journal '*Harijan*'. At the background of RTC was British Government's effort to weaken the Hindus by separating SCs/STs from the Savarnas (i.e. high castes).

After RTC, it was found the award of Prime Minister Ramsay McDonald was patently communal. It treated untouchables politically separate from Hindus and recognized the right of Depressed Classes to reserved seats. This was the biggest threat to India's unity. Gandhiji realized this in Pune jail and on September 20,1932, he went on an indefinite fast (unto death) against it and it stung the conscience of high caste Hindus and produced in them a wave of enthusiasm to rectify the situation. Ambedkar was persuaded to meet Gandhi and the two -Gandhi and Ambedkar-made a pact, known as Poona Pact, on September 24 which eliminated separate electorate and provided for larger representation for Harijans through reserved seats.(The role of Malviyaji has been mentioned in above para.) But Hindus and Muslims failed to reach a settlement. This was the result of the Second Conference. After the Third Round Table Conference, in which Congress did not participate, a joint committee prepared a report. On the lines of this Report, the Government introduced India Bill in July 1935 which became the Govt. of India Act, 1935.The Act offered the S.Cs. hardly anything worth while. Ambedkar was so bitter that in 1935, he announced his intention to convert the Depressed Classes to some other religion.( Missionaries and Maulanas are trying to convert them whereever possible.)

In 1939, when the British and India Governments declared Second World War, Congress opposed India's joining the Allies in the War. On this, Ambedkar again opposed the Congress claim to speak for the country's depressed classes. The political views of Ambedkar and Jinnah were alike. In 1940 Ambedkar expressed his views on Pakistan in his book *Thoughts on Pakistan* which was not against the formation of Pakistan. In 1942, he founded the People's Education Society with the object to uplift the Depressed. The same year he was invited by Viceroy to join the Viceroy's Executive Council as Labor Member. In 1946, Ambedkar was made a Member of the Constituent Assembly. His in- depth knowledge of constitutional law marked Ambedkar as one of the principal architects of India's Constitution. He combined in his person a sense of poetic justice and natural aptitude. The British authorities appointed him as the first Law Minister of the Government of India.He continued as Law Minister in Nehru's Cabinet for sometime.

Ambedkar presented free India's Draft Constitution in the Constituent Assembly in November 1948. He was also closely connected with the drafting of the Hindu Code Bill. In 1951, he resigned from Nehru's Cabinet and dissociated himself from the Congress Party. In the last days of his life, he was ill which hampered his normal activities. His bitterness towards Caste Hindus oppressed him.He felt persecuted by his own co-religionists which made him anti-Savarnas He wondered whether being a Shudra was really synonymous with being an undesirably different kind of person so despicable that people wanted to avoid him. Disgusted, with thousands of S.C.s, he embraced Buddhism.

Bhimrao Ambedkar married Ramabai, daughter of a Railway porter. They had four sons and one daughter. On her death, he married a Saraswat Brahmin lady, Dr. Sharda in 1948. He had no child from this marriage.

On the night of 5-6 December, 1956, Bhimrao Ambedkar passed away in sleep at Delhi.

Besides being a Constitution expert, Ambedkar was also a social reformer. He sacrificed his casteist interests for broader national interests. Through constitutional provisions, he tried to make up for the injustice from which the people from scheduled and depressed castes suffered. He drafted, with other committee members, the Constitution of India to promote democratic changes in the country. The Constitution has certainly proved a tool of subtle change, though slow. None can deny that the caste system continues to retard human dignity and the reality of casteism has not changed. Members of a caste work in their hereditary profession, they marry in and eat with their own caste groups and look up or down the other castes. In North India, where Tulasidass's *Ramacharitamanas* has a social sway, the poet's reproach that 'an insult to one's caste is the worst insult'or that 'a Shudra, rustic,cattle and woman deserve reprimand' is literally followed,.intimate contacts like marital relations with other castes are not acceptable as it is thought that a man's or woman's birth in a caste is the result of divine persuasion, and only good conduct might lead to the individual's rebirth in a higher caste, which means abiding by the precepts of the faith. Finally, it means no change. Even the Holy *Bhagvatgita* supports the Varna Vyavastha.

The food habits of Hindus have got of late mildly relaxed. Only some Savarnas in cities don't mind eating food cooked by other castes, while in past they did not eat; the schedule castes could not draw water from wells in use by upper castes nor could they live in an upper caste locality. These conditions are somewhat relaxed. Similarly , earlier only caste Hindus could worship in temples. In South India a SC member had to be cautious that his shadow should not fall on a Brahmin. In some places, only upper castes could twirl their moustaches upwards, and lower caste women had to keep their breasts bare. Exploitation of lower castes by upper castes was a normal practice. They had to tolerate oppression.Times are changing and demand giving up orthodox practices and being more liberal.

What happened to the followers of those great men who opposed caste system in the past? Buddha, Mahavira and Nanak had exposed discriminatory practices of Hinduism; and had also evolved new philosophies and religions - Buddhism, Jain,and Sikh. They had great many followers abroad also. Buddhism moved out to Central Asia, China, South East and Far East Asia. Lately, Dayananda and Vivekananda raised their voices against orthodoxy. Casteism had side effects. It is strange that the Portuguese Church in Goa took the Brahmin way. They had separate doors for Brahmin Christians and lower caste converts. Raja Ram Mohan Roy's Bramho Samaj, Narayana Guru's saintly life and Gandhi's crusade against caste system have not succeeded in eradicating caste barriers.. City life (travel by bus and eating in restaurant) have mellowed down the rigidity. It is good that the stigma of caste is disappearing, never mind at a slow pace.

Several social horror stories originate from the pernicious caste system. Reported in Press, dismal accounts hurt people. A Dalit woman was stripped and paraded naked in her village; a peasant girl and an untouchable boy and his friend intending to elope were burnt alive. A few hundred Dalit families suffered as they demanded higher wages. Such cases are not rare. The bright side is that prospects for change appear on the way; the gloomier side is that they take society to ransom and protect criminals. This reflects that the link between caste and occupation is disappearing, that politics is affecting the caste system, and that the affirmative action initiated by Dr. Ambedkar is moving ahead.

In independent India, there are signs that people are determined to undo the injustice to socially backward classes - Scheduled Castes and Schedule Tribes who were guaranteed some favor out of the way like admissions to schools and colleges even when their performance did not justify. A certain percentage of jobs (22.5%) was reserved and 85 Parliament seats were set aside for them so as to ensure their adequate representation.

The recommendations for reservations (besides SCs/STs) for OBCs by the Mandal Commission were not taken kindly by caste Hindus : The upper caste opposition was against the assurance given by Malviyaji before the Poona Pact. The OBCs form 24% of Indian population - they are the thrusting lower middle castes whose claim to reservations was proposed and supported by the Mandal Commission in 1980, and their recommendations after acceptance by the Government were implemented by VP Singh Government in 1990. These affect a state policy which is beneficial to Backward castes. Benefiting from these provisions, Mayawati of the Bahujan Samaj Party (BSP) became the Chief Minister of UP. H.D. Devegowda, from a backward caste, became the Prime Minister of India, and Uma Bharati became the Chief Minister of Madhya Pradesh. The Dalits and Backwards need to throw up good, competent and selfless leadership to compete with others.

It also needs to be noted that despite the constitutional protection, there are inequalities and there are no signs that these will disappear in the near future. Affirmative action has benefited a minority of the suffering people- sons and daughters of the underprivileged have come up on the strength of their caste affiliations. But this needs to have a limit. The Supreme Court expressed its disquiet at the benefits bagged by the creamy layers at the top of the bottom ranks of society. To call the top of them as Shudras, which they want to continue doing, for monetary gains, is not appropriate.

The increasing importance of castes in elections is augmenting mobilization of votes. Candidates are picked up for caste loyalties. VP Singh said, "Try to see what people within all parties are (and) you will find a deep change has taken place." The lower castes have acquired higher political status, in Bihar and UP, and Upper Caste Hindus are subordinates and supplicants to them. Some people think that globalisation will undo the caste difference and benefit the menials; it will be good if it does.

An assessment of Ambedkar's personality is not easy or simple. Nehru once said that Ambedkar's life was a protest against Hindu conservatism and orthodoxy. It was a symbol of revolt against oppressive features of Hindu religion. Arisen from the poor background, there is no dearth of such characters; he stood up with the education he had earned against great men - Caste Hindus - like Gandhiji and Madan Mohan Malviya- and made them to realize the gross injustice the Shudras suffer at the hands of Hindu obscurants, mainly the Dwijas. Look at the situation closely, it was the Brahmins alone who were accused of perpetrating injustice on Depressed and SCs. For the first time the Vaishyas, because of Gandhiji, also came to be held responsible. Of course, the Kshatriyas were perhaps more to be blamed for the condition of the Shudras for malpractices, like Begar. Ambedkar was not swayed by the professions made in the scriptures, particularly the Mahakavyas, Ramayana and Mahabharata, which are full of stories of atrocities against low castes by heroes so that they could be projected bigger than life size.

Many people were angry with Ambedkar, rightly so, for his statements in the Round Table Conferences against the saintly person of Gandhiji. But on going through some of his works published by the Maharashtra government, the readers realize the reality of the depressed against their tormentors, most of whom are unwilling even now to change their behavior. Through numerical strength, the SCs are trying to assert their rights but their voice is suppressed, even stifled. When VP Singh was Prime minister, the entrenched classes did not like giving them even a small slice of employment. And, no less to be blamed is the leadership of SCs and depressed who squander state funds on wasteful things like putting up statues of their leaders. It is also alleged that they pass on some of the money received as collection to their children or relatives in the name of party funds. However, nothing justifies using foul words against Gandhi and other caste leaders. The authors were shocked to learn that it was one of the so called high caste journalist who in a T.V. program called Gandhiji a 'bastard bania'. How could one stoop so low to utter such foul words for a saintly person like Gandhi?

The fundamentals of castes in India possess three qualities: membership by birth, marriage within the goup and social hierarchies. Caste has an elaborate theory of ritual purity and pollution.

According to the Current Biology (Vol 9, december 1999 R999) genetic researches, archeological and DNA evidence link India's 80% population with two pre-historic movements. First, genetic resources: about 50000 years ago there was an outward movement from Ethiopia and Africa's Horn. Most of the rest of India's genetic variation stems from a second ancestral group of West Asian descent. Their genes entered the Indian population roughly 9000 years ago.

**Annexure :**
What is caste? Caste has been variously defined as

(1) "a close corporation in theory at any rate rigorously

hereditary: equipped with a certain traditional and independent organization, including a Chief and a Council, meeting on occasion in assemblies of more or less plenary authority and joining together at certain festivals; bound together by common occupations which rebate more particularly to marriage and to food and to questions of commercial pollution, and ruling its members by exercise of jurisdiction the extent to which varies but which succeeds in making the authority of the community more felt by the sanction of certain penalties, and above all by final irrevocable exclusion from the group."- Senalb, French authority.

(2) "a class of community which disowns any connection with any other class and can neither intermarry nor eat nor drink with any but persons of their own communities". - Nesfield

(3) "as a collection of families or group of families bearing a common name which usually denotes or is associated with specific occupation, claiming common descent for a mythical ancestor, human or divine, professing to follow the same professional callings and are regarded by them who are competent to give an opinion as forming a single homogenous community."- Sir H. Risley

(4) A social group having two characteristics : membership is confined to those who are born of members and include all persons so born; the members are forbidden by an inexorable social law to marry outside the group. Dr. Kelkar.

Ambedkar thinks that the people of India form a homogenous group and endogamy is the essence of caste system. (Endogamy is prohibition of intermarriage. Marriage among Sapindas i.e. blood - kin or sagotras i.e. of the same class is sacrilegious Superposition of endogamy on exogamy creates a caste. This results into an equal number of members of sex - men and women. Though this is not possible, this can be possibly achieved in two ways: (i) Burning surplus woman on the funeral pyre of her deceased husband. No doubt there are widows, but they cannot be burnt. It is impractical. And (ii) Enforcing widowhood on her for full life, or man may be forced to remain widower throughout his life for an ascetic celibate is as good as burnt.

Caste and class are the same. A caste is an enclosed class.

The Brahmins (the priestly class) arrogated to themselves certain customs and social superiority and from them originated the unnatural institutions like caste system. The docile people took this as divine dispensation. Thus grew the caste system. Manu gave the humanity the law. Ambedkar says caste system existed even before Manu who was an upholder of caste system.

The Westerners think that castes originated for occupation, survival of tribal organization, rise of new belief, cross breeding, migration.

At the outset there were four classes - Brahmin, Kshatrya, Vaishya (merchant), and Shudra (artisan and musicians). Some closed the doors, others found it closed.Persistent efforts are being made to do away with this unnatural institution. Such attempts at reform have aroused a great deal of controversy regarding its origin.In Twentieth Century Jat -Pat Todak Mandal made efforts in this direction but it hardly made a dent.

Is caste a religion? No. It has nothing to do with religion. Varna and Ashram are not castes. Varna teaches that every one has to earn his bread. The object of caste system has been to preserve purity of race and blood. This biological defense has proved unsuccessful in the face of stronger sex urge in man. In the shrinking world of scientific developments, the division of society on ground of purity will not stand.

India is a democracy and Indians should feel proud of their country being multiracial, multi-religious and multilingual.. The British rulers succeeded in their policy of divide and rule. Muslims asked for Pakistan and they gave it. The leaders of Depressed Classes and of Sikhs asked for Achhutistan and Khalistan, respectively, but their leaders proved wiser and their patience is paying. Which other country in the world can say it has a Muslim President, a Sikh Prime Minister, a Christian heading a political party with the majority of seats in the Parliament. And, it should not be forgotten that it was Ambedkar who refused to fall in line (or for bait) for Achhutistan. Democracy provides opportunities to every single individual, it is for him to avail?" Can a satisfactory balance be found between tradition and modern world?

# 6
# JAYA PRAKASH NARAYAN
(1905 - 1979)

Not all politicians are manipulative by nature. The simple souls amongst them who serve humanity selflessly donot hanker for power or office. Jaya Prakash Narayan was one such person. On return after his education in USA, he devoted himself to the cause of freedom of his country. After Independence, he was thought of as number two, next to Nehru, cut for P.M.'s office. But he turned into a Gandhiite and renounced politics. Next time when an opportunity came his way after Indira Gandhi's downfall, he dissipated it by selecting some one else - one who proved an utter failure. Anyway, what distinguished J.P. was his sacrificing nature, a rare quality among politicians.

Jaya Prakash Narayan, or JP as he was popularly known, was a gentleman politician. In his dealings with humankind, he adhered to ethical norms. From his very school days, he set freedom of the motherland as the goal of his life, and when in 1947, the British left India after partitioning the country and effecting the 'transfer of power' in Indian hands, Jaya Prakash Narayan said 'transfer' was not independence from imperial hold. Whereas to Congress leaders, including Jawahar Lal Nehru and Sardar Patel, the bait appeared worth acceptance, Jaya Prakash was not willing to consider the offer anywhere near 'Towards Freedom,' as Indian historians would define it.

J.P. was tired of the trickery, the British power had been playing by creating divisions in India's pluralist society. Successive steps like the division of Bengal during the very year JP was born, manipulating the Muslim League to create discord in the unity of people of India, Jalianwalla Bagh and other tragedies, followed by RTCs (Round Table Conferences) had shattered people's faith in the hollow promises of the British. J.P's incarceration in 1940s was his personal experience, and not a hearsay of British brutality. The struggle should continue was his natural reaction, which would cost him, he knew, dearly soon - interrogation by Intelligence in the Lahore Jail (1943-46). When the British intellectual Harold Laski asked J.P. whether he was tortured in the jail, he did not flinch from confirming it that torture was inflicted by the British rulers. Later, even in independent India, the treatment meted out to him by the indigenous version of authorities during detention in Sohna (in Haryana) and at Chandigarh was not less reprehensible. Should such a thing be allowed to transpire in democracy? This remark invited sarcasm from the authorities who called JP's theories like that of Total Revolution as bizarre and said it was responsible for anarchy in Bihar. There are people who blame J.P. for the anarchy in Bihar during the past two decades and even at present. How were the youth inspired to improve the lot of their compatriots and how did they learn the lessons of patriotism ?

Jaya Prakash Narayan's life is a saga of courage and it evokes an empathy amongst the youth. JP was born in an ordinary middle class family on October 11, 1905 at Sitabdiary, a village at the confluence of Ganga and Ghaggar, in the interior of Bihar. Once floods unsettled even the location of the village; shifting it from Bihar to the Balia District in UP. His father Harsu Dayal was a revenue official in the canal department and mother a religious minded lady given to rituals. Narayan was the eldest child in the family. He had two sisters and one brother. Family members called him 'Boul', meaning 'simple'. A studious child, he made a mark in his school. He won an award for his Hindi essay on 'The Present State Of Hindi in Bihar.' At the age of 11, he went to Patna to join the Patna College School and stayed in a hostel. He learned about Gandhiji's *Satyagraha, Asahayoga* and *Ahimsa*, which the leader was applying to gain the freedom of the country from the British tyranny. The arrest of an 11-year old hostel-mate of his for revolutionary activities left a mark on J.P.'s mind. Soon, he also suffered punishment by his disciplinarian English principal for boycotting classes on Raksha Bandhan (Sister's Day), which had been so far a holiday but suddenly declared a working day. In the hostel, he came to know about Bihar's patriots, like Rajendra Prasad and Braj Kishore. One day he met Braj Kishore who was so impressed by JP that he married his daughter Prabhavati with Jaya Prakash. This relationship would influence J.P.'s personal and political life..(Those days child marriage was in vogue.)

Narayan passed his matriculation creditably and was awarded a scholarship of Rs. 15 p.m., which was by the standard of that time a good amount. He joined Intermediate course in the Patna College. One day, he listened to a speech of Maulana Azad who asked students aged 15 years or more to leave their studies in institutions funded/aided by the government. Majority of outstanding students of the Patna College, including JP, were so much influenced that they decided to leave the College. But before doing so, JP sought for his father's advice. The father bid him to appear at the Intermediate Examination from the Bihar Vidyapeeth, a private body. He fared very well in the examination but did not seek admission in B.A./B.Sc. He declined to join the Government-aided Benares Hindu University. Nor was he willing to go to England for higher education. His parents and in-laws gave him $600 to go to USA. As J.P.left for USA, Braj Kishore Babu sent Prabhavati to the Gandhi Ashram.

Jaya Prakash Narayan left for USA in a boat for Japan. Being a vegetarian, he found life difficult on boat . From Yokohoma (Japan) he left by a liner for San Francisco. He was impressed by the Japanese cleanliness and efficiency. In the ship, he took up small jobs, such as proof reading, to earn some money.

One of Jaya Prakash's class fellows was studying at Berkley (in California). So, after landing at San Francisco, he proceeded on October 8,1922, to Berkley hoping to work in a restaurant or elsewhere to earn money to meet expenses on his studies. He joined the Nalanda Club, an inexpensive hostel. He worked hard and secured 'A' grade in all subjects. But as he had failed to get job regularly, he had failed to pay the fees that were increased mid term, and also as he fell short of attendance which his professor refused to condone, he had to leave Berkley. He learnt of the possibility of earning and learning in Iowa State University and left for Iowa. But in Iowa too, he faced the same difficulty. He fell short of attendance in German which he had taken as an optional subject,and though he secured 'A' in it, he could not be declared successful. JP never forgot this irrationality of conventional education. He was depressed and moved on to Chicago and joined the University of Wisconsin at Madison. He found a job and stayed with a West Indian family. Unfortunately, he fell ill and was unable to stir out for six months which loaded him with a deficit of $900. He had to ask home for money. In Wisconsin, he found even highly placed persons indulged in corruption. Its reputation for a clean government suffered in his eyes.

J.P. left the place with a friend and joined the University in Columbus. There he studied for BA and then for MA with special studies in Marxism. His thesis on 'Social Variation'was declared the best essay of the year. J.P.'s teacher, Prof. Edward Ross was happy with his progress and gave him excellent testimonials. He was to take up a job but misfortunes never come alone. He received a cable about his mother's serious condition. He at once left for India via London. doing odd jobs, on November 23, 1929, JP reached home. At mother's instance, to please her, he performed a *puja*. He had researched on Marxism but now he learned to see things from a detached mind and distanced himself from Marxism and power politics. In fact, modesty had got ingrained in him and he left arrogance for good. To him, now freedom meant freedom from hunger, poverty, and ignorance.

Gandhiji's effort  was to make the country self- reliant, honest and disciplined; grabbing power was not his goal because he was convinced that once Indians were ready to rule themselves, freedom would automatically follow. Jaya Prakash's view tallied with Gandhi's reformist, constitutional approach. He differed from Subhash Chandra Bose and Nehru who were in favor of quick freedom. JP believed in encouraging grassroot organizations and their democratic functioning . Gandhiji apprehended that possession of state power without the counter balance of grassroot democracy would not help improve the plight of the average underprivileged Indians. It would only promote unscrupulousness among dominant groups so as to get positions of power. Gandhiji was right. (We are witnessing his apprehensions come true.)

After meeting his parents and relatives, JP proceeded to Wardha to meet Prabhavati in the Gandhi  Ashram. She had accepted Gandhi's views on celibacy as also on women's role in the social-economic progress. For JP, celibacy had a different meaning. Yet, JP and Prabhavati had many things in common. Also, JP was drawn to Gandhiji. In December,1929, the couple traveled to Lahore where the Congress pledged for the first time for full independence.

In certain matters JP and Nehru had identical views. Nehru took a liking for JP. (JP addressed Nehru as Bhai i.e, Brother). When on April 6, 1930, Gandhiji launched a country-wide Civil Disobedience movement, all of J.P.'s doubts and disenchantment about non-violence disappeared. With Gandhi's permission, he went to visit his mother who was seriously ill. But by the time he reached home, she had passed away. Soon his father was also gone. To add to his worries was his joblessness. On Ganndhiji's advice, J.P. got an appointment to work as Birla's private secretary. But JP did not like the job. Jawahar Lal then asked JP to write the History of Civil Disobedience.

Civil disobedience had created uneasiness for the government and the Governor General invited Gandhiji for talks. For an appreciation of the demands of various political parties, a Round Table Conference was organized in London. But nothing emerged and Gandhiji returned to India. To receive Gandhiji, Jawaharlal Nehru went to Bombay but the moment he landed there, he was arrested. In Nehru's absence, JP acted as the General Secretary of Congress. But on September 7, 1932, he also was arrested and sent to the Nasik Jail.

Congress was that time composed of several parties and there was no consistency in its ideology. Communists pulled out of Congress when the Communist International under Stalin denounced Gandhi. JP's confidence in Moscow and CPI was shaken; yet he remained a Marxist. Obviously, the loyalty of the communists was to Russia and their united front was a ruse. After his release from Nasik in January 1934, JP organized a relief mission in Bihar which was devastated by an earthquake on January 15, 1934. JP did not like the slow pace of work of the Congress which was largely supported by lawyers, landlords and industrialists who were interested in electoral and legislative activities and in taking over privileges enjoyed by colonial masters. The Socialists formed a

Congress Socialist Party (CSP) with JP as its secretary. The group's policy was to organize peasant and labor unions and help them develop in a mass movement.

As against CSP, neither the Communists nor the Congress wanted to disturb the status quo of social justice and economic immobility that shackled Indian society. Whereas during Civil Disobedience, peasants had lost everything and their families suffered, the rich paid the fines imposed on them and saved their property. The CSP finally broke with the Communists whose goal was monolithic communist rule and who would not share power, except with convenient allies.

JP analyzed the situation. Britain would not loose its grip on India. No doubt war looked imminent but that would be between rival forms of imperialism. Despite his sympathies with Russia, an ally of Britain, JP saw no reason to relax the struggle against foreign rule over India. None-the-less Nehru was sympathetic to Britain in its hour of agony and wanted India to participate in war against Hitler. Azad was less emotional and would not mind to extend cooperation to British authorities as a bargaining point. Rajaji wanted a slow and phased transfer of power with minimal repercussions on Indian society. He pressurized the All India Congress Committee (AICC) to cooperate in the war in return for installing a national government with statutory power without any say in the conduct of war. To J.P., Rajaji's views appeared against the interests of the Congress as also against the country's interests. The demand for India's independence and drawing of a constitution by a Constituent Assembly elected on the basis of full adult franchise came up in the Tripuri Congress. But the Congress leadership retraced in favor of transfer of power. To JP, the attitude of the Congress looked reprehensible. He wanted the matter to be discussed in the Ramgarh Congress but two days before the Congress session, JP was arrested allegedly for making a seditious statement. Gandhi criticized the arrest as a provocative action of government and warned the Viceroy about its consequences.

Sometime earlier, Britain had declared war against Germany. The Viceroy declared that India too had joined the war. Gandhiji opposed the government's action. JP wrote to Nehru that Rajaji had stabbed in the back. The Congress ministers in provinces resigned in protest. M.A Jinnah and the Muslim League grabbed the opportunity. Gandhiji planned Civil Disobedience and asked Vinoba Bhave to be the first volunteer, relegating Nehru to be the second volunteer in the CD agitation as he did not like his stand.

Towards the year's end, JP had completed his sentence and was released but as he came out of jail, he was arrested under Defense of India Rules. He was sent to Deoli, 80 miles from Ajmer. Finding condition in Deoli Jail horrible, JP went on hunger strike. After 30 days, the government accepted J.P's demand for closing the Deoli Jail. Nehru and moderate leaders were released but JP continued to languish in the jail. Nehru did not like Gandhi's non-violent fight against Germany, nor did he like Subhash's cooperation with Japan and playing a second fiddle to Japan. President Roosevelt pressurized Churchill to reach an agreement with the Congress. But Churchill did nothing more than sending Stafford Cripps to India. As Gandhi placed freedom first, the Mission failed. JP and Ram Manohar Lohia escaped from Hazari Bagh Jail to Nepal. The Government tried to arrest them but the police failed. When J.P. tried to revive the Quit India movement, some one informed the police and he was arrested on September 19, 1943 at Mughalpura, near Lahore, while he was proceeding from Amritsar to Rawalpindi. The police took him to Lahore Jail where he was tortured but JP refused to reply to any question relating to the underground activities. He was kept in prison and would be released from the Agra Jail on April 11,1946 after the Cabinet Mission's arrival in India.

The Mission agreed to set up a Constituent Assembly. The Muslim League was determined on creation of Pakistan. and took to direct action which in its wake brought Calcutta killings—communal massacre. The Cabinet Plan was placed before AICC at Bombay. JP opposed negotiation with the League and predicted that Partition would not be a correct solution because the root cause of communal trouble was economic and political rather than religious. Moreover, the Congress was not fully representative of the population. Only 15% population elected members indirectly, which meant there was need of strengthening the organization. "When we are sure of our strength we can compel them to quit India". JP regretted that Congress was being converted into a parliamentary party without any constructive program. Its present policy was 'compromise and constitutionalism'. Congress and League were becoming successors to the British who were playing role of mediator. The League held all cards because it could withhold negotiation on one or other plea. Earlier, when the League had walked out of Constituent Assembly, JP said Congress was not capable of drafting Constitution of India, and it would be better to call another Assembly of elected people who could consider the matter.

According to J.P, negotiations with Cripps and Cabinet Mission were the greatest national upheavals since 1857, caused by outside pressure and world situation. He did not see any goodwill of the British in negotiations. He had justified the Quit India movement and considered Congress's constitutional and parliamentary approach as wrong. He asserted that unless Congress was prepared to launch another struggle, they would not get real independence. The bulk of Congress did not like JP's advice. Now that power appeared within grasp, some of the intelligentsia were bold to say that leaders were tired and hungry for power and prestige of office. The negotiations with Missions had shown that the leaders could be persuaded to compromise on basic issues, especially when Gandhi was out. The Muslim League adopted intransigence as their last strategy to push the Congress to accept the Mission Plan of Partition. The League pulled out of the Plan and threatened direct action.

JP advised the Socialist Party to adhere steadfastly to revolution. He saw no conflict between democracy and revolution. In the AICC meeting, JP and Lohia had repeatedly clashed with Nehru and Patel. Gandhi advised the Socialists not to launch any agitation or protest and added that unity was the need of the hour. The result was the Socialists abstained from voting. The Mountbatten Plan was approved by 153 to 29, with 36 abstentions:

As for communal riots, JP held that these were the results of a conspiracy between the Muslim League and the British government and that the Congress had fallen in the trap of negotiations instead of conducting mass agitation. JP said, "Every Englishman was a Leaguee". About Punjab riots, he said, "the disturbances were carefully planned and were part of the conspiracy to install the Muslim League in office as a step towards the final installation of Pakistan." The conspirators included the

Governor and his colleagues. It could not be accidental that riots had broken out only in the districts that were ruled by the British officers.

Attlee gave the final signal for creation of Pakistan on February 20, 1947 when he announced his govt.'s decision to transfer power to two dominions - India ruled by Congress and Pakistan by Muslim League. To push the idea, Lord Mountbatten was appointed the Viceroy of India. For League, any constitutional change meant a step towards the creation of Pakistan and its trump card to achieve it was direct action and communal riots. Hindu Mahasabha was not interested in creating a secular India. Nehru's reformative steam would result in barren negotiations. Gandhi's advice was not acceptable to Congress leaders. Nor was JP's extra constitutional pressure acceptable to the Congress. To some J.P. symbolized the spirit of uncompromising resistance to foreign rule. He was opposed to constitutional and communal hurdles that came in the path of freedom. Long solitary confinements had detached him from routine human desires and ambitions. Some thought authorities had released leaders because of their genuine interest in handing over power to Indians.

An impression was created that rhe reins of government were to be handed over to Indians by the British within a set constitutional framework. This ignored the need of change in style and values in administration from colonial rule to democracy. JP was not in favor of accepting such independence

Gandhi and the Socialists did not join Independence Day celebrations. Congress explained that riots had occurred because they could not get time to reorganize colonial system of administration inherited from the British. But the fault lay with the Congress in that they adopted the style and values of the British system. The new rulers moved into big houses vacated by senior British officials. Nehru himself set the pace. He entered the C.-in-.C. House. The repercussions of this are seen even today amongst politicians and MPs and senior officers who vie with each other and the stronger ones manipulate to get whatever they want. Some manage to secure in irregular manner places for cremation and burial, for memorial houses and some even name streets, hospitals and public places after the leaders who did not deserve such a consideration.

Gandhiji had tendered a very sagacious advice that Congress convert itself into a social service organization. It was ignored and its repercussions are being experienced now. The Congress has become a source of power and political advancement. Vested interests have grown and are growing within it with corruption and jobbery in tow. Party elections, beginning with enrollment of members, have become a racket for the self seeking. Power politics is rampant. This condition prevails not only in the Congress but in other parties also. Gandhiji had wanted JP to take over as President of the Congress when Kripalani resigned because members of the new government did not consult him. But Sardar Patel 'flatly refused' to have JP as president. Finally, Rajendra Prasad was made president.

ii

Some important events in J.P.'s life after 1947 are briefly mentioned here.

January 29, 1948: JP told Gandhiji how difficult it was to work in the Congress. The very next day, on January 30 Gandhiji was assassinated. JP blamed government of callousness in protecting Gandhiji and added that it would be proper for the Home Minister to resign. Patel did not like the advice. J.P. was antagonized.

1949:Some Socialists were of the view that Nehru had made use of JP and Socialists, only to counterbalance the group headed by Patel. Although Lohia had been critical of JP, the latter did not like any harm done to Lohia. When in May 1949, Lohia was arrested for demonstrating in front of the Nepal Embassy in New Delhi, JP sarcastically said, "There are more restrictions on the liberties of the citizen in free India today under the Congress rule than there were under the worst British despot."

Nehru met JP, Kripalani and Narendra Dev to explore the possibility of their joining the India Government. JP invited Nehru's attention to the welfare aspect of citizen's life and said there was a need that India present a good picture because if India failed, the appeal of China would be irresistible which may change the course of history. JP sent a 14-point program to Nehru. Nothing happenrd

1957: JP gave up basic membership of the Party to form

another party. JP was getting disenchanted with party politics and after the Pachmarhi conference, he joined Vinoba's Bhoodan movement and set up an ashram in a village near Gaya.

JP was critical of Nehru government's double standards in respect of peace and communists. Nehru had closed his eyes to the repression in Hungary. Similarly, and perhaps more ominously, from the point of India's interests was to let China grab Tibet. JP frankly stated that we were not serving the cause of peace by closing our eyes over aggression.

1965: JP favored maintaining good relations with Pakistan. He set up an India-Pakistan conciliation group and took a goodwill mission to Pakistan and met President Ayub Khan. But the initiative was lost after Pakistan invaded India in 1965.

1968: A noteworthy effort of JP was to bring peace in Nagaland. He helped to set off confrontations that were disturbing peace. He also tried to end the problem of Naxalism and its violence. Similarly, in Kashmir he made efforts to eschew communal passions. He addressed a convention in Srinagar at which Sheikh Abdullah was present. JP advised that Pakistan's war on India in 1965 had changed the situation. No India Government would accept a solution of Kashmir that kept the state out of India. He chastised the participants in the Second Annual Convention against communalism and that their parties professed faith in secularism but had done nothing to educate people and to the contrary had adopted a policy of accommodation of communal parties to share the political power. Thus, they had spread communalism.

JP was awarded the Magsasay Prize for his outstanding services to people.

1971: JP took deep interest in solving the problem of dacoits (armed bandits) in the Chambal ravines which had been their base and hideout for generations. A small group of dacoits surrendered to Vinoba Bhabe in 1960 but there was no follow up. In 1971 Madho Singh, a notorious dacoit approached JP, identified himself and expressed his resolve to surrender but in a way that dacoits did not lose face and also would not face death sentence. JP agreed to contact the governments of MP, UP, and Rajasthan. The State governments responded favorably and JP went into the heart of dacoit land for their surrender. JP persuaded the dacoits to surrender their arms and report their crimes. In a touching gesture, Madho Singh touched Prabhavati's feet, while she put a *tilak* on his forehead. The outlaws surrendered their arms and ammunition before a statue of Gandhiji. More than 400 wanted dacoits followed the example in the next few days A declaration was made by dacoits: "We the inhabitants of the Chambal Valley whose activities have brought much suffering to people surrender ourselves today in the service of the society. With Vinoba Bhave's and Babu Jaya Prakash Narayan's blessings, we start from today a new life. We have committed many mistakes and misdeeds for which our hearts are full of genuine remorse. We ask (for) forgiveness from all those who suffered on account of us and pray God to grant (us)moral strength to walk on a path of righteousness and may He make us worthy members of the society in this life".The authors learned that the surrender of the dacoits could be possible with the significant aid to JP in this noble cause by Mr. Jagannath Prasad Gupta, Senior Advocate, Gwalior who kept himself in the background.

JP Narayan set an example that moral persuasion can have far reaching effects. (One critic opined that it could not be denied that the Police had made dacoits' lives so uncomfortable that they thought it better to surrender)

Students in Bihar sought solution to their grievances but the government ignored their request. Their agitation took violent form. A Students Action Committee sought for JP's help and guidance to solve the problem. JP agreed to lead mass movement. He wanted people to go back to Mahatma Gandhi's days: (i) to bring about total revolution based on people's welfare (Sarvodaya), and federal village republics as centers of the country's political and economic life, and (ii) to establish a party-less democracy .When he found people's protests about price rise of commodities had no effect on the government, he joined the agitation and became a rallying point. JP added, "If the problems of people cannot be solved democratically,"I will take to violence."(This angered Indira Gandhi.)

1974: In May 1974 the Socialist Trade Union leader George Fernandez organized a country-wide railway strike. More than two hundred thousand workers were arrested and their families were thrown out from railway quarters, causing them suffering. She tried to crush the strike. The JP movement was temporarily forgotten for the reason that a landmark event of great importance occurred. Indian scientists detonated an underground nuclear device at Pokhran in Rajasthan. Indira Gandhi met criticism by saying that the nuclear experiment was peaceful.. She was given credit for that development. In spite of this, her government misused MISA (Maintenance of Internal Security Act) against her opponents, though the Act was meant for use against smugglers.

Indira Gandhi taunted JP for alliance with RSS. JP replied that if RSS was communal, then he did not mind being called communal, and added that he wanted to usher 'total revolution' which had a good purpose. Some people criticized that total revolution would lead to anarchy and did not like such undignified confrontation. They arranged a meeting of Indira Gandhi and JP. The two met in November 1974 at PM House. Unfortunately the meeting proved a disaster. There were sharp and acrimonious exchanges. She said JP movement was being funded by wealthy people under American influence. JP retorted that Mrs. Gandhi was leading India towards Soviet-backed dictatorship. JP then in private handed her a bundle of papers wrapped in a folder. This contained letters written by Kamala Nehru (Indira's mother) to Prabhavati. The meeting did not arrest the descent of their confrontation. JP accused her of murder of democracy.

Indira Gandhi, in a letter to one of her friends in US, described JP a frustrated man. Inder Malhotra, in his biography of Indira Gandhi, commenting on a similar situation says that JP was "sometime a naïve – as for instance, in welcoming and commending to his countrymen the 'basic democracy' of Pakistan's Field Marshal Ayub."

When Mohan Dharia, a Minister, condemned police brutality on agitators, Indira Gandhi asked for his resignation which he submitted. JP led a protest march on Parliament.

1975: The Nehruites considered Party-less democracy and total revolution as self contradictory. On June 25, the President of India declared a national Emergency. JP was arrested along with most of the political leaders. There was severe criticism of Indira Government. The Emergency lasted two years and was withdrawn and General Elections were announced.

J.P. invited political parties to work together and as a first step of *lok-niti* to overthrow the indira government. At JP Narayan's initiative, the existing four important political parties (Congress, Jana Sangh, Bharatiya Lok Dal and Socialist Party) submerged their identity and formed the Janata Dal.

Jaya Prakash Narayan, was the last lingering link with the stalwarts of India's freedom movevement. He renounced power and active politics and took self-exile. He turned the protests into a national cause. They challenged Indira Gandhi's formidable power. JP criticized her government's actions, especially the supercession of three Justices of the Supreme Court and expressed his apprehension that it might even destroy the foundation of Indian democracy. She curtly replied that Jayaprakash Narayan's letter was part of a concerted attempt to decry her and the very policies for which her father Jawaharlal Nehru had stood.

JP movement began, as already menti ned, in Bihar and spread over other parts of the country. Its aim was to secure the resignation of government of Congress (R) and dissolution of the State Assembly in Bihar. Other parties joined it, though initially Jana Sangh gave it muscle power in the hope that JP's towering personality and leadership may intensify the struggle and forge opposition unity. But Indira Gandhi was determined to suppress the movement and she saw to it that student violence was met with stronger counter violence. The crusade turned into a distortion of democratic process.

On 12 June, 1975, Jagmohan Sinha, a judge of the Allahabad High Court in Raj Narain' case set aside Indira Gandhi's election of 1971 from Rae Bareli constituency and debarred her from contesting elections for six yeas. She said the country was in danger.

On June 26, Indira Gandhi declared National Emergency. J.P was arrested along with most of the political leaders. J.P.was confined to a rest house. There was severe criticism of the government.Because of his ill health, he was transferred to hospital first in Delhi than to PGI in Chandigarh. In November, 1975, he was released. During the rest of Emergency, he was confined to bed in Bombay's Jaslok Hospital and it was in a wheelchair that he took part in a rally after Indira Gandhi's fall from power. At the time of release, it was alleged by JP's supporters that something had been done to him which had aggravated his kidney ailment.

The Emergency lasted two years and was withdrawn and general elections were annonced.( B.B.C. sarcastically reported "Empress of India has fallen.down.")

A meeting was neld at the Ramlila Grounds at which JP announced that he would launch a movement against Indira Gandhi's Government. The hitherto squabbling groups had all agreed to merge in to form a Janata Dal and fight Indira Gandhi. People contributed generously. Indira lampooned the Janata as *Khichri*, a hotchpotch, and asked people to choose between 'stability and progress' and 'confusion and instability'. The Janata leaders said that Indira had failed to remove poverty and hunger, which she had promised. Janata will provide 'bread and freedom'(if elected). A Muslim supporter of Congress remarked about Sanjay Gandhi's Family Planning campaign, 'These vasectomies have become for us the greased cartridges of 1857'.

Jayaprakash Narayan wielded a good pen and he authored many books, and booklets on social, political and economic problems.

On 18 January 1977 Mrs. Gandhi broadcast that General Elections would be held in March 1977. Jaya Prakash flew to Delhi on 22 January. On 24th, he went back to Patna for having dialysis. During his visit to Delhi, JP met Jagjivan Ram. This shook the government. Mrs. Gandhi and her party was defeated. J.P. urged the new government leadership to move swiftly and provide clean and responsive government. He wanted extra constitutional power to be repealed and the coercive machinery to be dismantled.

The new Janata government was to take decisions. To be present on the occasion, J.P .changed his dialysis schedule to be in Delhi on 23-24 March. The main contenders were Janata Chairman Morarji Desai and CFD leader Jagjivan Ram. Desai was known for his rigidity and self righteousness but it was said that after release he had changed. Jagjivan Ram was an astute politician and a good administrator but his reputation was not unsullied.. On 23 rd, it was decided that the newly elected Janata MPs would indicate their preference for prime minister to JP and JB Kripalani. Majority was for Desai. The Parliamentary Party confirmed the decision in favor of Desai.

JP tendered the most beneficial advice to the minorities in

his convocation address to the alumni of the Aligarh Muslim University in March, 1968. A gist of the address is given here:

At the height of the Mughal power, the issue of 'Muslim power versus Hindu power' appeared settled. But with the rise of the British power it became alive. There were two ways of resolving the issue. One, each contending community allied itself with the foreign power to secure for itself the maximum benefit which meant continuance of the British rule, and, two, the two communities combined to throw the foreigner out. In AMU too, there were contenders for the two philosophies, the overall bent being towards the first. The British kept it under its wings but it did not succeed as is evident from the contribution of the alumni to the national movement, and eventually one of them became the President of India, the highest office in the secular and democratic state. Yet, despite Partition, the issue remains there. The reason is that the feudal mentality persists. In the feudal system the religion of the overlord settles the issue. In it sharing of power is limited. Power can be shared only in a democracy. As long as the feudal mentality lasts and the past dominates the minds, the question of 'Hindu power versus Muslim power' will remain. Pakistan decided in favor of a Muslim state In the minds of some people there is the hangover of the two nation theory. The role of the AMU should be to lead the intelligentsia out of the dilemma. Both India and Pakistan should get out of that feudal mentality and stagnation into the modern, democratic, secular mind and radical, social and economic transformation and development. The solvents of communal reaction are democracy, secularism, and socio-economic development.

Jaya Prakash Narayan breathed his last on October 8, 1979

# 7
# LAL BAHADUR SHASTRI
(1904-1966)

---

When the Prime Minister of India, Jawahar Lal Nehru suddenly expired on May 27, 1964, the ruling Congress Party leadership searched for a suitable successor. Senior leaders like Morarji Desai, G.L.Nanda, and others waited in the wings. Rumors were afloat that Nehru had groomed his daughter Indira Gandhi for the office. Being in grief, she maintained her dignity and did not rush to press her claim but looked for someone to fill in as a stop gap from whom she could take over at a later date. TheCongress leadership looked for someone malleable and who could be manipulated. The general impression about Morarji Desai was that he was rigid, haughty and not accommodating. As for Nanda, he was conservative and weak. Further search took them to Lal Bahadur Shastri , who they thought could be the candidate they were looking for. He possessed several qualities of head and heart. He had been Nehru's confidant. He was courageous, considerate, dignified, and modest. Hyperbole was an anathema to him; he never prevaricated from implementing a decision. Also, he showed no passion for power, greed or lust. On January 2, 1965, Shastri was elected as the new leader of the Congress Parliamentary Party and was sworn in as the Prime Minister of India, much to the disappointment of Morarji Desai who thought he was the one most eligible.

Lal Bahadur was born on October 2, 1904 at Mughalserai son of Ram Dulari Devi and Sharda Prasad Verma who was a school teacher at Allahabad. Their ancestral home was at Ramanagar, near Benares, across the Ganga. At the age of 4, Lal

Bahadur lost his father. Grandfather Munshi Hazarilal took the family to Mughalserai. Another tragedy befell. The grand-pa also died. Who says joint family system is useless.Grandpa's elder brother Munshi Darbarilal came to the bereaved family's rescue.

Lal Bahadur was initiated to learning at an early age. He took lessons in Urdu and *tehjeeb* (courtesy) from a Maulvi and in other subjects up to sixth class from teachers in the Railway Middle School. To give her son higher education, Ram Dulari moved to one of her cousin's house at Benaras where Lal Bahadur joined the DAV School. Here, he came under the influence of a nationalist teacher, Nishkameshwar Mishra. who inculcated patriotic feelings in him. About this time, the news of the Jalianwalla Bagh tragedy shook every Indian and when Gandhiji asked students ( of age 16 and above) to withdraw from schools run or aided. by government, Lal Bahadur left the school and became a volunteer for the Congress Party.

In 1925, Lal Bahadur passed the Shastri examination from the Kashi Vidyapeeth, and deleted his end name Verma and added instead Shastri. Now onwards, he was to be known as Lal Bahadur Shastri. He was conscious of his poor financial condition but as advised by his teacher Mishra, he never let poverty be an ornament to be exhibited. In future, gossips grew (when Shastri came to occupy a position) that he was so poor that he could noy pay ferry charges, and therefore used to swim across the Ganga. When a journalist enquired of him whether this was true, Shastri replied that only once he swam across the Ganga as he had no money to pay for the ferry. After his education, young Shastri went about in search of a job. He was interviewed for a job in the Servants of India Society by the Society's President Lala Lajpatrai at Lahore on a salary of Rs. 60 per month. He was selected and posted at Muzaffarnagar (UP). His duty was to uplift the untouchables. The next year when Lala Lajpat Rai died and Purushottam Das Tandon (of Allahabad) succeeded him as the Society's President, in the interest of work  Shastri was transferred to Allahabad.  Shastri though diminutive was tough and hard working. Tandon was pleased with him and praised his efficiency. Though deeply religious, Shastri was not communal, not even sectarian; yet he was critical of caste system. However, he believed in disseminating knowledge about India's cultural heritage.

On May 16, 1928, Lal Bahadur was married to Lalita Devi at Mirzapur. The two made an ideal couple and shared their joys and sorrows so long as they were alive.

Shastri's volunteering work brought him in contact with Jawaharlal Nehru. The latter was impressed by Shastri's dedication and devotion to work and thoroughness of completing it.Confidant of both Nehru and Tandon,.Shastri was liked by common man. At one time when some differences cropped up between Nehru and Tandon on the selection of general secretary of AICC, Shastri tried to remove their misunderstanding and to bring them together. Unfortunately, he did not succeed.

In 1929, the AICC organized a big show at Lahore. Shastri went there to help in the organizational work of the Congress session. He was thrilled to see the goings-on of the session and happy that a resolution about India's independence had been passed by the Congress.

In 1930, after participating in the Round Table Conference at London,Gandhiji returned to India and landed at Bombay. He was dismayed at the British attitude and launched a Civil Disobedience (CD) movement. The Salt Satyagraha. attracted world wide attention. At Allahabad, Shastriji participatesd in the no-rent agitation. He was arrested and sentenced to two and a half years imprisonment. But the situation improved and his sentence was reduced. Gandhiji and Viceroy Irwin met and made the Gandhi-Irwin Pact that diffused the situation.

The RTC talks failed when Gandhiji pressed demand for control over Defense and Foreign Affairs. The Congress Working Committee met on January 1, 1937 and decided to resume the Civil Disobedience movement and to boycott foreign goods. Once again Congress leaders, including Shastri, were arrested and sent to jail. Between 1930 and 1934 Shastri was imprisoned several times.

In 1935 Nehru became president of the UP Congress Committee with headquarters at Lucknow. Lal Bahadur was appointed its general secretary. (Besides holding these offices, Shastriji was also member of the Allahabad Municipal Committee, the Allahabad Improvement Trust, and the Allahabad Distt Congress Committee). Shastriji continued to carry on the work of Provincial Committee from Allahabad. He came in contact with the top leadership of Congress in UP. He toured the rural areas and studied the conditions of labor and peasants and realized that without introducing land reforms their condition would not improve. Shastri worked out a land reforms report which recommended changes and the need of a new legislation. It was appreciated by Nehru and others.

The British could no longer ignore the conditions and passed GOI Act 1935. General Elections were held in 1937. Shastri was also elected from one of the Allahabad constituencies. The Congress formed government in UP. The Congress ministries in provinces were doing good work when the Viceroy proclaimed that India would join the Allies in world war. This upset the Congress as the Governor General had not taken the political parties in confidence. The Congress started agitation. Shastri and other office bearers were arrested. The British Government tried to pacify the Indian public and sent a mission led by Cripps which reached India and offered minor concessions. The Congress Party turned these down. Gandhiji derided it as 'a post dated check on a crashing bank.' The Cripps Mission failed and returned

In August 1942, the AICC met at Bombay and adopted the Quit India resolution. The Government promptly arrested Congress office bearers. Shastriji went underground to help run the agitation but was arrested on August 19 at Allahabad. He was held in prison up to August 1945. This meant a suffering for Shastriji's family which somehow survived. In 1945, the World War was over. Wavell went to London to seek orders about the release of the agitators. Chruchill agreed to their release but turned down the Viceroy's proposal to form a new representative Executive Council composed of equal number of Caste Hindus and Muslim League and a Schedule Caste Member. The Muslim League was adamant on its demand that the League should be treated as representative of all Muslims. This was not acceptable to the Congress. This meant the Council could not function. Similar difficulties were experienced in provinces. In 1946, when a new government was formed in UP, Shastri was made Parliament Secretary to the Chief Minister. Later, he became Transport Minister. He found the bus services in U.P. were unreliable and inefficient. To improve the transport services in future, he would establish a state bus service which proved a boon to the people.

The Attlee government which now replaced Churchill's ministry, declared its decision to partition India before the transfer of power. The Muslim majority areas were to form Pakistan and the rest of British dominion, India. However, the case of princes was to be separately handled. On March 24,1947, Wavell was replaced by Mountbatten. On 15 August 1947 the country became independent and was divided into India and Pakistan. In India, Nehru formed the government .

In 1951, Nehru brought Shastri from Lucknow to Delhi. At Delhi, Shastri was designated the General Secretary of the Congress Party. Nehru asked Shastri to look after the work of elections of the Congress. He did a commendable job which was appreciated by every one. In 1957, after elections, Shastri was inducted as Minister of Transport and Shipping. Under his stewardship, shipping and ship building improved. In 1958, he was appointed Minister of Commerce and Industry. The same year, he suffered a mild heart attack but recovered soon and joined Heavy Industry Ministry. He combined Industry with Agriculture, and Village Industries with Small Industries. His reputation for integrity soared high.

Whichever Ministry Shastri joined, he left his mark on it. As Railway Minister, his new charge, Shastriji improved rolling stock and tracks, planned to abolish third class,and improved the quality of food served in the trains. When two major Railway accidents occurred, Shastrijii resigned on moral grounds. This was the first time that a Minister had voluntarily given up office. It set a healthy trend for future.

In 1961,when G.B. Pant fell seriously ill, Shastri took over as Home Minister. He brought peace to Assam where language riots between the Assamese and Bangla – speaking Assamese had disrupted public life, mainly in the Catchar region. A formula, evolved by Shastiji, satisfied all parties and restored amity.

As Home Minister, Shastri advised the Police to do their duty but with humanness. For instance, if they had to disperse off a mob, they should use a water hose in place of lathi. Also,they should be imbued with a spirit of fairness and be subject to discipline.

In Punjab, the demand of a Punjabi Suba by Master Tara Singh was creating  serious problems. Shastriji dealt with it with reasonableness which saw Master Tara Singh's 48-day fast peter out. The Government set up a commission comprising of Justice SR Das, Sir CP Ramaswamy Aiyer and Justice MC Chagla. The Commission found that no injustice was being done to the Sikhs, as alleged by Master Tara Singh.

In 1963, under the Kamraj Plan, Shastriji was one of the Ministers who resigned with the object of invigorating the Congress Party. In 1964, he was recalled by Nehru to join the cabinet as Minister Without Portfolio. Nehru died in May 1964 and a search for consensus candidate for the Prime Minister's office found Shastri as the most suitable candidate. On June 2, 1964, Shastiji took the oath of the office of Prime Minister. He evolved a low key style for the governance of pluralist India. He persuaded Indira Gandhi to join his cabinet as the Minister for Information and Broadcasting.

With the object of making India strong, the Constitution had laid a democratic structure based on universal suffrage and made provisions for elections for Parliament and State Assemblies, Parliamentary system of government, free speech, free press, and faith in secularism. The government had been fighting the shortcomings of illiteracy, religion, orthodoxy, casteism, regionalism, secessionist tendencies, conservative and traditional practices that stood in the path of India's progress.

On India's northern and western borders, China and Pakistan were unfriendly with India. Pakistan thought Shastri was weak and they could snatch Kashmir from India. President Ayub Khan reasoned that Pakistani army equipped with sophisticated and modern weapons would have a cake walk over India. As a probe Pakistani army attacked Indian outposts in the Rann of Cutch. After their tanks had rolled 10 miles unhindered inside Indian territory, they proposed a cease fire. Their strategy was to capture some territory, talk peace and thrust a war on India. This was the same tactic they had adopted in 1947-48 in Kashmir.

The British had left behind an administrative set up which was excellent for status quo. After independence it had to be development oriented. The pace of cumbersome administrative decisions had slowed down action which bred corruption. The rules and procedures were outdated and dilatory and overcautious. Shastriji set up an administrative reforms commission under the chairmanship of Morarji Desai. Beside, he set up a Central Bureau of Investigation (CBI) for dealing with corruption, and a code of conduct for Ministers and officers. Also, Shastri set up a National Integration council whose aim was unity and cohesion of the country. Shastri steered an Official Language Bill. It was passed. He gave attention to staff matters to remove the irritant, and excessive restraint by officers, free expression of views, need of improvement in relations between ministers and services, action on oral orders and instructions by officers and ministers, involvement of officers in evolving policies, code of conduct for officers, processing of cases through proper channel etc.

During Prime Minister Nehru's time, on Prime Minister's behalf, Shastri had introduced some reforms and pacified agitated public.Though not the senior most minister, he had moved a resolution on democratic socialism before the subjects committee. Shastri explained that to him democratic socialism meant a polity dedicated to the welfare of common man which required tempering of idealism with realism, adding that timely and proper action was important. He made it clear that government should not trade in grains unless it was ready to carry it out satisfactorily, as otherwise it would increase corruption and add to people's miseries. The resolution was adopted unanimously.

Pakistan had been trying to incite people in Kashmir to agitate against India. During Nehru's time in Srinagar a hair from Prophet Mohammed's body, which was preserved in a case, was found missing. Later, it was restored. But some people suspected its genuineness. Shastri brought the matter to a peaceful conclusion by seeking the opinion of a group of learned Muslims.They confirmed.the genuineness of the hair.A new ministry under GM Sadiq was set up. The public in Srinagar demanded Sheikh's release. Shastri persuaded Nehru to release Sheikh.Sheikh Abdullah was released on April 8,1964. Abdullah made volatile statements for a few days and then sobered down and expressed a wish to bring India and Pakistan together on the question of Kashmir. He wanted to go to Pakistan to meet Pakistani leaders. Nehru did not object to his visit to Pakistan. He did not want conflict with Pakistan. He knew it was not only China but the USA and the Western countries also were pro-Pakistan.

The US's Pakistan policy decisions were influenced by the

opinion of British officers to groom Pakistan to fill in the vacuum created by British withdrawal from India. The U.S. administration ignored its prior commitments with India. For instance, President Eisenhower had assured Nehru on February 24, 1954 that military aid given to Pakistan would not be used against India but during his very presidency, Pakistan had received substantial military aid. The US- Pakistan Pact (1954) had compelled India to review its national priorities and to augment its defense capability. USSR had cautioned India to be more careful about its borders.

Pakistan's foreign policy was designed and developed by Zulfikar Ali Bhutto. He believed that Pakistan could regain initiative in its foreign policy by taking decisive diplomatic, political and military action. Which in simple terms meant, snatching Kashmir from India. Much though India might have liked to have friendly relations with Pakistan, Pakistan's intentions were maleficent. Still Shastriji wanted to explore the possibility of improving relations with Pakistan. In October 1964, he was to participate in a summit conference of non-aligned nations in Cairo. But Pakistan's President Ayub Khan was not a member of the conference, and was therefore not going to Cairo. Shastri took the initiative and suggested to President Ayub that he would like to meet him on his way back from Cairo. Ayub extended him the invitation. In Karachi, Ayub and Shastri drove together to President House and held talks on India- Pakistan relations and how to improve them. Shastriji formed the impression that Ayub had a practical approach, but Zulfikar Ali Bhutto, Ayub's Foreign Minister, was a different type of man.

Soon after Indian PM left Karachi, Bhutto set up a 'Kashmir Cell' under Pakistan's Foreign Secretary. The two had concluded that Shastri was unlikely to loosen India's links with Kashmir and to revive the Kashmir question, Pakistan would have to initiate an overt action. President Ayub went with Bhutto's analysis, despite warnings from some of his friends that Bhutto could bring disaster on Pakistan by invading India. Ayub approved of General Musa's plan of invasion on Kashmir. It was in four phases: infiltration, probing encounter in the form of disguised invasion; guerrilla warfare camouflaged as revolt by local population through propaganda, a massive and lightening armored attack to capture Amritsar and some other territory to be exchanged when defeated India begged for peace.

Pakistan's generals and politicians thought that the present was the most opportune time for Pakistan to snatch Kashmir from India. India had a new prime minister. India was experiencing food shortage and economic hardships, morale of Indian army was low and part of India's army was bottled up on China border while Pakistan had a powerful friend in China – which was inimical towards India.

Pakistan's Operation Desert Hawk was the first probe in the Rann of Cutch to raise a claim for 3500-sq mile area in adverse possession of India though the boundary was well demarcated. As planned, Pakistani army men intruded, already mentioned above, but they were apprehended. When questioned, how they had entered the Indian territory, they explained that they had lost their way. They were let off without any action. But on January 20, 1965, Pakistan Border Police was seen patrolling. Indian police expelled the intruders. Then on February 18, the Pakistanis again violated Indian border. When India Government complained, Pakistan denied and said that the area near Kanjarkot was Pakistan's and it had been in its possession since 1947 and now they were establishing a post at Kanjarkot. Shastri had a talk with his Chiefs of Army and Air Force who advised that it was not worth fighting a war on that spot and if there is to be a trial of strength, let it be elsewhere. But some suitable place. The British Prime Minister intervened and the matter was settled by the International Court of Justice in favor of India.

Ayub was ebullient. He concluded that Pakistan Army's high quality armor and power of fighting men were in a position to hurt India irreparably. By May 26, Pakistan's 30000 armed men constituting the Gibraltar force gathered at Murree for their clandestine invasion on Kashmir. Pakistan appointed Maj.Gen. Akhtar Hussain Malik as Supreme Commander for Operation Gibraltar. In July 1965, it was given go-ahead order. The Army would breach the Cease Fire Line (CFL) to keep the pot boiling, especially on Srinagar-Leh highway. The disguised invasion began on August 5. Shastri had no intelligence about it. The infiltration continued from August 5 to 8 using arson, murder, destruction, stain guns. Thereafter, Sadai Kashmir (clandestine radio within Occupied Kashmir) was to broadcast on Abdullah's arrest anniversary that Kashmiris had risen in revolt, established a Revolutionary Council, canceled all agreements with India; a national government of Kashmir had been set up and denials of infiltration were to be made. India's attempts to suppress Kashmir's independence were proving futile; as Pakistan's army had launched massive attacks across CFL in Chhamb and captured Akhnoor. An attack by Patton tanks was now to follow to capture Amritsar. Pakistan Army said the attack would change the course of history.

Pakistan had not learned from its past defeats and used the stale methods : Every time they sent their army men as patriots or freedom fighters in the garb of tribal. They were strangers to terrain, and bribed shepherds for information. Indian action also followed a set pattern. The tribal informed the Indian army about entry by strange faces and the invaders were crushed. The world too had become accustomed to the flop of operations. This time India adopted a different policy. India retaliated and occupied two important posts in Uri sector. The Prime Minister of India said that when our freedom was threatened and territorial integrity endangered by an enemy, there is only one duty- meet the challenge with all might. In his broadcast to the nation, Shastri apprised his country-men that Pakistan had probably taken a deliberate decision to keep up an atmosphere of tension; and added that when the nation's freedom and sovereignty were threatened loyalties of every citizen have to be ultimately to the motherland.

Seventeen days later, Pakistani Army in massive numbers invaded Kashmir. From 15th August Pak Army stepped up violation of CFL, including Kargil sector. India retaliated by capturing three Pakistani posts in Kargil sector. Shastri clarified, "If Pakistan continues aggression, India will not limit herself to defensive measures. It will strike back and carry the fight to the other side". General Chaudhary, the Indian Army Chief met Gen. Nimmo (U. N. representative) and informed him of the violations by Pakistan's Army which had entered in some sectors, including Mendhar, near Poonch to dislodge Indians from the Indian posts.

On 28 August, Indian forces crossed CFL in Uri sector to check Pakistani infiltration in Kashmir Valley. They drove away the Pakistani army from nine Pak bases in Uri-Poonch loop and captured the Hazi Pir Pass.

Pakistanis continued inciting Kashmiris. Pakistan's

Information and Broadcasting Minister asked Pak nationals to make sacrifices to liberate their Kashmiri brethren.(Among those killed by Pak army were mostly Kashmiri Muslims!) Within a few hours operation Grand Slam began on September 1.Their objective was to capture Akhnoor.Indian position was precarious. Indian Army and Air Force Chiefs met Shastri who told them to go ahead with their plans of entering into Pakistan's Lahore, Sialkot and Barmer sectors.

India's Army Chief Chaudhary had already apprised Gen Nimmo about Pak infiltration. The matter came up before the Security Council. The Security Council took note that India had attacked on September 6 only after infiltration of Pak troops in India, and Indians took defensive action. That very day, Gen. Chaudhary informed PM Shastri that Indian army had moved inside Pakistan and some units were reaching outskirts of Lahore. Indian Air Force was making supplies to ground forces. Now it was a general war. India under Shastri had crossed rubicon. This electrified the nation. To save Lahore and Sialkot, Pakistan Army gave up its push towards Akhnoor .

On September 6, the Security Council, aware of the position expressed its apprehension that the conflict might become global. Kosygin (USSR) offered his good offices for negotiations between the two. Pakistan asked U.S.A. for aid of arms and equipment which the latter refused. Surprisingly, Harold Wilson (UK) urged Shastri and Ayub to order cease fire but held India responsible for the new situation, created by its attack on Punjab. This was biased and partisan. Operation grand slam had failed. As for the British attitude this should not have surprised India because Britain had most of the times taken anti-Indian postures in the world bodies. But India's diplomat CS Jha, especially sent to USA by Shastri, by his diplomatic skill manged minor innocuous changes in the resolution that was passed. This was in favor of India. On 11th , U Than, Secretary General,U.N.visited Pakistan and India. In India, he met the President of India, PM Shastri and E.A. Minister Swaran Singh. India had kept the war limited to West Pakistan and had not taken any action on the East Pakistan border.

By September 11, Pakistan's offensive had been beaten back. A Pakistani journalist Altaf Gauhar wrote : Pakistan's policy of counter offensive ran aground. With that collapsed Pakistan's entire military strategy. For Pakistan war was over. Shastri made a statement about the situation in Parliament which was received with warmth by all parties. In the India-Pakistan conflict, China maintained silence for sometime. They supported Pakistan but their support was theatrical, meant to boost up Pak morale. This did not disturb India. Both China and India knew that any Chinese action against India would attract US action. On September 13, USSR issued a warning to all those who wanted to fish in troubled waters. Shastri in a letter to China clarified the position.

Pakistan decisively lost two battles : the battle of Asal Uttar in Khem Karan sector and the 15- day tank battle in the Sialkot sector. (This was the graveyard of Patton tanks.) Pakistan totally failed in achieving its objective- capture of Kashmir. Pakistan Government offered two reasons for its failure : larger numerical strength of hostile Indian forces, and no support to Pakistan by its allies. The Pak Army was disillusioned. They had failed to steamroll into India.

As against Pakistan, India met its objective : It defeated Pakisan's effort to seize Kashmir, destroyed Pak armor and occupied some Pak territories. Because India had met its objective, Shastri did not press for capture of Sialkot and Lahore. Also, Pakistani propaganda that Kashmiri brotherhood was impatiently waiting to be liberated by Pakistan was given a lie, both inside and outside India as well as in Pakistan. As a result of defeat, the Pakistan Army developed a healthy respect for Indian Army. The wrong notion it nourished that a Pakistani soldier was equal to three Indian Jawans was dispelled. The Pak Army was cut to size and they learnt that it is man behind the armor that matters in battles. Shastri was greeted as the architect of a successful and triumphant policy.

Pakistan should have realized that this frail little man had proved the real successor and heir of Jawaharlal Nehru. He defended Indian's liberty bravely and heroically.

The Government of Pakistan ordered cease fire effective 0300 hours West Pakistan and 0330 New Delhi Time on September 23, 1965. If that was to be the fate, why did Pakistan attack? One of the reasons was that Pakistan was emboldened from India's defeat by China in 1962 War and Indian Army was stretched along its frontiers of China and Pakistan. This was a miscalculation of Pakistan. Its second mistake was to assume that Muslims of India, including Muslims of Kashmir, would help Pakistani soldiers. The assumed Chinese political and military help also did not materialize.

The serious looking Shastri could be light and jovial, people did not know. He reminded that President Ayub had declared that he would walk through Delhi. Shastri said President Ayub is great, high and mighty." I thought he should not undergo the travail of such a long walk. We should ourselves march towards Lahore to greet him". Another one: Some people presented Shastriji a giant cake in the shape of a Patton tank on his birthday. Symbolically, the Prime Minister destroyed the tank putting a knife through it. He then asked the cake to be sent to Jawans. One more : I am not a marshal. I wear a *dhoti*. May be for this reason Pakistan considers India weak. Defense Minister Chavan also wears a *dhoti*. *Dhoti*-clad people have defended their country and marched up to Lahore.

We heard an amusing anecdote about Shastriji's Vidyasagar-like behavior. Shastrji got down at the Lucknow railway station and saw a big crowd. He went to the exit and asked the ticket collector why there was such a crowd. The official told him to clear off. The Police Minister is coming. But as he was moving a *neta* recognized him.Shastriji was Home Minister. The poor ticket collector regreted his behavior.

At the invitation of Kosygin, Shastriji went to Taskent to meet Ayub. Ayub stressed on establishing a joint self- executing machinery and turned down 'no war pact' suggested by India, little realizing that 'no war pact' was an affirmation of UN Charter.

At Taskent, there were dramatic moments. Bhutto had great capacity for theatrical performance. To some extent he was responsible for the 1965 ( and later 1971) wars . Shastri told Kosygin Indian army had taken Hazi Pir after a great sacrifice of its men and won't leave it. Kosygin with cogent reasons convinced Shastri that for the sake of peace, India should accept Security Council's resolution regarding restoration of August 5, 1965 position. The night the Taskant Declaration was signed, something untoward happened. Shastriji died of heart attack. When the news reached India the entire nation was plunged into grief. People remembered that during the War with a sense of gratitude that Lal Bahadur

Shastri had provided the nation a bold, decisive,wise and admirable leadership.

Later, the Bharat Ratna award was conferred upon Shastriji posthumously.

Shastri had kept it to his heart that poverty was not a badge to be hung on the chaste This was the lesson his teacher had taught him while he was a child. He never flaunted poverty to curry any favor from any one. No doubt, democracy has many merits one of which is equal opportunity to develop, and Shastri is one of the finest examples how a man from an ordinary background rose to the highest position in the land.

# 8
# INDIRA GANDHI
### 1917-1984 )

"She (Indira Gandhi) was stoned, jailed and reviled by her enemies but she was also admired, honored and revered by her supporters in India and around the world. Indira Gandhi has been called a mother figure, charming and dedicated. She has also been derided as arrogant, dominating and ruthless. Gandhi was a controversial ruler. To many of her loyal admirers, she is remembered as a woman of courage who was devoted to making sure that India survived as an independent democratic nation".

*- Heroes of Conscience*

In the history of modern India, Indira Gandhi cut a striking figure.There is no woman comparable to her. During her prime ministership of 15 years, in two broken periods – 1966-1977 and 1980-1984 , she was elected three times. She has been described as intelligent, courageous, brave, bold, witty and generous. She performed many good and bad deeds that affected a vast mass of humanity. Some of her regime's good and controversial deeds were: nationalisation of banks, abolition of privy purses, adverting famine, meeting global oil flow and economic slump, explosion of atomic device, successful blasting of SLV (Satellite Launching Vehicle), strengthening India's defense by procuring Mig-72 and T-72 tanks, sea Harriet Pump sets and submarines to match Pakistan's one billion worth armament obtained from USA and victory over pakistan in Bangladesh War. The measures taken by her kept India's unity and integrity in tact.

For India's victory over Pakistan, Indira Gandhi was called a Devi (goddess). But her obstructive and obstreperous critics thrust on her the epithets of evil, oggress, harsh and cruel. In justification of her harshness, her supporters said she needed it for the sake of self preservation. It was circumstances that made much of her what she was in life.

Indira Gandhi was born daughter of Jawaharlal Nehru (son of Motilal Nehru who was a leading lawyer) and Kamala Nehru, on November 19,1917 at Allahabad. An interesting anecdote relating to her birth is : Grandmother Swarup Rani received the news of the birth of a grand daughter. Very coolly, she said, "It should have been a boy." Motilal reacted, "The Nehru family makes no difference between a daughter and a son. Don't you love your son and daughters equally?" He added " May be Jawahar's daughter does better than a thousand sons."She did not disappoint the grandpa and made the Nehru family proud. Motilal named the child "Indira".To this, parents added a middle name 'Priyadarshini' (meaning beautiful to the sight). After she grew up, entered into adulthood and married, the end name of her husband, Feroze Gandhi, was added to hers, which made her name quite sizable- Indira Priyadarshini Nehru Gandhi. From Motilal, she imbibed self respect and from Jawaharlal fearlessness. Of her childhood, a few memories stood out: Kamala's unfair treatment at the hands of aunt Vijayalakshmi (father's sister) and Jawaharlal's indifference to Kamala for the reason, he thought, Kamala was orthodox and theirs was an arranged marriage.But if such marriage was backwardness, he too was equally orthodox. for he had abided by his father's wish to marry a girl of his choice.

Indira, as a child, found the entire Nehru family was involved in the freedom struggle. The family members went off and on 'on pilgrimage' to jail, which affected Kamala's health and deprived Indira of adequate care and security. Her early education, according to biographer, Inder Malhotrai "was episodic, uneven and nomadic." We can quip that Indira changed her school as her father, the anecdote goes, got his shirts laundered from Paris. The schools were : ST Mary's Convent; Pupil's Own School (in Pune), L'ecole Nouvelle at Bex in Switzerland, where she learnt music, skating and French, Shanti Ntketan ( where she had opportunity to meet Rabindranath Tagore),and Badminton School. The learning in schools was supplemented by a series of letters written her by

Jawaharlal..These were later published in the form of a book titled *Glimpses of World History*. Most of the letters went over her head. The father's advice to daughter was : Never do anything secret nor wish anything you may need to hide or feel ashamed, for fear is a bad thing. Indira always kept this advice in mind. She got opportunities for recieving practical training in politics from her family in the Anand Bhawan which was always full of political activities. At the  end , she  would go to Somerville College, Cambridge, where she studied Modern History.

In 1929, Indira accompanied the family to Lahore where she witnessed grandpa Motilal passing the Congress presidential crown to Jawaharlal. The next day, people took pledge to India's independence. Indira would later see the family participating in the Salt Satyagraha (1930), and  Kamala Nehru being arrested and taken off to jail (1931). She was now the only member of Nehru family out of jail and took charge of activities in the Ananda Bhawan. She nursed the victims of the lathi charge. She donned the mantle of Joan of Arc and with other children became the conduit for running messages, making flags, putting up posters.

Motilal passed away on February 6, 1934. Indira felt she was deprived of the company of the person who loved her most. Jawaharlal took her to Shanti Niketan. But Kamala again fell ill and had to be taken to Bhowal Sanatorium and later to Switzerland. Kamala passed away on February 28, 1936 at Lausanne, Switzerland. Indira who had accompanied her mother went to Cambridge. There, she came in frequent contact with Feroze Gandhi. (a young Indian Parsee student at Cambridge) and Krishna Menon, a prominent Indian acquaintance of her father. Finding World War hotting up, Indira and Feroze left for India without completing their courses. On reaching Allahabad, she met her father in the jail. She sought his permission to marry Feroze Gandhi. Nehru  tried to dissuade her in view of Feroze's unstable financial condition. But as she was resolute,he gave his consent.  Indira and Feroze were married on March 26, 1942.

At Allahabad the couple lived in a rented house. Feroze took up insurance business and  freelance journalism. In August 1942, they went to Bombay to attend the Congress Session. Gandhiji asked the British rulers to Quit India and gave a call ' do or die' to his countrymen. Early next morning, the police cracked upon and arrested most of the leaders. Feroze went underground and Indira left for Allahabad. Both were arrested at Allahabad. Indira was released on May 8, 1943 and Feroze sometime later.

In August, 1944, Indira gave birth to a son at Bombay. He was named Rajeev. Jawaharlal was released on June 15, 1945. Next year, she gave birth to a second son. He was named Sanjay.

The world war was over in 1945 and all around there was talk of India's freedom. The Congress under Gandhi's leadership demanded a United India; the Muslim League under M.A. Jinnah insisted on a separate homeland for Muslims to be carved out by partitioning India. Congress and League failed to reach an understanding and elections were held to find out public opinion. Congress swept the board and won majority of seats. The League won almost all the reserved Muslim seats.

The Governor General Wavell invited Nehru to join the Viceroy's Executive Council as its Vice President. Nehru accepted the offer on September 2, 1946 and joined the Council as its Vice Chairman.. The League also joined but with the clear intention to wreak it from within.

Nehru, burdened with additional responsibilities, asked Indira, who was at Lucknow, to join him as his official hostess and political aide at New Delhi. She moved to New Delhi to live with her father as 'she wanted to be near the seat of power', commented someone. Or, was it Nehru's desire to groom his daughter as his successor to P.M.office? Or, was it that Nehru wanted to help her in her estranged relationship with husband Feroze Gandhi? Some people account her coming to Delhi to her desire to escape a miserable marriage to 'a very likable but crude man, a skirt chaser', and jealous of his wife's connections with growing success in political life.

In Britain, Attlee replaced Churchill as prime minister. He told the Parliament that power would be transferred in responsible Indian hands by June 1948. To expedite the transfer, Wavell was replaced as Viceroy by Mountbatten. The new Viceroy announced that the British would withdraw from India on August 15, 1947. On June 23, the British Plan of Partition was published. On August 15, 1947, India was partitioned into two dominions- India and Pakistan.

Nehru became the Prime Minister of India. Mountbatten continued as the Governor General of India at the request of the Nehru Cabinet. MA Jinnah became the Governor General of Pakistan and left for Karachi.

Indira, while living with her father, had gained political experience, in Party's work as well as in Government's activities. In 1950, she was made a member of the Central Committee of the Congress Party. Elections for Parliament were held. Feroze won from Rae Bareli. As a Member of Parliament, he moved to a government allotted accommodation. As Indira had been actively participating in Congress Party's work, in 1955, she was made in-charge of the Woman Wing of the Congress.

Indira Gandhi campaigned for her father from Phulpur constituency. In 1958-59, she was made Congress President. This completed the circle – from Motilal to Jawaharlal to Indira. Next, she took keen interest in Kerala politics and went to campaign there.In Kerala, she unearthed CIA's hand in anti-communist and anti-state government propaganda, and noticed that the Church in Kerala was receiving funds from CIA. In the 1960 elections, Muslim League, aligned itself with Congress and, won elections with majority The League projected itself as a party different from the old League and made progress among Muslims in the country. On October 20, 1962, when China invaded India, Indira organized a Citizen's Committee for distributing cloth, drugs and food as aid to the Army. She rushed to Tezpur and organized administration which was abandoned by officers. The Committee built up the morale of Jawans and citizens. While the Chinese perfidy failed the non-alignment policy of India Government, it affected prime Minister Jawaharlal Nehru's health and he died of a stroke on May 27, 1964.

## II

Lal Bahadur Shastri formed the new cabinet. Indira joined it as the Minister for Information and Broadcasting. In 1965, Pakistan attacked India, Indian Army beat back Pakistan's invasion. To conciliate the two estranged parties, Soviet leader Kosygin played a broker and on his invitation Shastri and Ayub met at Taskent. An agreement was reached which the three leaders signed. but that very night Shastri died of a heart attack. Morarji Desai staked his claim for the Prime Minister's office but he lost the contest to Mrs.

Indira Gandhi by 169 to 344. Kamaraj and other Syndicate members had supported her under the impression that she would be weak and amenable. They were soon in for disappointment. She had a steely will and proved a super strategist. She dealt with the situation in a deft manner.

In 1966-67, lack of rains created famine like conditions in parts of the country.There was already    shortage of grains. To meet the situation, Indira Gandhi visited USA and met President Johnson. Her pleadings proved so effective that the President promised to give to India 3.5 million tons of wheat and $900 million as aid. But USA asked India to devalue the Rupee. Which India did by a hefty devaluation of the Rupee by 35.5%. The devuation annoyed the leftists in India as also the Soviets. To placate the communists, Mrs. Gandhi visited the Soviet Russia.

Beside the famine, communal friction was also creating problems. One cause of friction between Hindus and Muslims was the slaughter of cows for meat. Hindus regard cow as  sacred and worship her whereas Muslims eat the beef. To draw public attention to cow slaughter,  Sadhus organized a big demonstration in Delhi. The mob turned rowdy and caused loss to property. Home Minister Gulzari Lal Nanda proved ineffective and failed to handle the situation. Mrs. Gandhi eased him out of the Government and made Chavan the Home Minister. She felt  something drastic was called for to change the people's social outlook and to improve the country's political situation. She ordered abolition of privy purses (of princes), nationalization of Banks and holding of fresh elections. She ignored. objections of all her detractors, irrespective of the fact these were raised by opposition parties or by her own party members. The country was stirred.

President Zakır Husain died in May 1969. A search for a candidate brought forth three names : Reddy, Giri and Deshmukh. Reddy was supported by Kamraj, Nijlingappa , Sanjeeva Reddy, Atulya Ghose, SK Patel, Morarji Desai, YR Chavan, and Congress Parliamentary Board and they signed Reddy's nomination papers. Indira Gandhi also appended her signatures. But when it came to voting, she did not vote for him as he was aligned to her opponents, the Syndicate. She supported Vice President of India VV Giri. The third candidate, CD Deshmukh was supported by Swatantra Party,

Jan Sangh and Kranti Dal.Congressmen were free to vote according to their conscience. Indira Gandhi's candidate V.V.Giri won.

Indira Gandhi noticed that Morarji Desai was aligned with the Syndicate. She stripped him of the Finance portfolio. To give the Party a shock,and to attract the poor, she announced nationalization of 14 Banks. While people lauded her as a savior of the down trodden, Rajaji criticized her of dictatorship and announced that he would back Congress(O).For the elections her slogan was '*garibi hatao*', that is 'eliminate poverty.' The Syndicate and others mocked that Indira Gandhi was eliminating poor instead of poverty. The Syndicate lost. Mrs. Gandhi's Party won.

India's neighbor, Pakistan thought that Indian leadership was divided and that it was an opportune time to invade India and snatch Kashmir. But Pakistani politicians did not realize that theirs was a divided house. East Pakistan had many grievances against West Pakistan. Finding that the authorities were not removing their grievances, East Pakistan rebelled. President Ayub, incited by by his Foreign Minister,Bhutto, decided to settle the score with the rebels in East Pakistan militarily. The result was repression of Hindus and immigration of East Pakistanis in large numbers as refugees to India. Pakistan refused to solve the refugee problem and a war between the two nations ensued.

On December 4, 1971 Pakistan launched the first series of air strikes from West pakistan against Indian airfields.India did not suffer any loss and gave a good reply. US President Nixon and Kissinger posed a threat to Indian action in East Pakistan and, to back up the threat, US sent 'Encounter', the mighty US ship, towards the Bay of Bengal. Mrs.Gandhi ignored the threat and the Encounter pursued by the Russian fleet moved away. In the war,the three wings of India's defense forces performed several acts of bravery and courage. Mrs.Gandhi did not bother about Chinese threats on India's borders in support of Pakistan. Indian strategy was well organized and succeeded. India won the war. A question agitated for long: Did Kissinger give Pakistan a signal to attack or it was a desperate move by a beleaguered nation to attack? When Kissinger saw Pakistan losing badly, he thought of stopping the war to help Pakistan but the move proved ineffectual. On December 7, the general Assembly resolved to call for an immediate cease fire and tocreate condition for the return of refugees.Pakistan accepted it on 9th but India rejected it on December 12. US charged India for the deterrioration of the situation. Zulfiqar ali Bhutto, Pakistan's foreign Minister, dramatically tore up a draft resolution and stormed out of the Assembly. Pakistan lost the war.The War was decisive. On 16th, the Pak Army surrendered unconditionally.Next day followed cease fire.Bangladesh became independent. If Jinnah had created Pakistan,much of credit for creation of Bangladesh , a new Muslim country, should go to Indira Gandhi. Nixon lost his credibility.The foul language he used for Gandhi punctured US moral authority in the Third World.

Indians were overjoyed with their country's victory. The enemy forces surrendered in Dacca. Indira Gandhi's popularity soared high. People called her 'Devi.' Congress President, DK Barooah said, 'Indira is India' which was sycophancy at its worst.

Though India won the war, its effects started telling on the country's economy. Radical slogans coined by Mrs. Gandhi's party did not fill people's stomachs. They wanted food and a control over spiraling food prices. They forgot their victory in Bangladesh. Instead they derided her son, Sanjay's fraternizing with the profiteers. There were demonstrations by the frustrated, unemployed and educated youth. In 1973, half a million people took part in a march on Parliament against corruption and deteriorating economic conditions. In 1974, Indira took severe action to break a Railway strike which shattered what little was left of her socialist image. Her authoritarian and corrupt practices eroded democracy. and social values. She was blamed for the country's travails.

The insurrection against Indira Gandhi began in Gujarat and then followed in Bihar where youth violence and mass agitation caused a breakdown of law and order, leading to dissolution of State Assembly. In Bihar, JP Narayan , a Socialist converted to Gandhism, came out of retirement to lead a mass national movement to topple Indira Government, which was responsible for factionalism, communalism, corruption and waste. He asked people to go back to the days of Mahatma Gandhi and bring 'total revolution', based on Sarvodaya (welfare of all), in the country and to establish village republics which should be the centers of political and economic life. His aim was to establish a party-less democracy. The agitation paralyzed the country. He invited opposition parties to throw out Indira government. This appealed to political parties. They united and formed a Janata Party according to Jaya Prakash Narayana's appeal. They received help for village based economy from industrialists and support from urban middle class. On the other hand, Nehruites and Congress leaders criticized JP's party-less Democracy and Total Revolution as ambivalent and self contradictory.

About this time Indira Gandhi was found guilty by the Allahabad High Court for violation of election code in 1971 elections. (Raj Narayan, an M.P., had accused her of electoral malpractice.) Her election became invalid and deprived her of her seat in the Parliament. Without a seat in Parliament, she could not continue as Prime Minister. She prayed for stay which was granted. On appeal, the Supreme Court allowed her to remain PM until her appeal was heard but disallowed her from taking part in Parliament's proceedings. This meant that if she wanted to remain active, she should step down from office. But her son Sanjay and the Congress High Command thought differently and considered Mrs. Gandhi's leadership indispensable for the country and therefore they advised her against resignation.

In Delhi, at a mass rally, JP and other leaders denounced Indira Gandhi for establishing a fascist dictatorship and demanded that she must resign and threatened that if she did not, people would start a national movement. J.P. asked police and military officials not to obey her government's orders and to revolt. The supporters of Indira Gandhi blamed JP of undermining the national government She added that Mahatma Gandhi had conducted a movement but that was against alien rule and not against the national government. Now Mrs. Gandhi's government, not an alien, had to meet anarchy with the inchoate amalgam: DK Malviya, traditional politician (Jagjivan Ram), family friend (Uma Shankar Dixit), fiery idealist (Chandra Shekhar), regional boss (Bansilal), Office Seeker (VC Shukla) and leftists and ex-communists in search of power (Mohan Kumaramangalam).

Sanjay argued that Mrs. Ganhi's resignation would not solve the country's problems. She should discard whatever impedes government directives. It was by totalitarianism that China had improved the lot of its poor. He said freedom of Press, independence of judiciary and such other concepts did not fit in with Indian democracy and must be curbed. Sycophants compared Mrs. Gandhi's son Sanjay with Jesus Christ, Adi Shankar, Marx and Einstein. The wise young man's advice was that she need not resign. Constitution expert Palkhiwala confirmed that she need not resign. Sanjay emerged as the heir apparent and became the extra constitutional authority. Mrs. Gandhi, accompanied by Siddhartha Shankar Ray, a leader of high stature and Constitution expert met President Fakhruddin Ali Ahmad with a draft order for proclamation of Emergency. The President signed the order. With this, Emergency was proclaimed all over India from June 26, 1975. Emergency introduced an era of authoritarian rule which would last 19 months.

Indira Government introduced a constitutional amendment in the Parliament. Civil liberties were suspended. Press freedom was curbed. Normal democratic processes were suspended. Social equality had to wait economic development. The lot of the down trodden had to be improved. Sanjay issued instructions to Chief Ministers, party bosses and bureaucrats. What good was democracy if it could not feed, clothe and shelter people, he questioned.

Noticing all applause around her, Mrs. Gandhi thought she was embodiment of popular will and people should adhere to her way of working. She saw herself as a natural successor of Nehru who was popular among people. She thought those who criticized her were irresponsible, incapable and conspirators. She reduced the cabinet to a rubber stamp. Accountability rested on her. Mrs. Gandhi undermined judiciary, presidency, press, cabinet, Parliament, Congress Party. She proved to being an autocrat.

After promulgation of Emergency, Parliament amended the Constitution and exonerated Mrs. Gandhi of the offense. Court's power to review was taken away. 42nd amendment permitted govt to prohibit anti-national activities. The Emergency factors were latent. Failings of democracy were publicized It was said that democracy bred corruption and violence and led to criminalisation of politics which had become rampant. Sanjaya's stress on family planning by sterilization and demolition of slums embittered people's feelings. They were angry with her, her son and her government.

Soon after promulgation of Emergency, sycophants started

giving encouraging reports to her. She remained unaware of the harm Maintenance of Internal Security Act (MISA) was doing and how police and other officials were terrorizing people. She felt secure.

In January 1977, Mrs. Gandhi, thinking that she had consolidated her position, announced that General Elections would be held in March 1977. She released the opposition, lifted censorship and permitted rallies and public meetings. The political parties did not have time to make preparations for election. But JP saw to it that the four main opposition parties ( Congress O, Jana Sangh, Bhartiya Lok Dal and Socialist Party) submerged their identities and formed the Janata Party. That meant the Janata Party would put up one candidate against each Indira Congress candidate and thus avoid a split of votes. Jagjivan Ram formed a party – Congress for Democracy. It also collaborated with the Janata Party.

In the elections held in March the Janata Party secured 298 seats as against Congress's 153, out of 539 Lok Sabha seats. Both Indira Gandhi and Sanjay Gandhi lost.

The Janata Party was led by Morarji Desai (Congress O). He became the PM. He chose Charan Singh as Dy PM. The Janata Dal called Mrs. Gandhi to account for her excesses and turned it into a vendetta. The Desai Government proved fractious and the constituent parties could not keep together and lost power. While Mrs. Gandhi had become and was seen as a martyr by the sheer mistakes and ineptitude of the Janata Dal, the latter lost power perhaps because of their smear campaign to assassinate her character. In November 1978, Mrs Gandhi won a by-election to Lok Sabha. Morarji Desai fell from power. Charan Singh succeeded him with the help of Sanjay Gandhi. But Sanjay took his revenge and pulled down his government.

Mrs. Gandhi came back to power. But then a great tragedy occurred in her life. One early morning a plane that Sanjay was flying crashed. Sanjay died on the spot. He was very young. Mrs. Gandhi's life became unhappy and miserable. To overcome her grief and make her dream of dynastic rule come true , Indira Gandhi groomed her elder son Rajeev. He had so far been reluctant to join politics but now at his mother's persuasion, he joined.Sanjay's widow, Maneka, however, added bitterness to Mrs. Gandhi's life.     Proud of her family,Mrs.gandhi called it a dynasty, which many detested.In the Western world dynasty refers not only to princes and kings but also to those families which have amassed wealth for a few generations and live in a style. They call their family a dynasty. For instance, Kennedy Dynasty, which does not mean that Kennedy's ancestors were kings or princes. They had settled in US long back and amassed wealth. Their family is therefore referred to as Kennedy Dynasty. Similarly, Motilal amassed wealth and enjoyed a social status, his son Jawaharlal became PM. Jawaharlal's daughter also became PM. If in that sense Indira Gandhi with pride called her family as Nehru-Gandhi Dynasty better to ignore rather than taking it as her personal pride, as her opponents think.

Indira Gandhi was all for national unity and strove for it. But the policy she pursued to achieve the goal left deep scars on the communal, regional and political framework. She created several problems and convinced many that she alone could handle these. Mrs. Gandhi is gone but the problems she created are still there. Some critics compared her achievements with those of other Indian PMs, particularly her father's. Whereas Jawaharlal sought popular and secular appeal, Indira often aroused people's charismatic sentiments. In Mrs. Gandhi's words, "My father was a statesman, I am a political woman" For her political survival,she moved from Nehru's policy of consensus to that of confrontation which took her opponents off-guard. She created such situations in Punjab, Kashmir and Andhra Pradesh. In the end, she fell victim to the very poison she had injected into the Indian system.

It is true that for long Indira Gandhi enjoyed matchless popularity. But some people think that she was a woman of unbridled ambition who would not stop at anything to gain and consolidate power. Jawaharlal Nehru had mishandled Kashmir and Tibet which proved fatal for him. For Indira Gandhi, it was Sanjay's acts, especially relating to Family Planning and Slum Clearance, and after 1980 involvement to end religious fanaticism, which proved disastrous.

Punjab was restive because of problems created by the Akalis. To create a dissension among the Akalis, Giani Zail Singh, then the Chief Minister of Punjab, and Sanjay selected a fanatic, fundamentalist preacher Journail Singh Bhinderawale, from amongst the Akalis who were agitating for Khalistan. But the preacher instead took up the cause of Khalistan. Almost every day murders took place.Mrs.Gandhi found the Khalistani proponents indulged more and more in violence. Finding no way to reconciliation, on June 1, 1984, the Prime Minister gave her generals orders to go ahead for operation Blue Star. On June 5, the Army assaulted on the Golden Temple where the terrorists were hiding and had taken position to fight. Army was asked to save as much damage to the Golden Temple as possible but the terrorists had so fortified and were so entrenched that some damage did occur to the Akal Takht when the army stormed the Temple. There were protests from Sikhs everywhere. Some Sikh soldiers of the Regimental Center at Ramgarh (Bihar) shot dead their commander, Col. S.C. Puri. A conviction had grown in Mrs. Gandhi that Sikhs would take revenge, and she would be a martyr at their hands.

On 30 October, 1984, while Mrs. Gandhi was addressing a political rally at Bhubaneshwar about the dangers of communalism and threat to India's security, some one threw a stone at her. It hurt her nose but ignoring the hurt, she said, "I am not afraid and will make the nation strong." She told an interviewer, " I have lived with danger all my life and I have lived a pretty full life and it makes a pretty little difference if I die in bed or standing up." Was it a premonition? The next day on October 31, 1984, she was assassinated brutally by two of her own bodyguards in her own lawns. There was an alarm about the brutal murder across the country.The assasinators were Sikhs. Within hours of Indira Gandhi's death, Rajiv Gandhi was given the oath by Giani Zail Singh, President of India, and he became the Prime Minister of India.

Mrs. Indira Gandhi was an exceptionally courageous woman. She looked serious but could be witty whenever she wanted. Once Zia-ul-Haq, President of Pakistan, told her, "Please do not believe in whatever appears in Press about you". Indira replied, "Even when Press says that you are a democrat and I am a dictator." It is a pity that she was not spared from gossip, and worse people accepted them as true, not realizing that rumors are spread by people to project themselves as associates of sensitive women. Mathai, Dinesh Singh and Dhirendra Brahmachari fall in this category

Mrs. Gandhi was knowledgeable about arts and cultural

affairs. She had a blend of scientific mind and a heart that cared for Indian's cultural heritage and traditions. Under her, popular culture flourished. Mrs. Gandhi was secular to the core. She had a completely secular attitude towards minorities. She had married a Parsee, Feroze Gandhi. Her elder son Rajeev married Sonia,an Italian Christian.The younger son Sanjay married Maneka, a Sikh girl. Indira Gandhi was an enigmatic person. She was bold but towards the end of her life she turned religious and superstitious. Disgusted at the atrocities being committed in the name of religion, she made an appeal, "Don't shed blood, shed hatred" Mrs. Gandhi regretted that she had to order the army to act and when the Army stormed into the Golden Temple, many men were killed and Akal Takht got damaged.

"Perhaps Mrs. Gandhi's greatness lay", says Pranay Gupte, "not so much in what she did but in what she wanted to do for her country." Another journalist, Aroon Purie said, "It was a job that Prime Minister Gandhi did at a great personal sacrifice with seemingly effortless grace, style, stamina and above all with guts." She was an accomplished politician and a leader of unmatched stature.

# 9
# C.V. RAMAN
(1888-1970)

**Scienceis my God and work my religion. - C.V.Raman**

    Chandrashekhara Venkataraman (popularly known as C.V. Raman) was the first Asian to win the Nobel Prize in Physics. Raman imbibed love for Physics and research from his father Chandrashekhara, a Physics and Mathematics teacher in a Tiruchirapalli (or Trichy) school and a musician. It was from him that Raman developed a taste in music and musical instruments as also in acoustics.

    Raman was the second child of Chandrasekhara and Parvathi Ammal born on November 7,1888. The parents aspired that Raman should become, like his elder brother, C.S.Ayyar an IAAS (Indian Audit & Accounts Service) officer They were proud that the elder child occupied a position in the civil service of the Government of India, and they earnestly wanted Raman also to qualify in that service which was considered next only to the Indian Civil Service ( ICS). Raman met their expectations and brought the family greater laurels. He qualified in IAAS and joined the Service but gave it up to take over an academic job in a college. His dash would bring him greater recognition and satisfaction.

    Raman grew up in an atmosphere of music and science and was recognized a prodigy. A story about his student days in the Presidency College, Madras, is endearingly told. One day, Professor Eliot saw a small boy in the B.A. class. Thinking that he might have strayed, the Professor asked him, "Are you a student of B.A.?" "Yes, Sir" replied the 14-year old Raman. (Madras University that time gave B.A.\ M.A. degrees both in Arts and Science subjects.)

In 1905, he passed his B.A. in first class and won a gold medal. In 1907, Raman was married to Lokasundari Ammal, a few years younger to him.

Raman joined M.A.(Physics) in the Presidency College. He was full of curiosity and enthusiasm and wanted to learn every thing new. He did not feel shy of making a query, if he did not understand something or had any doubts about it. He would set questions like "How?", "Why?" Acoustics interested him most and he developed keen interest in the study of 'sound'. By the time he was 18, two of his research papers were published , one in the Philosophical Magazine, and the other in Nature,one of the most prestigious scientific journals, both published from England.

Raman passed M. A. recording highest marks of all times in Madras University. He passed the IAAS competitive examination also and was appointed as Assistant Accountant General in the Finance Department at Calcutta (Kolkata).At Kolkata, he continued taking keen interest in research. One day, he met Dr. Amritlal Sircar, Secretary of the Indian Association for the Cultivation of Science, and sought his permission for research which he gave. Raman started conducting experiments in the Association's lab.But after sometime, he was transferred to Rangoon (renamed Yangong).This caused a set back to Raman'sresearch.

In 1915, the Calcutta University opened a Science College and created a chair for physics. Raman was appointed Professor in the Physics Department. This gave him an opportunity of closer association with the Indian Science Congress. At the 'first' session of the Science Congress, when Ashutosh Mookerjee, the Vice Chancellor was the Congress President, Raman chaired the Physics section . ( He would preside the Science Congress's annual sessions in 1929 and 1948.) At the age of 29, Raman became the Palit Professor. He was deeply interested in the working of musical instruments. Around 1918, he explained the complex vibrations of the strings of the musical instruments. Later, he found the characteristic tones emitted by instruments, like Tabla, Mridangam etc. In 1919, when Amritlal Sircar died, Prof. Raman became the Honorary Secretary. of the Indian Association for the Cultivation of Science. He was also in-charge of its two labs and was deeply immersed in experiments and research in accoustic.

In 1921, the Congress of the Universities of the British Empire held its meeting in London. Raman participated in it as the representative of the Calcutta University. He was invited to lecture in the Physical Society of London. He observed a strange phenomenon. A whisper, in the St. Paul's Church was clearly heard at two different points? This effect was produced by the reflection of sound. The phenomenon was similar to the scattering of light in ice and quartz system.

Raman's curiosity was aroused by an ordinary phenomenon we see almost every day: Is the deep sea water really blue? On his return journey from London , he would sit on the deck and enjoy the beauty of the sea and pondered: Was the deep blue of the sea due to reflection of the sky? If so, how could it appear in the absence of light? As he thought over the problem, it occurred to him that the blue color may be caused by the scattering of the molecules of the sun's light by water. Within a month of his return, he prepared a paper and sent it to the Royal Society of London. Next year he published a lengthy article on the molecular scattering of light. The Royal Society of London was so impressed by the article that in 1924, it honored the scientist by electing him as its Fellow-FRS. He visited USA and looked into the telescope on the Mount Wilson in California. In 1925, he went to Russia to attend the bicentennial of the Russian Academy of Sciences. Raman's research on sound had made him famous all over the world. In 1926, he started publishing 'The Indian Journal of Physics'.

On March 16, 1928, he announced the discovery of a new phenomenon , now known as the Raman Effect. To explain it in simple language: "Sometimes a rainbow appears and delights our eyes. We see in it shades of red, orange, yellow, green, blue, indigo and violet. The whole ray of the sun includes all these colors. When a beam of sunlight is passed through a glass prism a patch of these color bands are seen. This is called spectrum. The spectrameter is an apparatus used to study the spectrum. Special lines in it are characteristic of the light passing through the prism. A beam of light that courses a single spectral line is said to be monochromatic. When a beam of monochromatic light passes through a transparent substance the beam is scattered." Raman studied the scattered light. On February 28, 1928 he observed two low intensity spectral lines corresponding to the incident monochromatic light. The incident light was monochromatic but the scattered light was not monochromatic. Raman had discovered a new phenomenon lying hidden in nature.

The successful research brought Raman honors from all over the world. In 1928, the Science Society of Rome awarded him the Mattencci Medal. In 1929, the British Government Knighted him and he became Sir C.V.Raman. In 1930, the Royal Society of London awarded him the Hughes Medal. Several Universities awarded him Honorary Doctorate. In 1930, the Swedish Academy of Sciences awarded him the Nobel Prize, the highest award a scientist or writer can be honored with. At the award ceremony, Raman demonstrated his finding 'Raman Effect' by the use of alcohol. (Raman was a strict abstainer.)

The Raman Effect explains the diffraction of light by ultrasonic waves in a liquid. (Diffraction is the very slight bending of light around cones. Ultrasonic waves are invisible high frequency sound waves.)

In 1933, Raman joined the Indian Institute of Science, popularly known as the Tata Institute famous for its crystals. In 1934, Raman established the Indian Academy of Sciences. The objective of the Academy was to bring into existence a center of scientific research where the keenest intellectuals of India can probe into the mysteries of the universe. The Mysore State government gave it 24 acres of land. Raman established at Hebbal, Bangalore, a Raman Research Institute, to which he gave away all his property. He became its Director. It is surrounded by a garden and tall eucalyptus trees. Raman expounded , "A Hindu is required to go to the forest in old age but instead of going to the forest, I made the forest come to me." (It is like mountain coming to Mohammed.) There, he conducted research on varied subjects like sound, light, rocks, gems, birds, insects, butterflies, seashells, trees, flowers, atmosphere, weather and physiology of vision and hearing. His research covered different fields of science like Physics, Geology, Biology and Physiology with particular reference to sound and colors.

Raman's collection of rocks and precious stones includes different objects like sand (that melts due to lightening), rock, including lava flow during a volcano, diamonds, rubies and sapphires, fluorescent minerals. To make his research interesting for the lay man, he bought different kinds of objects like diamonds, butterflies, flowers and plants. The discovery of Laser (Light Amplification by Stimulated   Emission of Radiation) revived interest of popular scientists in Raman Effect.

Raman used to announce his new research at a session of the Academy. In one of its sessions held in Madras in 1967, he discussed the influence of earth's relation to its gaseous envelope and in 1968, put forward the theory of the Physiology of Vision.

Raman was a delightful speaker. Once, while addressing a conference of doctors, Raman humorously called himself a 'General Practitioner of Science.' ( A doctor is a practitioner of Medicine. Why the general practitioner of Science be called a Doctor?) The color of the sea interested him more than the forest. He remained a student throughout his life and used to say that if a research worker is not inspired from within, no amount of money can bring success in research. He said the equipment that brought him the Nobel Prize did not cost more than Rs.300 and that all his research equipment could be managed in a table drawer.

Raman said, "Research is a strange work. Success in research brings limitless joy whereas failure pushes one to deep despair."He added  that Science was his God and work his religion."On God, he said, "New discoveries confirm the existence of God, and if there is God, we have to find Him in the Universe." In 1970, he spoke on his new thesis of hearing and eardrum. This was his last lecture.

In 1970, Raman suffered a mild heart attack. He recovered from its attack but that was not for long, On November 21, 1970, he passed away peacefully.

Below are excerpts from the Presentation Speech of Prof. H. Plaijel, Chairman of the Nobel Committee for Physics of the Royal Swedish Academy of Sciences on Deecember 10, 1930 on the  award of Nobel Prize to Sir Venkataraman:

"The diffusion of light is an optical phenomenon. A ray of light is not perceptible unless it strikes the eye directly. If, however, a bundle of rays of light traverses a medium in which extremely fine is present, the ray of light will scatter to the sides and the path of the ray through the medium will be discernible from the side. The small particles of dust begin to oscillate owing to electric influence from the ray of light, and they form centers from which light is disseminated in all directions. The wavelength, or the number of oscillations per second, in the light thus diffused is the same as in the original ray of light. But this effect has different degrees of strength for light with different wavelengths. It is stranger for the blue part of the spectrum than for the red part. Hence it is a ray of light containing all other colors of the spectrum passes through a medium, the yellow and the red rays will pass through the medium without appreciable scattering, whereas the blue rays will be scattered to the sides. The effect has received the name 'Tyndall Effect'.

"A closer examination of scattering in substances in liquid or gaseous form showed that the scattered light did not in certain respects follow the laws which should hold good for the Tyndall Effect while the sides were polarized. But this did not prove to be the case.

"This divergence was made the starting point of the nature of scattered light. Raman took an active part and sought to find the explanation of the anomalies in asymmetry observed in the molecules. During these studies of his in the phenomenon of scattering, Raman made, in 1928, the unexpected and highly surprising discovery that the scattered light showed not only the radiation that derived from the primary light but also a radiation that contained other wavelengths, which were foreign to the primary light.

"In order to study more closely the properties of the new rays, the primary light that was emitted from a powerful mercury lamp was filtered in such a way as to yield a primary light of one single wavelength. The light scattered from that ray in a medium was watched in a spectrograph in which every wavelength or frequency produces a line. Here he found that, in addition to the mercury line chosen, there was obtained a spectrum of new sharp lines, which appeared in the spectrograph on either side of the original line. When another mercury line was employed, the same extra spectrum showed itself round it. Thus, when the primary light was moved, the new spectrum followed in such a way that the frequency distance between the primary line and the new lines always remained the same.

"Raman investigated the universal character of the phenomenon by using a large number of substances as a scattering medium, and he found the same effect.

"The explanation of the "Raman Effect" has been found by Raman with the help of the modern conception of the nature of light.It cannot be emitted from or absorbed by material otherwise than in the form of definite amounts of energy or what are known as "light quanta". Thus the energy of light would possess a kind of atomic character. A quantum of light proportionate to the frequency of rays of light, so that in the case of a frequency twice as great, the quanta of the rays of light will also be twice as great.

"In order to illustrate the conditions when an atom emits or absorbs light energy, we can, according to Bohr, picture to ourselves the atom as consisting of a nucleus, charged with positive electricity round which negative electrons rotate in circular paths at various distances from the center. The path of every such electron possesses a certain energy, which is different for different distances from the central body. Only certain paths are stable. When the electron moves in such a path, no energy is emitted. When, on the other hand, an electron falls from a path with higher energy to one with lower energy – that is to say, from an outer path to an inner path – light is emitted with a frequency that is characteristic of these two paths, and the energy of radiation consists of a quantum of light. Thus the atom can give rise to as many frequencies as the number of different transitions between the stable paths. There is a line in the spectrum corresponding to each frequency.

"An incoming radiation cannot be absorbed by the atom unless its light quantum is identical with one of the light quanta that the atom can emit. The Raman Effect seems to conflict with this law. The positions of the Raman-lines in the spectrum do not correspond, in point of fact, with the frequencies of the atom itself, and they move with the activating ray. Raman has explained this apparent contradiction and the coming into existence of the lines by the effect of combination between the quantum of light coming from without and the quanta of light that are released or bound in the atom. If the atom, at the same time as it receives from without a quantum of light, emits a quantum of light of a different magnitude, and if the difference between these two quanta is identical with the quantum of light which is bound or released when an electron passes from one path to another, the quantum of light coming from without is absorbed. In that case the atom will emit an extra frequency, which either will be the sum of or the difference between the activating ray and a frequency in the atom itself. In this case these new lines group themselves round the incoming primary frequency on either side of it, and the distance between the activating frequency and the nearest Raman-lines will be identical with the lowest oscillation frequencies of the atom or with its ultra red spectrum. What has been said as to the atom and its oscillations also holds good of the molecule.

"In this way we get the ultra red spectrum moved up to the spectral line of the activating light. The discovery of the Raman-line has proved to be of extraordinarily great importance for our knowledge of the structure of molecules.

"So far, indeed, insuperable difficulties have arisen in the way of study of these ultra red oscillations, because that part of the spectrum lies so far away from the region where the photographic plate is sensitive.Raman's discovery has now overcome these difficulties, and the way has been opened for the investigation of the oscillations of the nucleus of the molecules. We choose the primary ray within that range of frequency where the photographic plate is sensitive. The ultra red spectrum, in the form of the Raman-lines, is moved up to that region and, in consequence of that, exact measurements of its lines can be effected. In the same way, the ultraviolet spectrum can be investigated with the help of the Raman Effect. In fact we have obtained a simple and exact method for the investigation of the entire sphere of oscillation of the molecules."

Raman  and his fellow workers have investigated the frequencies in a large number of substances in  solid, liquid, and gaseous state. Investigations have been made as to whether different conditions of aggregation affect atoms and molecules, and the molecular conditions in electrolytic dissociation and the ultra red absorption spectrum of crystals.The Raman effect has yielded important results about the chemical constitution of substances; and in future it will deepen our knowledge of the structure of matter.

# 10
# Dr. V.N. SHIRODKAR
( 1898-1971)

*Susruta was the greatest surgeon in Indian history. Shirodkar was the greatest innovative surgeons of modern India.*

Ever since the female generally experienced the pangs and joys of child birth, there have been some women the world over who suffered despondency of pregnancy loss, preterm delivery, placental abruptness, fetal growth and other abnormalities. And, medical practitioners had been continually trying to eliminate these anomalies but in vain. Superstitions and religious dicta also hindered the efforts and studies. Sometime the knowledge accumulated over centuries turned out faulty. It was believed in the West that the male fetus sat in the right side of the uterus and the female one in the left side. This misinformation was corrected in 1543 A.D. by Versalius when it wes proved that the uterus had only one cavity for male or female. The organ Uterus was identified and so named. Similarly, the concept of 'Cervical Incompetence' came in vogue in 1648. But its application and detailed placental anatomy and fetus's relationship to the gravid uterus had to wait until the completion of their documentation by William Hunter in 1865. The last two centuries are a witness to the explosion of information and comprehension of human conceptions, early fetal organ genesis , embryology of the reproductive organs leading to the development of adnaxae and uterus. .

Medical science has achieved success in eliminating many of the anomalies. Experts have successfully evolved devices that have corrected uterine anomalies. A pioneer in this field was an Indian, Dr. V.N.Shirodkar: His device known after him as Shirodkar Operation has helped (and continues to help) innumerable women the world over. It has filled their lives with joy. No more can they be stigmatized by superstitious people, specially mother- in- law, as barren as was done in the past.

The uterine anomalies that develop during various gestation periods are:

6-Week: Multi potential germ cells appear in the endoderm ( cell groups) of the yolk sac and migrate along the dorsal mesentery (a developing stage) to invade the gonads (ovary) ridge in the absence of Y chromosome . The fallopian tubes form extensions of the paramesonepheric cuts and ducts.

8-Week: Fusion of the masonepheric ducts is complete and the mid line portion becomes the uterus body.

10.5- Week:: Resumption of the fused medical walls with a single created uterus cavity is complete.

11-12- Week: The caudal tip of the fused ducts projects in the posterior wall of the urganogenital sinus and forms the vaginal fornices as well as 1/3 rd vagina

20- Week: The process of vagina canalization is complete.

Defects can occur during the periods of gestation or even prior to 5- week gestation. Defects in developments of female organs lead to absence of paramasonic ducts, no formation of uterus, fallopian tubes, or of upper vagina. Also, ovarian germ cells may migrate and develop into lower vagina in case the patient has a blind vaginal pouch with hormonally active gonads but no active end organ. When reproductive potential is absent and there are no menses, after successful vaginal plasty, heterosexual intercourse can be initiated.

The 5 to 9- week gestation allows paramasonapheric duct formation without proper mid line uterine fusion. ovaries , fallopian tubes and lower vagina may be  present but without the uterus, cervix or upper vagina. The remnant fallopian tubes may be unilateral or bilateral.

During 10-12 week gestation a variety of fusion and resorption disorders occur. Ovaries, fallopian tubes and a lower vagina may be present with mild to severe malformation. Variations in uterine form may be accompanied by a double cervix and possibly double upper vagina. The severest anomaly leads to uterine and cervical duplication (known as didelphys) with a double upper vagina. The least severe anomaly can lead to an arcuate uterus.

There is a possibility that an aberrant uterine fusion sagittal or transverse septa of the upper vagina may exist in conjunction with other Mullerian defects.

A vaginal defect may also be identified in a suspect case of coexistent uterine anomalies which impact during labor on reproductive function through dyspareunia, obstruction of menses and dystocia. Transverse septa are possible anywhere along the vaginal canal but these are common at the junction between the middle and upper thirds of the vagina. During childhood an obstructive transverse vaginal septum may be encountered, necessitating incision to avoid destructive hydromucoco plus. It is possible that a patient with an incomplete vaginal septum that does not impair menstruation or intercourse may conceive and deliver without obstruction.

The incidence of uterine anomalies approximates 0.25%. These anomalies are encountered in one in 300 women and in one in 1000 deliveries. Most of the obstetric manifestations of uterine anomalies are: abortion, preterm delivery, abruption placenta, fetal malpresentations, dysfunctional labor, and postportum hemorrhage in women with two or more consecutive pregnancy losses.

Surgical repairs in pregnant as well as non-pregnant cervix who had habitual spontaneous abortions became popular in 1950s. Dr. Shirodkar made a landmark contribution in this. In 1955, he reported that cervical cerclage which was painless dilation and effacement followed by a rupture of the membrane, rapid labor and expulsion of the fetus during the late second or early third month was the cause of habitual abortion. He clarified that those women who repeatedly abort between 4th and 7th months and whom neither rest nor hormone treatment helps in retaining the product of conception suffer from cervical incompetence. It implies lack of lower uterine integrity in retaining the uterine pregnancy. Biochemical and hormonal influences play a major role in incompetent cervix. Its symptoms are: a watery vaginal discharge (sometime bleeding) prior to an atypical mild cramping or pressure in the lower pelvis.

Only when a diagnosis has determined, therapeutic alternatives are considered. These could be: surgery (Cerclage or

Lash or Mann procedures) or non-surgical modalities (bed rest, tactile agents, hormonal therapy).

The basis for cerclage repair is reinforcement of junction between fibrous cervix and muscular uterine isthmus (internal cervical). There are many cerclage techniques amongst which Shirodkar's is most popular. This places a submoucosal suture at the level of cervicovaginal junction. It was advised that the needle up should be blunt so as to avoid perforation in cervical vaginal mucosa. Its therapeutic advantages include a high cervical suture placement and an absence of directing the needle toward the amniotic membranes.

Uterine anomalies are divided into seven classes: Hypoplasia Agenesis, Unicorniate, Didephys, Bicornuate, Septate , Arcuate and Des-related.

Class I : The hypoplasia has 5 subdivisons

Class1A.: The presence of transverse vaginal septum prevents an adequate outflow tract for menstruation and is diagnosed when menarche does not follow the larche and adrenarches.The vagina can be connected by both surgical and non surgical means. Patients with a normal uterus have a fair chance of live births.

Class I B : Cervical agenes prevents passage of sperm making pregnancy unlikely. But once pregnancy is achieved, term delivery is a possibility.

Class I C : Uterine agenes is rare.

Class I D : Tubal agenes is seen in conjunction with a unicornuate uterus without a rudimentary harm.

Class II : Malformations involve the unicornuate uterus and have several forms, namely, one, pregnancies in unicornuate uteri with a spontaneous abortion rate of 33 to 48%, a pre term rate of 17 to 29% and a live birth rate of 40 to 66% (have been reported). The presence of a firm, solid pelvic mass contralateral to a deviated uterine fundus are diagnosed. Two, if the pregnancy is implanted in the rudimentary horn, it is a potential surgical emergency; 89% cases occur at 20-week gestation after uterine rupture. Pregnancy in a unicornuate uterus is at risk for interrogative growth retardation, pre term labor and abnormal pressurization of the fetus.

Class III - Uterus Didephys (Uterine and cervical duplication.

Class IV : Biocornuate uterus has wide variation of morphology with complete (type IV-A) and partial (type IV-B) forms. The uterus is characterized by two fundal bodies. Outcome is variable with spontaneous abortion in 35% patients, early delivery in 23% and Caesarian birth in 70 to 90%. Viable birth rates range from 40% for complete lesions to 90% for milder partial forms.

Class V : Sepate Uterus : This is the most common uterine anomaly. The sepate and biocornuate have to be distinguished. In a sepate uterus abortion occurs upto 67% of cases (as compared to 35% in bicornuate).

Class VI. Lesions include arcuate form of uterine cavity.

Uterine anomalies in complete cervix is reported in 17 to 30% patients.Genetic considerations are called for. Fetal concerns should also be examined Urinary tract anomalies may be present in patients. In some cases ceasarian section may be required.

Dr. Shirodkar was also known for turboplasty. (Incompetent cervix is the cause of repeated second trimester abortions.)He devised two operations for genital prolapsed and improved the results of turboplasty. He was gentle to the tissues and quick and precise in work and tirelessly worked for 14 to 16 hours a day. An expert surgeon informed the authors that no surgeon ever did as many turboplasties as Dr. Shorodkar did. He was involved in family planning work also. He stood for liberalization of indications for abortion. (Abortion is the termination off pregnancy before 20th week of gestation.) Spontaneous abortion may be threatened , incomplete, complete or missed.

Dr. Shirodkar was widely traveled and he lectured in USA, UK and other Western countries on the themes that benefited humanity. He visited Japan and South East Asia also. Several universities bestowed honors on him. In 1960, he published his vast experiences in "Contributions to Obstetrics and Gynecology." In 1961, he along with others founded the Indian Akademi of Medical Sciences. That very year, he was awarded Padmashri and a decade later, in 1971, Padma Vibhushan. He was a versatile - painter, sportsman and violin player.

Vithal Nagesh Shirodkar was born on April 27, 1898 in village Shiroda, in Goa. After schooling in Hubli, he did his M.B.B.S. with special studies in Obstetrics and Gynecology from the Grant Medical College, Bombay, in 1923. In 1927, he had his M.D. from Bombay University and in 1935, F.R.C.S. from England. On his return to India, Shirodkar held a surgical appointment for a while and was soon thereafter appointed Hony. Obstetrician and Gynecologist to the JJ Group of Hospitals. In 1940, he was appointed professor in the Grant Medical College. He was attached to the Wadia Maternity Hospital also. Of the four Cerclage techniques in vogue, the two most popular are those devised by Shirodkar and Mac Donald; the other two are known as Emergent and Transabdominal. The Shirodkar Cerclage places a submucosal suture at the level of cervicovaginal junction.The surgery requires of a surgeon to gently clean the vagina to avoid trauma to the cervix or membrane. The theoretical advantages of the Shirodkar technique include a high cervical suture placement and absence of the needle toward the animiotic membranes. One of Dr.Shirodkar's students, Dr. Shakuntala Gheewala writes, "His lectures were always informative and his method of teaching interesting.He would introduce jokes in between serious topics so that it registered with students.If he wanted to say, ' cauterization is burning ', he would say, "I will burn you a little".' He was conservative in outlook, and did surgery as a last treatment, not as a shortcut He invented a simple operation for prolapse coming down of vaginal walls and cervix of uterus.He advocated a simple round stitch around cervix to prevent repeated abortions. He was popular among students."

Authors' search for a beneficiary of the Shirodkar operation took them to a very happy couple Kanubhai Shah and his gentle wife Kusumbehn, formerly of Bombay. Kanu is a witty guy and rather than intruding into a lady's sphere, he asked Kusumbehn to narrate her experience about the birth of their son, by Shirodlar Operation. We were wondering that the lady might feel shy.But no, she described her experience in detail. After the loss of two male children of eight days and two days, respectively, by premature birth, followed by three miscarriages, the couple was worried. Kanubhai discussed with doctors and on their advice met Dr. Shirodkar, who carried out an operation and a bonny baby was born. The doctor congratulated Kanubhai. Their son Suraj is now

43, healthy and doing well in life. Kanu and Kusum Shah live in Santa Clara with Suraj and his family. That day we met four other families who had benefited from Dr. Shirodkar's expertise.

Dr. Shirodkar passed away on March 7, 1971.

GLOSSARY

abortion : termination of pregnancy

Technical before 20th week it may be threatened, incomplete, complete abruptic placenta : bleeding when placenta separates from uterine wall.

adrenarche : deviation in menarche

agenesis : defective/ incomplete uterus development

arcuate: curved like a bow.: tiny crescent line within the gestation sac in first trimester.

Bicornuate uterus: uterus with two horns in  embryo that failed to attain fusion.

Caudal: analgesia or anesthesia that result from solutions into caudal canal.

Cerclage: a type of surgery.

Cervical intelligence ; incapability to retain the product of conception.

Cervix : lower part of uterus

corpuscle : a cell of blood

didalphys: uterine and cervical duplication dorsal; position used for examination of chest and abdomen

dyspereunia  : pain during sexual intercourse in patients with a double uterus caused by a vaginal septum dystorcia : difficult, slow or painful birth endoderm : innermost of the three germ cell layers of the embryo fundus (uterine) ; the bottom or area farthest from opening of a hollow organ

gestation : conception between fertilization and birth

hypoplasia : defective/ incomplete

development  incompetent cervix : uterus incapable of retention conception lesion : localized abnormal structural change caused by injury or disease

menarche : first menstruation marks on set of puberty in female ( 11to 13)

mesentery: double layer of peritoneum extending from abdomen to pelvic, conveys blood vessels and nerves; holds and supports abdominal pelvic organs

morphology : science dealing with form and structure of body

mucosa : mucous membrane of tissues lining cavities opening to out side of body

nephron : functional unit of kidney

obstetrics : medicine concerning management of women during pregnancy, child birth and puerpernum

para masonepheric : cuts, ductsrelating to uterus

postpartum hemorrhage : excessive bleeding from or into genital tract in 24 hours of birth

resorption :removal of bone or structure by pressure

sagittal : plane running vertically dividing body into right and left parts

septa : septum is dividing wall, partition or membrane

septate uterus: Partial or incomplete uterus

sinus : a hollow cavity connected with nasal passages

submucosa : layer of tissue that connects mucous membrane

thelarche : enlargement of breast indicative of onset of puberty which takes 5 stages

transverse : plane separating body into superior and inferior parts

tubal pregnancy : ovum fertilizes in outer part of tube, passing along tube in 3 to 4 days. It reaches uterus in early blastocyte stage and gets embedded into endometrium between 6th and 7th day. The free passage of fertilized ovum may be arrested due to mechanical factor resulting in tubal pregnancy: the main cause is sulpingitis. The formation of embryo proceeds in the same manner as in uterine pregnancy. Tubal rupture may shock the patient.

Unicornuate: one horn

uterine agnesis : defective uterus

urogenital sinus : hollow of genital and urinary organs

uterus : hollow muscular reproductive female organ Fertilized ovum gets enmeshed in it.

In India creditable work is being done at various centers by eminent doctors. Some named by Dr.R. Meera are: Dr. Ramamurthy (Neurophysician,Chennai),Dr.Srinath Reddy (AIIMS, New Delhi), Dr.Shah (Beach Candy, Bombay), Dr.Venkataswamy (Opthalmologist, Arvind Eye Hospital, Chennai).

# 11
# Homi  J.  BHABHA
( 1909-1966)

*A few nations that have grown very strong technologically over the past few centuries have wrested control for their own purposes. These major powers have become the self proclaimed leaders of the new world order.What does a country of one billion people,India, do in such a situation?We have no other option but to be technologically strong.But can India be a leader in the field of technology?My answer is an emphatic 'Yes".*
*—A.P.J.Abdul Kalam with Arun Tewari in* Wings of Fire

A stream of thought similar to that of Abdul Kalam, the present President of India, were nurtured decades ego in the mind of another Indian, Homi J.Bhabha, who while studying in England had witnessed fast scietific developments taking place in Europe. On return to his motherland, imbued with enthusiasm, he had tried to do whatever he could to hasten developments in the sphere of science in India. Homi Bhabha thought that like the Western countries, India should create opportunities for latest nuclear research. But giving the idea a concrete shape was not easy. It required finances which were ever in short supply in India. He surmised that finances could be procured from a big industrialist, perhaps from the Tatas. The Tatas were men of  foresight and vision and would agree to invest finances.The Tata Institute of Fundamental Research (TFIR),  one of the most prestigious and renowned organizations, originated primarily with Bhabha's efforts at Bangalore in 1935. The same year, it was shifted to Mumbai, then known as Bombay.

Homi Bhabha was born in 1909 at Bombay. He received

his early education at the Cathedral School and passed the School Leaving Certificate examination in 1925. Two years later, in 1927, he proceeded to England for higher education. Bhabha studied Mechanical Science at Cambridge from 1927 to 1930 and passed Tripos in 1930. But after graduation in Mechanical engineering, he switched over to Theoretical Physics and in 1935, received Ph.D. in Physics. Why he took to Physics has a story behind it. In 1928, Homi had clashed with his father J.H. Bhabha, an Oxanian and Bar-at- Law and working as Director of Education in Mysore State, who wanted Homi to become an engineer. But the son wanted to study Physics.The father had taunted 'You are not Socrates or Einstein'.

At Cambridge Bhabha was exposed to scientific developments in the substructure of atomic nucleus and fission of uranium nucleus. Between 1935 and 1939, he conducted research on cosmic radiation, with John Cockraft and Paul Dirac in the Rutherford lab. He had opportunities to meet with other distinguished researchers. He befriended W.B.Lewis, Neil Bohr (at Copenhagen), Wolfgang Paul (from in Zurich), Enricho Fermi (from Rome), and James Franck. He identified muons present in cosmic rays and learned about the discovery of fission material.

That time, high energy physics was the great expanding science.The notion of a man made explosion of colossal power was implicit in Einstein's special Theory of Relativity. Uranium 235 was the new material of quest and there was a race to secure it. There was a symmetry in the develpment of atomic knowledge.There was a fear that Hitler might first come in possession of the atomic device. In 1932, J.D. Cockraft and T.S. Wilson used a 500 Pound piece of equipment to split the atom. (The Director was outraged at this expenditure). Their colleague Sir James Chadwik discovered the neutron,consisting of proton and electron holding energy of 1to 2 million electron volts.In 1934, Joliet-Curie of France made radio-active isotopes artificially and Enric Fermi, in Italysuccessfully slowed down neutron.He went on to produce tranceuranic elements with even heavier masses . In 1939 scientists had become aware of the possibility of atomic explosion.

Bhabha wanted to continue his research but in 1939, he left for India hoping to return soon. While he was still in India, the

World War started and he was stuck up. In 1940, he was elected (in absentia) to the Fellowship of Royal Society ( F.R.S.). This was a great honor for the young Bhabha. Since he was unable to return to England, he accepted an appointment in the Indian Institute of Sciences (IIS) at Bangalore as a Reader in the Physics Department, which was headed by the famous scientist, C.V. Raman , the Nobel Laureate. After sometime, Bhabha was designated as the Professor of Cosmic Rays. Bhabha was well known amongst physicists. His name was already associated with electron scattering.

Bhabha wanted that India should keep pace with scientific developments that were taking place in the West. He had witnessed fast progress in nuclear research. He thought should India get involved in nuclear development, it would change the face of the country. But this required finance. The Tatas were one of the most advanced industrialists in the country. They had already established TISCO at Jamshedpur and had set up power plants in Bombay Presidency. In March 1944, Bhabha foresaw that if a chain reaction came out successful, rapid improvements could be expected.Tatas could help in this. Fortunately, the Bhabhas were closely related to the Tatas. Homi's paternal aunt was married to Dorabji Tata and to him Homi wrote a letter seeking his help in establishing a Center for fundamental research in emerging areas of Physics. Western countries were engaged in such work and were making rapid progress. Should India take steps in the right direction, it will develop nuclear energy for power production, and if a Center was set up for the purpose, it would initially serve as a nursery for growing atomic energy program and build a team of experts.The world soon experienced the effect of development in nuclear energy when US exploded the atomic device in Japan. The world became aware of the potential of atomic energy on August 6,1945, when US dropped on Hiroshima an atom bomb that killed one lac people. The plutonium bomb dropped on August 9 at Nagasaki killed 74000 people. The impact was so acute that Japan surrendered and the War came to an end..

Dorabji Tata gave Rs. 45000, an amount not small for those times.(Director of cavendish Lab had expressed his displeasure on expenditure of 500 Pounds.) In December 1945, the Tata Institute of Fundamental Research (TFIR) with Homi Bhabha as Director was set up.( A few months later the Institute was shifted from

Bangalore to Bombay.) Jawaharlal Nehru inaugurated it. Bhabha was entrusted with complete authority over nuclear affairs.

In a Note, Bhabha apprised Prime Minister Jawahar Lal Nehru of the developments and  summarized his atomic energy vision for India. The Note included 13 items in the Institute's Program, such as-Setting up Atomic Energy Establishment; Prospecting and Processing Uranium; Building Plant for Production of Heavy Water and Barium; Providing Plants for Uranium Enrichment and for Atomic Power ; Breeder Reactors; Plutonium Extraction. It also included Coordinating Research in Universities and Institutions; Developing and Promoting Use of Radioactive Tracers in Biology, Medicine and Industry.

The work called for expeditious processing and completion. Many hurdles, such as  bureaucratic delays and auditing of petty expenditure,could be avoided in the interest of  speedier execution of work. Provision of on-the-spot facilities to the scientists and technologists would facilitate their work. Prime Minister Nehru agreed to Bhabha's request  to legislate Atomic Energy. After this was done, an Atomic Energy Commission was created. Bhabha asked the government for a sanction of Rs. 10 lac (one million) for the atomic energy program during the first year, and later for  Rs. One Crore (ten million) for the next three years. (The current annual budget for the program  runs into hundreds  of crores.)

The Atomic Energy Commission was set up under the Ministry of Natural Resources and Scientific Research. Its functions related to atomic subjects including atomic research. On January 3, 1954, the Commission set up a Department of Atomic Energy (DAE). All work relating to application of nuclear power was placed under the Deparment. The construction work of its buildings started in right earnest at Trombay. The area was underdeveloped and workers had to be wary of uninvited guests the bushes were infested with slithering snakes. To fight with the menace, plenty of serum was kept ready and on the spot treatment given to the patients. Another serious problem was the lack of trained personnel To meet this shortage, it was decided that people at the top should do more than one job. Thus a multi-disciplinary atmosphere was created.

In 1955, Bhabha was made president of UN Conference on Peaceful Uses of Atomic Energy and Applied Physics. The

Deparment of Atomic Energy was formally inaugurated on January 20, 1957 by Prime Minister Jawaharlal Nehru. Bhabha was appointed as the Secretary of DAE. In 1962, when the construction work of the building was over, there emerged a magnificent building..

Bhabha is acknowledged as the founder and prime architect of Indian atomic energy program. His researches and talents were recognized world wide From 1960 to 1963, he was President of the International Union of Pure and Applied Physics.

All his life, Dr. Homi Jehangir Bhabha dominated both the scientific and policy spheres of India's nuclear affairs. First, he brought the nuclear program to life and then set its priorities and direction. In his letter to Dorab Tata Trust in 1944, Homi Bhabha had made the prophetic observation that "When nuclear energy has been successfully applied for power production, in say a couple of decades from now, India will not have to look abroad, for experts but will find them ready at home." His prophecy has come out true. Now a large number of Indian scientists and engineers are working abroad. In the country itself the number of technical personnel engaged in work is pretty large. Bhabha had personally recruited and sponsored many of India's principal scientists, such as Sethna, Vasudev Iya, and Raja Ramanna, who would play important role in the development and testing of nuclear weapons.

Bhabha's personal relations had helped in making the program successful. His rowing teammate in England, W.B. Lewis, who later became the Chairman of the Canadian program was helpful in building up the Cirus, the Canadian heavy water reactor-ostensibly for peaceful purpose .(Later it proved to be an ideal system for producing weapons grade plutonium ; later its capability was achieved and utilized.) In fact Bhabha had from the beginning planned to establish India's nuclear capability. Nehru had supported Bhabha's plan for developing an Indian nuclear weapons option. The validity of this decision was sharply illustrated in the wake of China's first nuclear test. Lal Bahadur Shastri had agreed with Bhabha's preference to withstand legislative and public criticism. Unfortunately, Shastri died of heart attack on January 11, 1966, and two weeks later on January 24,1966, that is a day after Indira Gandhi was sworn in as Prime minister, Dr. Homi J. Bhabha died in a plane crash in collision with Mount Blank

Bhabha had once told Ramanna, "We should first prove ourselves and then talk of Gandhi's non violence and a world without weapon." He meant the first need was the product and only thereafter discretion of its utility or use should be talked about. It also needs to be remembered that the core competence of the various units of BARC has helped in developing strategic technologies.

Giving nuclear capability was Bhabha's contribution to his country. In fact Bhabha knew  much about nuclear fission which he wanted to use in creating a nuclear device to end the monopoly of a few nations. Whatever that be , Bhabha was responsible for providing the wherewithal for India's nuclear device.His ingenuity helped India to be placed on the secure map of the world.

The Government of India in recognition of Bhabha's services, in January 1967, renamed the organization as the Bhabha Atomic Research Center (BARC). The Center provided facilities for research in technology for building nuclear reactors, fuel fabrication, reprocessing irradiated fuel, applications of radio isotopes in medicine, agriculture and industry. The Center has also set up schools of research in nuclear physics, solid state physics, chemical and life sciences, reactor engineering, instrumentation, nuclear radiation safety and nuclear medicine.

The BARC also provides research and development support in relation to concepts, designs, materials, reliability and safety.

# 12
# S. CHANDRASHEKHAR
(1910—1995)

---

The lumber years for scientists, as for athletes, generally come at a
young age. Isaac Newton was in his twenties when he discovered
the law of gravity, Albert Einstein was twenty-six when he
formulated special relativity, and Clark Maxwell had polished off
electro-magnetic theory and returned to the country by thirty-five.

— Alan Lightman in '*a sense of the mysterious*' (p.173)

Subramanyian Chandrashakher had by twenty-five done
significant original research in astrophysics for which he would be
later recognized as the foremost astrophysicist of his time. ( Recenly
we read about a child prodigy of 6 in India who was doing wonders
in computer science.) Also, Chandrashekhar is a unique example
of how the course of a man's life could change by the study of a
single book. The book was *Atomic Structure and Spectral Lines*
by Arnold Sommerfeld. The episode is worth telling.

Chandra (as Chandrasekhar was popularly known), born
on October 10,1910 at Lahore, was the first son (and the third of
10 children) of C.S. Ayyar, a civil servant, and Sitalakshmi, a lady
of high intellectual attainments. He was educated at home by his
parents and private tutors. Mother taught him Tamil and English
and father taught English and Arithmetic. In 1918, on C.S. Ayyar's
transfer, the family moved to Madras ( Chennai). There he attended
the Hindu High School, Triplicane from 1922 to 1925. In 1925, at
the age of 15, he joined the Presidency College and opted for studies
in Mathematics, Physics, Chemistry and Sanskrit, beside English

which was compulsory. Inspired by an Indian prodigy, Ramanujam who was then doing research in Mathematics at Cambridge, Chandra wanted to take mathematics in B.A.(Honors) but his father did not approve of the idea, since according to him, it was not a good scoring subject for I.C.S (Indian Civil Service). Chandra compromised with Physics Honors to which his father did not object as his own younger brother C.V. Raman, a Physics student, had qualified for IAAS (Audit and Accounts) Service and had later earned recognition in academia.

Chandra took Physics and was doing well but his heart was on Mathematics. Seeing Chandra's deep interest in Mathematics, he was allowed by professors to informally attend Mathematics lectures. Chandra was highly impressed by a book titled *Atomic Structure and Spectral Lines* written by Arnold Sommerfeld. It was based on Bohr's Quantum Mechanics. In 1928, Sommerfeld lectured at the Presidency College. Chandra attended the lecture and made it a point to meet the lecturer, Sommerfeld. The Author mathematician, Sommerfeld clarified that Quantum Mechanics had been superseded by Wave Mechanics of Schroedinger, Herisenberg, Dirac and Pauli et al. and the Pauli exclusion principle had replaced Boltzman statistics with Fermi - Dirac statistics.

Chandra studied the new Quantum Mechanics and Statistics and in 1929 wrote a research paper 'The Comptom Scattering and the New Statistics', and sent it to Professor H.R.Fowler for publication in the Proceedings of the Royal Society of London. In October 1929, Chandra attended Herisenberg's lecture at the Presidency College and discussed the subject with him. Chandra was invited by Professor Meghnad Saha to Allahabad where the scientific community appreciated Chandra's paper. However, the British snobbery treated Chandra just otherwise. He would suffer for his bold and brilliant approach and faced a serious problem at Cambridge. He had established a record score in the final examinationand for which he was awarded a special Government of India three-year scholarship for studies in England.

Chandrasekhar was hesitant to accept the scholarship as his mother was terminally ill. But Sitalakshmi asked him to avail of the scholarship and go to England. Chandra intimated the authorities that he wished to utilize the government scholarship to study and research at Cambridge with Professor R. H. Fowler, who had applied the new statistics to collapsed stars, that is white dwarfs, a subject of his interest. The office of the High Commissioner had proceeded to make necessary arrangements, as intimated.

Chandra departed from Bombay on July 31,1930. While he was on boat, he utilized the time in working out the statistical mechanics of the degenerate electron gas in white dwarf stars. He came to the conclusion that massive stars cannot fade out as white dwarfs as they become black holes. This was against the prevalent scientific view which was that all stars after burning up their fuel became faint planet sized remnants known as white dwarfs .He determined that stars with a mass greater than 1.4 times that of sun must collapse. He reached London on August 19.but to his horror and surprise , he found the Director of Public Instruction in Madras and the High Commissioner of India in London had bungled in his admission to Cambridge. The office of the High Commissioner realized the mistake they had made but rudely declined to rectify it. The situation was not only frustrating but distressing also. Fortunately, Prof. Fowler's intervention saved the situation and Chandra took up his three- year studies at Cambridge in right earnest.

Mother Sitalakshmi died on May 31,1931. Mother's death disturbed Chandrashekhar. He was heart-broken. In England Chandrashekhar attended the monthly meetings of the Royal Astronomical Society and got acquainted with E.A.Milne ,PAM Dirac and other famous people. Here is a brief account of what he did during the next three years:

1930-31: Chandra calculated opacities and applied the results to construction of an improved model for the limiting mass of degenerate star.

1931-32: He spent summer at the Bonn Institute of Gottingen on invitation from Max Bonn. In autumn he returned to Cambridge and continued to work on atomic absorption coefficients and mean opacities. In January 1932, he presented his results on model stellar photospheres at the meeting of the Royal Astronomical Society. He was complemented by Milne and Eddington.

1933-34 : He worked at the Bohr Institute at Copenhagen.

He was convinced that his real strength lay in developing and expounding the implications of the basic physical laws of nature as distinct from the pursuit of the new laws of nature. The scientific community evinced interest in Chandra's work in degenerate stars. He spoke on the theme at the University of Liege. He was presented a bronze medal. This set him on the firm path of theoretical physics. He passed the rest of the research period in writing four papers on rotating self gravitating polytropes which became his Ph.D. thesis.

The three-year scholarship was now coming to an end and Chandra faced a difficult situation. In August 1933 the government scholarship actually ran out. Unexpectedly, he got a Fellowship in the Trinity College for four years. Milne nominated Chanrashekhar as a Fellow of Trinity College. The meetings of the RAS had done him good. He had become familiar with leading scientists like Sir James Jeans, Sir Arthur Eddington and international visitors like Henry Norris and Harlow Shapley.

Chandrashekhar passed the summer of 1934 in Soviet Russia. A leading scientist V.A. Ambastenmian suggested to Chandra that he should work out with precision on dwarf stars. On return from Russia, he worked on white dwarfs with precision and completed the work by the year's end.

In January, 1935 Chandra presented the results at the meeting of R.A.S. After he had read his paper, Eddinton read his paper 'Relativistic Degeneracy' in which he vehemently criticized Chandra's conclusions. But some of Eddigton's assertions were wrong which none pointed out apprehending Eddington's malice Chandra was in a fix. The Eddington factor 's effect was that in England all the doors were closed for him. It is not known whether Chandra believed in luck or not. He found himself out of sympathy with the political nature of academia in India. His father asked him to return to India. Chandra did not want to return to India. At this juncture he received an invitation from Harlow Shapely to visit Harvard Observatory. At Harvard, Chandrashekhar gave lectures relating to his research. These were appreciated by scientists. Shapely nominated Chandra for election to the Harvard Society of Fellows. From the Chicago University Otto Struve invited Chandra to visit Yerkes Observatory. The office of Chancellor Robert Maynard Hutchins offered Chandra a position as Research

Associate for a year expecting it to become a tenure track appointment in a year's time. Chandra accepted the offer.

In August 1936 Chandra left for India. In Madras, he married his former class fellow, Lalitha Doraiswami. After a short while, the newly weds left for USA via england. After a sojourn at Cambridge, on December 21, 1936, the couple arrived Wisconsin. Yerves Observatory was not far. In 1938, when the University approved of his teaching a course in the Chicago University campus, Chandra joined the University of Chicago. It looks unbelievable that he taught there for 59 years. In 1952, when the Department of astronomy revamped its graduate curriculum, and Chandra's post was being eliminated, Enricho Fermi offered him a post in the Department of Physics. Chandra accepted the offer and henceforth confined himself to teaching there The same year Chandrashekhar became the Managing Editor of the Astrophysical Journal. The next year Chandrashekhar and Lalitha became naturalized US citizens. The Journal under his management made considerable progress. In 1967, he transferred it to the American Astronomical Society.

Chandrashekhar wrote about his creative life. He divides his life in seven periods during each one of which he contributed something specific: one, 1929-1939-stellar structure, including the theory of white dwarfs; two, 1938-1943-stellar dynamics, including the theory of Brownian motion; three, 1943-1950, the theory of radiative transfer , including the theory of stellar atmospheres and the quantum theory of the negative ion of hydrogen and the theory of illumination and the polarization of the sunlit sky; four,1952-1961 hydrodynamic and hydromagnetic stability, including the theory of Rayleigh-Bernard convection; five, 1961-1968 the equilibrium and the stability of ellipsoidal figures of equilibrium; six, 1962-1971 the general theory of relativity and relativistic astrophysics; and, seven, 1974-1983 the mathematical theory of black holes. Each of these produced its own monograph. In 1982 Chandra lectured on Sir Arthur's birth day centenary at Cambridge. In 1983, Chandrashekhar was awarded the Nobel Prize.

One significant contribution that Chandra made towards the end of his life relates to Newton's Principia. It was published in a book titled—*Newton's Principia for the Common Man.* This dispelled the wrong notion that Newton's theory of perturbation of the orbit of the moon is an error, or that some of his diagrams were incorrectly drawn.

Dr. Chanrashekhar passed away in 1995 at Chicago, leaving behind his wife Lalitha and brothers and sisters at Chennai. NASA honored him by renaming its Advanced X-ray Astrophysics Facility after him: the Chandra Xray observatory. This helps astronomers in better understanding the structure and evolution of the universe. Besides science, he took keen interest in literature, music and philosophy. His work *Truth and Beauty: Aesthetics and Motivations in Science* was highly acclaimed. In addition to the Nobel Prize,which was awarded jointly to him with astrophysicist F.A. Fowler, he received 20 honorary degrees and was elected to 21 learned societies . He was awarded the Gold Medal of the Royal Astronomical Society of London, the Rumford Medal of the Academies of Arts and Sciences and many other coveted prizes. Chandrashekhar always kept India's well-being in mind. He was associated with many scientific institutions .He was instrumental in establishing the Ramanujam Institute at Madras (Chennai).

What the great astrophysicist said about Science is worth quoting ," The pursuit of science has often been compared to the scaling of mountains. High and not so high. But who amongst us can hope, even in imagination, to scale the Everest and reach its summit when the sky is blue and the air is still: and in the stillness of the air survey the entire Himalayan range in the dazzling white of the snow stretching to infinity. None of us can hope for a comparable vision and of the universe around us. But there is nothing mean or lowly in standing in the valley below and waiting for the sun to rise over the Kanchunchunga.

# 13
# Dr. S. RADHAKRISHNAN
(1888-1975)

No person in the recent history of education is comparable to Dr. Sarvapalli Radhakrishnan. Professionally, an academician and philosopher, he rose to become the head of the Union of India. A philosopher as the head of state was the ideal of Plato, the ancient Greek Philosopher. In Radhakrishnan as the President of India (1962-67), the Greek philosopher Plato's dream became a reality.

Dr. Radhakrishnan was primarily concerned with two broader aspects of philosophy: one, should philosophy concern with interpretation of life only or should it also shape life? Contemporary thinkers view that philosophy concerns with the interpretation of life, and that shaping it is the concern of religion. It is religion that tries to find the meanings of life, spirit and freedom.

In the opinion of some scholars, Dr. Radhakrishnan was only an interpreter or at best a historian of Indian Philosophy. They also say that he was not an original thinker or philosopher ; he had no philosophy of his own. This is wrong others say. He was a creative thinker, besides being a scholar, they assert. He was aware of the difficulties that come in the way of historical interpretation of Indian thought and used the comparative method to clarify that indian philosophy was not an antiquarian pursuit. He wrote," Ancient Indians do not belong to a different species. They ask questions and find answers analogous in their diversity to some of the more important currents in modern thought."

Radhakrishnan was influenced by the Advait Vedanta of Shakar and Dvaita and Vishistadvaitavad of Ramanuja and

Madhvacharya. He was also influenced by Western thinkers like Plato, Plotinus and Immanuel Kant.

Shankaracharya (aka Shankar) was said to be a 'Prachchhinna Buddha', meaning Buddha in disguise. But in refutation of this and in support of Shankar, it is asked: Was Buddha, in repudiating empirical soul, not inclined towards the Upanishadic soul? As for the Bodhi of Buddhism, if the self is not universal, then what can Bodhi be? And, then in that case, what the universal self is?

Dr. Radhakrishnan had definite views on questions of religion and philosophy. According to him, human consciousness has three levels- perception, reason, and intuition. Perception helps in collecting observed data, reason helps in exercising rational reflection. On the other hand, intuition adds meaning, value and character. Radhakrishnan believed that scientific knowledge was dominated by perception and reason, and, therefore, it was inadequate, partial and fragmentary. It is the intuitive insight that gives fullness to man as a man, leads him to spiritual joy which is akin to aesthetic satisfaction and brings about fulfillment of his inner being. This is Radhakrishnan's idealistic view of life; an idea of a universal religion and a universal spiritual life for every being. It is connected with the third level of consciousness (i.e. integral consciousness). It adds meaning, value and worth of life and makes it purposeful. Devoid of it, civilization would be bankrupt. Dr. Radhakrishnan was optimist that cultivation of awareness would take man towards the quest for infinite joy of the absolute and away from materialistic pleasures.

Dr. Radhakrishnan's view of religion has also come in for criticism. It is generally thought that religion encourages man to take to dogmas and that it prejudices him towards other beliefs. A true believer claims that only his religion is true and its values are ultimate. But were it so, where would the common tie and underlying unity of different religious traditions stand? Radhakrishnan thought the world of spirit could be the basis. It may enable us to ignore formulations of the divine in different traditions and lead towards unity, for the divine though formless and nameless is capable of manifesting himself in all forms and names.

Dr. Radhakrishnan was not an Indianist (i.e one who

believes that India alone can save the world from disaster). He searched for a universal religion which is found in all lands and in all cultures, in all thoughts of Eastern as well as Western thinkers; in the thoughts of seers of Upanishads as also of Western thinkers like Plato, Plotinus, Philo, Jesus and Paul and in all men of God. He believed in the meeting of the Eastern and Western streams that reside in the spirit which alone can save mankind from the present meaninglessness.

Dr. Radhakrishnan has to his credit several works, of these the following are well known: *Indian Philosophy (Vol I, II, 1923,1927), Hindu View of Life (1927), An Idealist View of Life (1931), East and West in Religion (1933), Eastern Religion and Western Thought (1939), Religion and Society (1947), The Bhagwat Gita (1948), and The Brahma Sutra (1960).*

In the estimate of the Western scholars Radhakrishnan's interpretation of Hindu Philosophy is the best interpretation ever made. This evaluation is welcome. But it would have been better if these scholars had, before expressing their opinion, compared Radhakrishnan's approach with the approaches of contemporary Indian philosophers, like Dasgupta and Harianna, who have also conducted detailed studies and interpreted their views on Indian thought in their own ways. Some critics opine that Radhakrishnan was a better politician whereas others were more devoted to Darshan (Sanskrit term for Philosophy). As Radhakrishnan's thoughts are scattered in his works, the assessment of his standing as an original thinker becomes difficult..

Gopal, a historian son of Dr. Radhakrishnan, has authored an outstanding biography of his father. .He begins the absorbing work with the uncertainty of his father's date of birth. We admire the courage and honesty of Dr. Gopal when he says that "most of the major details about his birth are uncertain." The official version is that Radhakrishnan was born on September 5, 1888 son of Sarvapalli Veeraswami and Sitamma. The family led a life of grinding poverty. Radhakrishna himself believed that the date of his birth was "in fact" September 20, 1887. He had his early education at Tirutani. He received his first lessons in the Bible in the Mission School at Tirupati (in 1896) which supplemented his knowledge of Hindu religion. But child Radhakrishnan had 'nothing remarkable'.about himself. He would rather go wayward than make academic progress. However, in his matriculation examination he fared very well and was awarded a scholarship. In his school he had became familiar with the writings of Vivekananda and V.D. Savarkar and imbibed the spirit of nationalism.

In May 1903, at the age of 16, Radhakrishnan was married to a distant cousin Shivakamu (or Padma as Radhakrishna called her) aged 10. "They were chosen for each other because they seemed hardly fitted for anyone else". They made a dissonant couple. Shivakamu was devoted to him but he would not accept that "his loyalty to her was tarnished by his extra-marital adventurers"..

In 1904, Radhakrishnan passed his First Arts examination with distinction and won a scholarship to the Christian College, Vellore. He was extravagant and had to at times borrow money.To supplement his income he took up tutions and wrote articles for newspapers...He realized .that poverty was an obstacle to man's progress. In 1906, he got his B.A. and three years later, in 1909, his M. A. That time brilliant students were crazy about going to Oxford but not Radhakrishnan. He said that if ever he went to Oxford, it would be not to study but to teach there.Years later, this would come .true. He went to Oxford as a professor.

Radhakrishnan wanted that he should look different from others. He worked out a dress for himself - a long silk coat buttoned-up at the neck and reaching down to his knees, a white dhoti with a black border, black shoes and a turban of white muslin. This was his attire (in India) for the rest of his life. Along with teaching, he had an active social life. Radhakrishnan persevered with his studies, and never ceased to build on what he had learned. Readers are attracted by Radhakrishnan's smooth language, rigor and clarity of style, literary allusions and striking quotations in his writings. He had become familiar with the works of Tilak, Gandhi, and Tagore and wrote about them appreciatively. But his impressions about his meeting with Gandhi were rather poor. He was impressed more by Tagore who, he found, was more influenced by Vedanta. He made a comparative study of Vedanta and Christianity also. Like Western critics he expressed his views on a world order after the First World War which brought him to the notice of Western scholars.

Much to his dismay, Radhakrishnan was transferred from

Presidency College to a college in Rajamundhry to make way for a non-Brahmin teacher. But then he got a job of professor of philosophy in Mysore University and moved to Mysore in July 1918.

In his next work he made a comparative study of the contemporary Western metaphysics with Vedanta and found the latter superior. An American philosopher castigated Religion as intellectual measles and wild oats.He thought Religion should not be the starting point; it better be the terminus of Philosophy; and ethical and religious conclusions should not control the philosophical discussion. Gopal summarizes Radhakrishnan's view "True philosophy would result in true religion and this was to Radhakrishnan, the Advaita Vedanta". He thought that the well known contemporary philosophers-Bertrand Russell, William James and Bergson-were producing ignoramus of philosophy?

While at Mysore, he tried his hand on a novel *The Crime of Leela*. One may appreciate the novelist's effort at depicting the role of women through a media different from the one he was accustomed to but at best it was an effort.

On Religion, Radhakrishnan held definite views: There is no one way to God. True religion is not renunciation but love and service. Hinduism should discard dead ideals and lifeless beliefs and nurture the true values of spirit.The classical scriptures provide emotional satisfaction, moral inspiration and spiritual solace; but their vital essence was being almost smothered by accidental accretions which had to be chopped off. So long there was a premium as blind credulity, abject dependence and dumb acquiescence to authority, India would not be free.

In Mysore with relative success and an ampler life, he found time for flirtations. But self indulgence carried with it no emotional attachment. He gave due attention to students and was popular with them. He had powerful memory and recognized each one of his students.

While at Mysore, Radhakrishnan had not abandoned the idea of going back to the Presidency College. But that appointment did not materialize. However, he applied for, was selected and appointed as George V Professor of Philosophy in the Calcutta University. His farewell at Mysore turned out in a function. From his carriage horses were detached and students in harness pulled it to the station. At Calcutta the only one friend Radhakrishnan had was Dr. C.V. Raman.

In Calcutta , Radhakrishnan completed his work 'Indian Philosophy' in two volumes, which he had begun in Mysore. The volumes were published in 1923 and 1927 by George Allen and Unvin. This was an interpretative survey rather than a chronicle. In it, Radhakrishnan expounded Indian thought in terms relative to the Western tradition. The two volumes were a unique work of Indian Philosophy, creatively powerful, with density of content and highly sophisticated. The work won applause every where. But Christians in England as well as in India criticized that the work was anti-Christianity. In the opinion of the authors Radhakrishnan was secular and so was his work.

In 1926, Radhakrishnan attended the Congress of Universities of the British Empire in London. There, his lectures on Indian Philosophy made impact on the audience. He visited United States and delivered lectures. After hearing him, many persons changed their views about Hinduism.

Between 1931 and 1948, he held various assignments. From 1931 to 1936 he was Vice Chancellor of Andhra University, Waltair; 1936 to 1952 Spalding Professor in Eastern Religions and Ethics in Oxford University; George V Professor of Philosophy, Calcutta University from 1937-1941;  Vice Chancellor, Banaras Hindu University from 1939 to 1948; Chancellor, Delhi University from 1953-1962. During 1946 (and later in 1952), he led Indian delegations to the UNESCO, and in 1948. he was elected as Chairmain of UNESCO. During 1947-49 Radhakrishna was a member of India's Constituent Assembly. He was also the Chairman of the University Grant Commission. In July 1949, he was appointed India's ambassador to USSR after Vijaylakshmi Pandit relinquished her charge. He was unconventional and his unconventional diplomacy was highly appreciated. As an ambassador, he made a mark.

Radhakrishnan was a strict vegetarian and abstained from alcoholic drinks. Ever punctual and disciplined, he stuck to his time table. Come what may, he went to bed at 10 p.m. A critic said, "He had the wisdom of a sage, detachment of a philosopher, and maturity of a statesman. He could mold himself to any circumstance."

Radhakrishnan had the rare distinction of meeting Stalin twice: first time on January 14, 1950 when Stalin remembered that Radhakrishnan was not a narrow minded patriot. He was critical of the British policy of creating enmity, hatred and differences among Hindus and Muslims. He was opposed to India's partition, its becoming a dominion and wanted the British to quit India. He felt India should develop into a multinational state with a strong central government. It should satisfy common man's fundamental needs, safeguard the liberty of human spirit and provide scope for different cultures.

Dr. Radhakrishnan's exposition of the symbol of Indian tricolor was the best ever made. The message of the flag was: "Be ever alert, be ever on the move, go forward, work for a free, flexible compassionate, decent, democratic society in which men of various persuasions will find a safe shelter". On the midnight of 14-15 August, Nehru was to speak immediately after Radhakrihnan. The program was meticulously drawn and according to it, Radhakrishnan's speech was to conclude at the very precise moment.after he had called his fellow citizens to bear themselves humbly before God, grace themselves to the tasks confronting them, conduct themselves in a manner worthy of the ageless spirit of India, treat intolerance as the greatest enemy of progress, and develop tolerant attitude to see in a fellow being face divine. Ego is a stumbling block, he said. The call for service has an important purpose. Radhakrishnan laid down his charge of ambassador in 1952.

Dr. Radhakrishnan reminded the world, "It takes centuries to make a little history. It takes centuries of history to make a tradition. Politics is never an act of obtaining political power, it is an essential branch of the art of promoting human welfare."

In 1952, Radhakrishnan was unanimously elected as Vice President of India. He thought the spiritual values which were part of India's living tradition demanded social progress and the Indian people should advance into the modern age. He said history is on the march and if we are hesitant we will be thrust aside. He suggested to Nehru to abandon the show of a united Congress and place himself at the head of progressive forces.

Nehru and Radhakrishnan had close relations. Radhakrishnan did not let TT Krishnamachari resign in a huff. On his commendation MC Chagla, a secular judge of Bombay was taken in the cabinet. During the period he was Vice President (from 1952 to 1962), he maintained the decorum of the Rajya Sabha.. He spoke out finally and freely. He was President of India from 1962 to 1967.

On Jawaharlal Nehru's death in 1965, the question of appointment of a new prime minister arose. Radhakrishnan acted according to tradition and administered GL Nanda the oath of acting PM. Again, he kept himself aloof from manoeuvring for the election of the successor. Lal Bahadur Shastri was chosen and he was given the oath of office of PM. Radhakrishnan liked and respected Shastri but there was little common between them. As Radhakrishnan had some trouble in the eyes, he reduced his visits both outside and inside the country.

India had troubles with Pakistan and China. When Shastri was PM, Radhakrishnan said that it was essential to come to term with them with honor and dignity so that money spent on arms could be diverted for internal development. Abdullah, JP, and Communist Party welcomed the advice. Outwardly agreeing with this, Ayub Khan, President of Pakistan sent three thousand guerrillas for infiltration into Kashmir. The India Govt accepted the challenge and retaliated across the cease fire line. Pakistani forces lost the war and there was cease five on 23 September, 1965. Radhakrishnan visited foreign countries to seek support. As a result of his visits, Tito of Yugoslovakia said Kashmir was an integral part of India and he condemned China's interference.

Radhakrishnan was not happy with the Taskent Declaration. On the might of 11th January 1966 Radhakrishnan learnt of Shastriji's death due to a massive heart attack in Taskent. Radhakrishnan called GL Nanda and administered him the oath of an acting PM for a few days. After due selection, Indira Gandhi was appointed as PM The relations between Radhakrishnan and Indira Gandhi were cordial.They had met as back as 1937.and when time came, he advised her how she should conduct herself to become the prime minister.

JP Narayana and some other leaders wanted Dr. Radhakrishnan to be President for the second term.But Indira Gandhi had some other ideas, She wanted Zakir Hussain, VP, to be the President. When Radhakrishnan came to know of this , he thought it was an indication that he should retire from the office. He told the VP to take salute at the Republic Day Parade and be the Chief Guest on Beating of the Retreat on 29 January 1967. However, on 26th evening, he broadcast a message to the Nation In his address, Radhakrishnan stressed the need for national outlook, equality and democratic behavior. He thanked people for their affection and expressed his best wishes for a bright future. Indira Gandhi did not like the broadcast. Nor did Kamraj and Dinesh Singh who had lobbied against Radhakrishnan. Radhakrishnan had felt the hurt.

Dr. Radhakrishnan's philosophy in a nutshell is: The world consists of distinct objects. The purpose, values and qualities of existence of the world require an ontological foundation. Religion and Philosophy ascribe it to the Supreme or Brahman, who is eternal and is free from the distinction of subject and object. He is also beyond speech and mind. The sciences are unable to account for.Shankar explains this in his Vedanta Philosophy. According to him the world of phenomena, including Ishvara (personal aspect of Brahman or personal God) is an illusion (maya) or magic (indrajala). It is temporal, imperfect and dependent. Radhakrishnan differs from Shankar and treats the world as real since it is a creation of the Supreme which is not created and eternal. Maya has a standing in this world of reality. It is not so much a veil as the dress of God. And, Ishvara too is an aspect of the Absolute and not illusion. The subjec- object distinction is the mode of intuition, comprehended by perception influence. The comprehension of Brahman, according to Radhakrishnan, takes place through intuitive knowledge - it is the intimate fusion of mind with reality. In intuitive knowledge the subject becomes one with the object of knowledge. In this respect it differs from perception or inference. Since Radhakrishnan views intuition as a valid means of knowledge, he is led to hold that religion should be a concern of philosophy rather than of theology.He was awarded Bharat Ratna.

# 14
# PARAMAHANSA YOGANANDA
## (1891-1952)

The sole country under the sun that is endowed with imperishable
interest—, the one land all men desire to see, and having seen once,
by even a glimpse would not give the glimpse for all the shows of
all the rest of the globe combined.

Mark Twain in Eternal Circle

The ancientness of India gives it a halo of peace, happiness
and miracles. The last century threw up in India many great Yogis,
of flesh and blood, genuine miracle-makers, not rope tricksters.
Swami Vivekananda, Paramhansa Yogananda, Mother Teresa, Sai
Baba, Maharshi Mahesh, to name a few. Yogananda popularized
Yoga in USA and placed it on the world map. Yogananda has vividly
described his experiences, life events and Yoga in his
*Autobiography Of A Yogi* He was a spiritualist and differed from
materialists and philosophers. Whereas Philosophers have abstract
ideas to play with,a spiritualist has spirits and he can produce
something from nothing. It is like the phenomenon -once one has
achieved the crux,he continues with that or hovers around  its
ramifications.

Swami Yogananda was a perfect Yogi. On reaching USA,
he demonstrated that Yoga was an excellent aid for healthy living.
The message appealed to heads and hearts of Americans and from
a mere demonstration, Yoga became a  popular movement. It grew
to great heights and today it is accepted as a general health
improvement technique. Yoga has made inroads into educational
institutions and is popular among adults and children alike. Today it
is so widespread in USA that some say the West has hijacked

Yoga from India. The credit for popularizing Yoga largely goes to Yogananda. Vivekananda had seeded Yoga in USA, it was Yogananda who watered the sapling and saw it grow steadily. He passed away in 1952 but his message continues being carried on through Kriya Yoga by his disciples, prominent among whom is Kriyananda. Kriya Yoga is a source of spiritualism especially Indian spiritualism. Its veracity is confirmed by independent critical examination. The credit for further popularising in the san Frasisco bay Area, especially among Senior Indo-American goes to Vasanti Bhat.

Scriptures mention several miracles that were performed by Yogis but they did so only when it became inescapable to illustrate a point. The Hindu scriptures, the Holy Bible, the Kuran Sharif, the Jatakas, the Avesta, the Guru Granth Sahib and other sacred books are full of spiritual information, including miracles. Why, we think Yogananda's transplantation of Yoga in a distant land and in an alien culture is no less than a miracle.

The greatest miracle is man himself and man is full of curiosity. He wonders whether he owes his birth, maintenance and extinction to some super power; and assumes that should there be one, it should be omnipresent, omnipotent and omniscient and who would reveal himself only to his favorites. Disciples believe that the Swamis have acquired capability to interfere on their behalf with the Super Power. Yogananda never claimed possessing any such capability or power.

People generally expect of a Swami to show them something unusual. But a true Yogi does not indulge in stunts for cheap popularity's sake. However it is also true that he does not object nor discourages his disciples from such indulgences. A Yogi does not believe in promiscuously revealing the secrets of the creator. He would show a miracle only for some substantive reason and that too after inward sanction. He thinks every one has a free will and he does not therefore encroach on independence of others. Swami Yogananda propounded Kriya Yoga. Kriya is derived from the root *kri* meaning to do.The Kriya Yoga thus stands for Yoga of Action.

How do miracles occur? Physiology informs that different sensory stimulants—gustatory, auditory, olfactory etc —are provided by vibratory variations in electrons and protons which according to Yoga are regulated by *prana*, a subtle life force charged with fine distinct sensory idea substance. In support of his theory, Yogananda cited the case of Gandhi Baba (not Mahatma Gandhi) who could induce an auto suggestive state enabling him to materialize and detect fragrances. He could also produce an object out of air. Yogananda had developed this power but his Guru cautioned him to keep off such mundane affairs as these do not have inner sanction and are moreover produced hypnotically. Men who have realized divinity don't indulge in affairs like miracles.

Mukund (aka Mukund Lal Ghosh and later Yogananda) was born on June 5, 1892 at Gorakhpur (U.P), son of Bhagabati Charan Ghosh and Gyan Prabha. Bhagabati Babu was a senior officer with the Bengal Nagpur Railway (BNR in short). During his postings at different places, he had developed a cosmopolitan, spiritual outlook. So had Gyan Prabha. Once, while the family was residing at Lahore (now in Pakistan), a Sadhu came to their house and predicted that the 8-year old child Mukund would renounce the world. This prediction had strange affect on the boy. He started having session with Sadhus and at times absconded from home in search of God.

Once it so happened that when the family was living at Bareilley (in UP), Mukunda absconded and mother Gyan Prabha passed away. Mukund ever thereafter was remorseful that he could not be present at the time of her death. It pained him all the more when he learned that she had at the time of her death expressed a desire to see Mukund and left a Swami's message and an amulate for him. He put on the amulet. (It was lost somewhere which too caused him great distress.) The Swami's message was spiritual. He learned that the sound 'Om' derives from the cosmic sun raises power of atomic energy. One day he dreamt that he was going to the Himalayas to learn Yoga from Siddhas and with their help he would realize cosmic awareness. He came across another message that the devout should go to Dakshineshwar. Legends of miracles and lives of legendary Yogis like Babaji, Lahiri Mahashaya and others connected with the Temple interested him.

While he was staying in an Ashram at Benares, Mukund learnt by practice making distinction between the needs of body and mind. One day Swami Dayanand, the head of the Ashram, went out. During the day no one offered food to Mukund and he remained hungry throughout the day. When the Swami returned late in the evening, Mukund, asked him, "What should I do (in such circumstances)? Should I starve to death?" The Swami replied "Die, if you must, Mukund ! Never before that you lived by the power of food nor by the power of God. He inevitably sees that His devotee is maintained. Better you cut through the chains of agencies and perceive the cause. But remember 'soul' needs a healthy body which is an immutable and unqualified image of God."

Another day while Mukund was shopping for the Ashram in the bazaar at Benares, he saw a Swami gazing at him. It flashed in his mind that he was the same person who often came in his dreams. He hurried to the mendicant who told him, "Don't grieve over your amulet". This surprised the boy, how had the Swami come to know about the loss of the amulet, his prized possession that was bequeathed by his mother. Unless the Swami had realized God, the boy thought, he would not have known about the amulate. The Swami told him, "I have waited for you for many years", and took him to his place. He advised Mukund that he should go back to Calcutta (Kolkata) and see his father and then come and meet him at his hermitage at Serampore, a place near Calcutta. The Swami's name was Yuktananda. (He was also known as Yukteshwar.The Ananda of Palo Alto observes a Swami Yuktananda Day.)

Mukund, as advised by swami Yuktanand, went to Calcutta. His father was happy to see the boy come back home.It turned out a pleasant surprise that Yukteshwar and Bhagbati Charan were initiated into Kriya Yoga by Guru Lahiri Mahashaya. After a few days' stay at home, Mukund rushed to Swami Yukteshwara's Ashram at Serampore. When he reached, the Swami was in communion with the Divine Mother. As he came out, Mukund prayed him for his intercession and to introduce him to the Mother. Mukund was immature and the Swami did not think it wise to attach importance to his request, and, therefore, he put him off saying that he would convey his request to the Mother. Later,Mukund asked Swamiji whether he had talked to Mother and what her reply was. Yukteshwar kept quite but the next day he took Mukund to the Dakshineshwar Temple to have Mother's darshan. They had an acetate experience. The Swami impressed the boy that administrative experience forms part of Kriya Yaga and one need be well versed in it. A saint gives importance to dependence on Lord with humility. God blesses and the experience brings joy. The swami told Mukund that saints realize God through the concept of cosmic. "God is the heaven, organizations are training centers. Worldly duties have to be performed; man can do these only if he assumes responsibility for an extended family."

Yukteshwar initiated Mukund in Kriya Yoga and as the Swami touched him, he felt a bright light had broken upon him like the countless suns blazing together. A flood of blessings overwhelmed the inner- most of his heart. The master persuaded the disciple to go home, practice Yoga, and come back to Serampore Ashram after 30 days. He also told him that Patanjali's Yogasutras would guide his path.

What is Kriya Yoga? People think it as a miracle-making device. They are wrong. The term Kriya signifies duty, not work. As instructed by Krishna in Bhagwat-gita, Arjun understood it as Nishkam Karma, that is: Do your duty without anticipation of reward: Kriya Yoga is one of the methods, others are Bhakti and Gyan. They help achieve peace, with the grace of God. Practice fetches him anubhava (perception and union with God).

According to Yogananda, Kriya Yoga is not the same as Karma Yoga. People expect that a Swami will show them something unusual- a miracle. But, a true Yogi does not indulge in stunts nor does he believe in revealing promiscuously the secrets of the creator. He would show a miracle only for some substantive reason and that too after inward sanction. The Yogi thinks that every individual has a right to free will and independence. He does not encroach on independence of others. Anubhav (perception and union with God) is the ultimate object of the Kriya Yoga. Advanced and effective meditation helps in self realization and having session with the infinite.

Motivated by his guru, Mukund continued his education. He passed the B.A. examination as per his father's wish. In 1915, guru Yuktanand gave his disciple Mukund the name 'Yogananda', as he entered the Swami order and now onward he would be known as Swami Yogananda. He realized that only meditation and blessings of God would help him achieve his goal. He became aware of an unusual longevity of sages and miracles prformed by them. Nevertheless, the guru cautioned him that 'wonder working' might appear spectacular or entertaining, but these were spiritually useless. Spirituality, he admonished, was the goal of a Yogi.

Yuktanand's instructions to his disciples were, "Give the body its due and no more. Pain and pleasure are transitory. Endure all duality with calmness. A seeker should go beyond physiology of the body and investigate the science of soul. If he acts like this, he will find a suitable structure hidden behind the body mechanism. With practice, he will learn and gain control over it. Great souls win dominion over soul. Be a living liaison for humanity, and be a bridge between Eastern and Western virtues. Carry India's message to the West with 'accommodative patience and forbearance'. Saints transform the crude ore of ego-permeated humility with courage and compassion." Yukatnand taught Mukund to differentiate between Jal Yoga (i.e., Union with water) and Dhyan Yoga (perception and union with God )". Mukund also learned about miracles performed by great yogis." Whatever it be, one must remember that wisdom is the greatest cleanser." From another Yogi, Nagendra Nath Bhaduri, he learned how Vivekananda had generated interest in Indian culture among people in the West. He forecast that a day would come when Yogananda would go to America and acquaint the Americans with nuances of Indian culture.

Yogananda took keen interest in developing the school that was attached to the Serampore Ashram. Soon it started overflowing with students. There was no place for newcomers and more space was required to cope up with the increase in the number of students. In 1918, Yogananda thought of opening a branch at Ranchi. The Maharaja of Kasim Bazar, Sir Nandy gave place near Ranchi for the branch of the school. This gave Yogananda an opportunity to gain administrative experience which, Yuktananda had stressed.

At about this time Yogananda received an invitation to be an Indian delegate to the International Congress of Religions being held in Chicago under the auspices of the American Association of Religions. The time for departure of the mission had come. Yogananda accepted the invitation and sailed for USA by boat. He reached Boston in September, 1920, after two months. On October

6, he addressed the Congress on the subject "The Science of Religion" He maintained that religion is something unusual and that customs and conventions can not be made universal though a common religion could be, which all of us may seek, follow and obey. The speech was well received.

Wherever Yogananda went in USA he was received with warmth. President Calvin Coolidge received him in the White House. This was the first time an Indian was received in the White House. He was convinced that the concept of East versus West was irrational and the distance in thought should be removed. He talked to some people that he wanted to bring out a journal and asked if they could suggest a catchy name. They appreciated.the idea of the journal. Burbanks, a social figure, suggested a title "East West" which was liked by every one. A journal was started and an organization developed around it. East West is a unique organization. with multifaceted activities.

In 1935, Yogananda decided to return to India via Europe by a charter boat with the financial help from Self Realization Fellowship. He sailed from New York on June 9, 1935. At London, he addressed a meeting. Thereafter, he traveled to Bavaria to meet a miracle making female, known as Newmann of Kennersr, a true saint who bled from several parts of body including chest. Continuing his journey, Yogananda reached Bombay. Mr. Kishore Modi, a member of the India Community Center, remembers that Swami Yogananda had stayed with his (father's) family in Bombay and that a large number of people came to have Swamiji's darshan. He found Yogananda was ever cheerful. At child Kishore's request Swamiji wrote a message for him which Kishore has for seven decades preseved and has all the way long brought from Bombay to Sunnyvale.

In India, Yogananda visited several places  and trained people in Kriya Yoga. He met Gandhiji at Wardha and Tagore at Shantiniketan. He was impressed by Gandhi's devotion to the cause of Harijans, and by his method of non-violence, non-cooperation as an alternative to armed conflict. Gandhi had noted in his diary, "If there be a rebirth in store for me, I wish to be born a pariah so as to render them more effective service" Another important person he met was Nirmala Devi.

Yogananda had a memorable experience at Purulia in Bengal. He met a 70-year old lady, Giri Bala. She narrated her life's story which was full of miracles. She said,: "I have never had any child.. Many years ago my husband died and I became a widow. Now I sleep very little. I find no difference between the states of sleep and waking. I attend to my domestic duties on day time and meditate at night. I hardly experience changes in seasons. I have never been sick nor experienced any disease. When some accident occurs, I feel slight pain. I have no bodily excretions. I can control my heart beat and breathing. In visions I often see my Guru and other great souls. Questioned why she did not teach the control system to others, she said that her guru had told her not to temper with God' systems. Moreover, if I teach others not to eat food, farmers won't thank me as they would starve and curse me. The juicy fruits would fall down and rot. Misery, starvation and disease are whips of our karma that ultimately drive men to seek the true meaning of life."

The elderly woman finally recounted "I feel man is nothing but spirit", and she demonstrated that in various ways we can gradually learn to live by the eternal light, and without food." She employed a certain breathing exercise that affects the chakras in body.

Yogananda has described many such cases. Bhawal Sanyasi's case is well known. It was reported by law journals. It related to the mysterious death of the prince of Bhawal and his resurrection by a Sanyasi, Bengali Baba. The prince's dead body was taken for cremation to a river bank and while his pier was burning, fierce monsoon rains struck which put out the fire and the dead body was swept away into the river. It shored up at a spot and was seen by the mystic Bengali Baba living near the bank. The Baba asked his disciples to bring the flowing pier, which they brought. He asked the deceased to get up. The dead was resurrected. The Baba advised the resurrected person to devote himself to spiritual growth. But the prince did not abide by the Baba's advice and left for home. When the prince reached home, no one believed what he told them. They had already divided the property. The prince took the matter to the court to get his land holdings. But the physician's testimony stood against him. The Bengali Baba was known as a great spiritualist and people thought he could have done the miracle. He might have entered into dead body. The court gave verdict in favor of the prince who got his property back. This experience resembles to the fiction authored in the West by Alan Wolf and 'with miracles associated with Shankaracharya and Bhartrihari. They echo Hindu spiritualism, which regards yoga as a science.

Yogananda narrates miraculous performances of Swami Ram, a great spiritualist. He showed some miracle at the Manger Foundation Research Institute at Kansas, in USA. He demonstrated controlled heart, brain waves, body temperature, brain death, alternate breathing, and heart problems. These were confirmed genuine by scientists with the aid of latest equipment, although these were considered humanly impossible. Another unbelievable thing was that he could move a metal spindle by looking at it. Till then telekinesis was unknown in the West. On the Himalayan heights lived great miracle makers like Lokenath, who travelled thrice from India to Mecca and learnt Kuran to show that Hindus and Muslims could live as good neighbors.

In the USA Dr. Ian Stevenson of the University of Virginia Medical School has done considerable research into the realms of consciousness. (Among females Sharada Devi, and Upasani Baba are well known spiritualists.) Mr. Arya Bhushan of Palo Alto, an American of Indian origin, has also done research on rebirth.

The basic technique of meditation taught by Yogananda calms and clears mind, recharges man with fresh energy and ideas, and filters his heart from the function of inner strength. Practiced on a daily basis, meditation produces beneficial physical, mental, emotional and spiritual results. It connects man with his inner power of morality, clarity and love.

Yogananda returned from India to USA via London where he addressed a meeting organized by the World Federationon "How Faith May Save Civilization." In USA, he continued with his constructive work. He opened a Self Realization Hermitage at Encinitasin, California.

Yogananda passed away on March 7,1952 at Los Angeles. Yoga is an eight fold path: 1.Yam (moral conduct,observing Ahimsa i.e. non-violence, Satya or truthfulness, Brahmacharya i.e.celibacy, Asteya i.e.no stealing or greed, 2 Niyam (religious observance – pure mind and body, contentment, self control, swadhyaya and devotion., 3 Asan (physical fitness), 4 Pranayam, 5 Pratyahar (withdrawal of senses from external objects). 6 Dharana (concentration), 7 Dhyan (meditation), and. 8 Samadhi.

How does Yoga reconciles celibacy in the common man's life? Food and sex and wine are body needs for human beings. But as these could be two-edged, a Yogi considers these as vice. Hunger has a legitimate purpose, its satisfaction is necessary for the sustenance of the body. Sex, iingrained in man by nature, serves for the propagation of the species. But the desire for sex should not be insatiable for otherwise it becomes an obstacle. Saints therefore advise that the desire for sex must be destroyed. At the same time saints are aware that humanity will not survive if there be no sex. This truth holds good for every religion.

According to Hindu religion, sex is covered by a number of sheaths; therefore whether flesh is weak or strong, mind should be resistant. If temptation assails with force, it must be overcome by impersonal analysis and indomitable will. Yogis believe that every natural passion should be mastered and energy conserved. Renewed sex yearnings sap man's inner peace and activating a wrong desire is inimical to man's happiness. Yogis say with self control man can roam the world like a lion. A true Yogi and a true devotee can transform human affection towards God and they can free themselves from all instinctive compulsions. The saved energy can be constructively used.

The devotees use external marks. But they hardly serve any useful purpose. The marks, according to Yogananda, disfigure their faces and bodies. The scriptures do stimulate desire for inward realization but continual intellectual pursuit arouses vanity, sense of false satisfaction and undigested knowledge. Wearing ochre-robe without realizing God is meaning-less and misleading. May be, renunciation of an outward symbol may prove injurious to the renouncer as he can take false pride. Mukund had learnt from Swami Yuktananda that Kriya Yoga helps man in his steady spiritual progress, and this was the core of Yoganand's message and practice of Yoga in USA. Yogananda learnt that God is softer than flowers and stronger than thunder.

Kriya Yoga teaches that truth can be learnt in day-to-day

life and for this one need not go to the Himalayas. Were going to mountain so effective, many living on high hills would have perceived God. A wise man knows that masters are under no compulsion to live in mountains only. Nor have the Himalayas the monopoly of saints. Should a man look within, he will discover that it is no use to transport the body higher. A true Yogi says use your body like a room or as a cove and that is where you can find the " Kingdom of God."

A guru alleviates mankind through either spiritual means or intellectual counsel or will power. A master bestows cosmic consciousness on a disciple who has perfected meditation and strengthened his mind. He knows that mere intellectual willingness or openmindedness is not enough. Only enlargement of consciousness by yoga and devotion (bhakti) can prepare a person to absent himself in liberating the shock of omnipresence. The divine experience comes to the devotee from the realization of natural inevitability.

Why do saints say that God is unfathomable? Is it not strange that on the one hand they regard him as one who is dear and near and on the other unfathomable? Does devotion reduce the distance between the devotee and his God?

Saint- poets say that man is a sensor for other's sins. Did Christ's life prove this for Saint Frances? Even through his body was affected with many ailments, he healed others' wounds. To this Maharshi Mahashaya's response was, "It you don't invite God to be your summer guest, he won't come in the winter of your life."

The Sanyasis are generally called Swamis. The swami order owes its origin to Shankaracharya. Many monks who take vows of chastity, poverty and obedience are continually engaged in humanitarian work. A Swami follows precepts of universal brotherhood which is the core of Hindu philosophy. The sutra *Aham Brahmasmi* (meaning I am Brahma) is matched by *Taltvamasi* (i.e. That Thou Art). The Swamis are Dasanamis that is they are of ten categories such as Giri, Sagar, Bhagat, Puri, Saraswati, Tirtha, Aranya.

It is said Yogis have power to percieve God and have power to do miracles. How does a Yogi perceive God? How does he operate a miracle? God is absolute unity. He is the sole life. He appears in separate and diverse manifestations of creation. A Yogi identifies consciousness with the universal structure, not with a body. A master Yogi is not affected by the law of gravitation. He who knows himself as the omnipresent spirit is no longer subject to the rigidities of a body in time and space.The Yogi has divine power and can produce things like God.God commanded: Let there be light and there was light and light occurs in all divine manifestations in flames and lights that devotees testify. A Yogi who has merged his total entity with the creator perceives the cosmological essence as light, and sees no difference between water and rays of light. Free from emotional manifestations, a master transforms his body of light into the rays of earth, water, fire and air. This is miracle.

Anyone who has realized that the essence of creation is light can perform a miracle, and a master yogi is capable of employing his divine knowledge of light to project the atoms of light according to his wish, will power and realization. In his dream state, his consciousness has ego limitation, and in sleep he demonstrates his mind's omnipotence. He sees his dead friends, remote places etc. This is like the modern picture which can portray any miracle the producer wants.

Today US has a network of Yoga centers which impart training in Yoga. Kriyayoga is one of the extended schools of Yoga. Its objective is union with the infinite through action/rite. The Yogi offers inhaling breath into the exhaling breath and vice versa, and neutralizes both the breaths, and releases Prana from the heart and brings it under control. Or, he may arrest the decay of the body by receiving additional supply of Prana by quieting the action of the lungs and heart. He may also arrest mutations of growth in the body by control of Apaan (eliminating current) which neutralizes decay and growth and the Yogi learns how to control over the life force.

The Kriya Yoga directs the life energy that revolves upward and downward, and around the six spinal centers which correspond to the 12 astral signs of the Zodiac and the symbolic cosmic man. Half a minute of revelation of energy around the sensitive spinal cord affects subtle progress in man's evolution. The Kriya Yoga gurus claim that half a minute Kriya equals to one year of natural spiritual enfoldment.

# 15
# MOTHER TERESA
## (1910-1997)

Mother Teresa was one of those rare persons who in her life time was revered like a saint. Her intense compassion for the suffering, poor and abandoned developed into a cult of acceptance of poverty and suffering. In 1950, she founded in Calcutta the Missionaries of Charity that replaced the deprivation of the poorest of the poor with love of God and they temporarily forgot their suffering. The Missionaries grew into a world- wide humanitarian organization all due to her single minded devotion.

Truth is one which the learned call by different names, says the Rig-Veda, an ancient Hindu scripture. "If the thuth is in" me, said Pope John Paul, it will explode." The truth exploded in Agnes Bojaxhiu, not in a sudden detonation but in a sustained blast that lasted half a century. Agnes would later become famous as Mother Teresa.

Agnes Bojaxhiu was born the youngest of the three children of Nikola and Drana of Spokje, in Albania, on August 26, 1910.The children grew up and received their early education in a local church school. When Agnes was 8, Nikola passed away. This threw the burden of the family on Drana. To maintain the family, she started cloth- business. She was religious minded and kept doors open for the poor to come in and share dinner with the family whose social and religious life revolved around the parish of the Sacred Church.

After completing their early education in the church school, Agnes and her elder sister Aga attended the Skopje State Secondary School. As they were interested in music, they joined the choir of the Church as also the Albanian Catholic Choir. At the age of

12,Agnes expressed a desire to become a nun and joined Soladity, a group of Blessed Virgin Mary. There, she heard about the charity and work of Jesuit Missionaries among the poor and lepers of Calcutta and was inspired by their devotion to work. When she was 14, her brother Lazar left home to join the military academy and immediately thereafter the family went on a pilgrimage to the Shrine of Our Lady of Cervagore in Letnice in the mountains of Montenegro. The visit proved good to Agnes's persistent whooping cough from which she suffered. In 1928, at the age of 18, she confirmed her wish to become a nun to her mother, who did not deny the daughter the will of God and advised Agnes," Put your hand in His hand and walk all the way with Him."

Agnes applied to the Order of Loretta Nuns. In September, 1928, her request to join the Order was accepted. She and another novitiate, named Betike Kanje, met at Zagreb. The two bid good bye to their families and then journeyed to the Loretta Nuns Mother House, in Rathfarman in Ireland, whose epitaph was : To love the poor, preserve the same, live, die and rise with them. Agnes spent six weeks as a novitiate and learnt English and then left for India. She arrived at Calcutta on January 6, 1929 on the day of the Feast of Epiphany and joined the Order. After this, Agnes left for Darjeeling. It took her two and a half years to complete the training. On May 24, she took her first vows as a Sister of Loretta and chose Teresa for her name after her patron saint "Therese" of Lisieux ( Child Christ). The Spanish version is Therese. To distinguish herself, she adopted Teresa as her name. For the next six years, Teresa served as a novitiate. On May 14,1937, she took vows of poverty, chastity and obedience for life. Soon after her return from Darjeeling, she moved over to Entally, a locality in Calcutta, where Loretta Nuns had a large property.

In Entally, the Loretta nuns ran St. Mary's, a school for five hundred girls, mostly orphans, and a smaller school for Bengali girls under the guidance of Father Julien Henry, the priest at St. Terese's. The property was surrounded by a high wall. Teresa taught girls Geography and History and at the same time she learnt Bengali and Hindi. At Calcutta, she witnessed three disastrous tragedies. One, Calcutta famine of 1943 that cost at least two million lives; and, two, Direct Action Day at the call of the Muslim League which took a toll of equal number of lives in the violence that paralyzed the city and where Teresa saw in the streets stabbed, beaten bodies lying in dried blood.; and, three, partition of India in which about 1.76 million Hindus and Sikhs fled Pakistan to India while an equal number of Muslims from India headed to Pakistan. Calcutta became the house of a very large number of displaced and desperately poor people.These tragedies left permanent deep marks on people's minds.

Every year Teresa used to go to retreat at Darjeeling. During her retreat in 1946,on September 10, she experienced an inner command to renounce the convenient life, to go to slums,work and live among the poorest of the poor, and to love Him in disguise of the distressed. Throughout the retreat, she felt the call was pressing for her answer. After her return to Calcutta , she confided the experience and shared her idea of leaving the convent with other sisters and sought support of superiors, including the Archbishop of Calcutta. The Archbishop discussed the matter with her spiritual director, Father Celeste van Exem, and Father Henry. who conveyed his permission. She requested him to bless an ordinary sari, a simple cross and a rosary, the symbols she had chosen for her new role. The Archbishop suggested her to join the Daughters of Anne who were engaged in similar work but she felt that that type of work did not suit her because the Daughters after the day's work among the poor returned to the convent. Teresa wanted not only to work for the poor but also to live among them.The other difference was that she wanted to be released from the convent. She wrote to the Mother General of Loretta, in Dublin, seeking her permission to leave the congregation which meant she could leave the Order but still be bound by her vows. She got permission from Rome on August 7, 1948 to the effect that she could leave the convent but remain a nun bound to the Archbishop of Calcutta instead of Archbishop of Loretta.

Teresa's new life required that she should better take some medical training. For this, she went to Patna where she took necessary training from sisters who were trained in medical care and first aid. One of the nurses advised her that for the new life she was adopting, she must remain healthy; and for this, she must eat well, rest well, stay clean, and then only she would have extra energy to help the poor.They impressed that she should combine her spiritual life with a practicl approach. She deliberated and decided that compassion for the poor did not mean that she neglected her own health. After four months training at Patna, equipped with medical skills, she returned to Calcutta. She was happy that Father Exem had found a place for her stay at St. Josef's House. She moved to that place and devoted her time to the care of the House's elderly residents and poor of the bustee.(locality). One day in 1948, Teresa went out in search of a place where she could start her work She walked continually unil the evening. She was tired .but happy that she was successful in finding a suitable place in the slums of Motijhil.

When Theresa went over to the slums in the Motijhil area to start her work, the children became curious and came out to see what had brought the foreigner to their area. By gestures, she called them and in her broken Bengali told them she would teach them. By now the elders had also come out. They appreciated her object. She had no board and chalk to write with. The ground became the board and her stick as the chalk.The first lesson was the alphabets. The children evinced interest. Teresa's school had started. When people came to know about her project, donations started pouring in. Chairs and tables came as donation . People of the bustee showed enthusiasm.

She noticed that some people were unwell. She decided that something needed to be done to restore their health. But treatment required medicines. She went to a neighboring drug store and sought for medicines for the poor. The store asked for payment but she had no money to pay. However, she was determined and sat outside the store the whole day. In the evening the druggist relented and gave her everything on her list.

The news of Teresa's school traveled fast. Two of her former students came forward to offer help in teaching. The number of students also increased. So they rented a hut to serve as school. Sister Teresa started her own Order and her own group of nuns. She named it the Missionaries of Charity. As the head of her own Order, she became Mother Teresa. In 1953, they moved to a big house and called it Mother's House. The Sisters had a daily routine. They rose at 4.45 A.M., prayed, ate breakfast, cleaned the house and while some of them worked in the House from 8.A.M. to

12.30 P.M,some left for work.. They returned for lunch and after rest, they went back to work up to 6.30 P.M. The day ended with dinner and prayer. and then to bed.

One day Mother Teresa found a woman lying in the gutter breathing her last. She felt distressed and asked herselft why should people who are on the verge of death not have loving care? She was agitated and carried the woman to a hospital. But the hospital won't admit her. It hurt her and she decided that people would not die alone or without care. So Mother Teresa opened a house for the dying and dead ,and named it Nirmal Hriday or Pure Heart. She always had time to wipe one more fevered brow and to say one more prayer. She loved babies and elderly, the sick and the dying and the poorest of the poor. For her, every person counted. But about family planning, she had her own views .She was opposed to contraception and abortion as methods of family planning, though both the state and central governments had been helpful to her in every respect. Even so, to smoothen her work, she took Indian citizenship. As her name and fame spread around, her projects also increased and she decided to open houses of Missionaries of Charity.

Mother Teresa once said, " Calcutta can be found all over the world, if you have eyes to see." There are in every country countless people , neglected and unwanted, who suffer from loneliness. Her first mission outside Calcutta was established in Patna. In 1960, she made an extensive tour of USA. She saw people staggering and dying from alcohol. About them, she spoke to the audiences. Those who heard her, generously, donated money for the cause. She traveled to Rome to seek Pope's official recognition to the Missionaries of Charity. The recognition came after a long wait in 1965. A House of Charity was organized in Cambodia, others were opened in Latin American countries and one in Rome itself. An International Association of Co-workers of Mother Teresa was formed with the assistance of Anne Blakie, a British woman. Another group for the sick and suffering was formed. In 1965, Pope Paul gave her a Caddilac, a big car, to facilitate her work. But instead of making its use for herself, she turned it into an ambulance and used it for the welfare of the poor.

In 1971, Mother Teresa was awarded the first Pope John Peace Prize. With her own resources, she set up a center for the

Aborigines of Australia. The same year when millions of people escaped for their lives from the oppression of the military regime of East Pakistan, she helped organize relief for refugees. After the war of Bangladesh, she went to Bangladesh and established four relief centers.Three million of Bangladeshis were killed. In 1972, presenting her with the Nehru Award, President V.V.Giri admired her as an emancipated soul that had transcended all barriers of race, religion, creed and nation. About her, a film titled Something Beautiful for God was produced. On December 9, 1979 Mother Teresa visited Oslo ( Norway) to receive the Nobel Peace Prize. The Peace Prize had so far been awarded to only to two persons. Albert Schweitzer and Martin Luther King. Three months later, she was awarded Bharat Ratna, the highest award given by the Government of India. In 1985, President Reagan gave her the Presidential Medal of Freedom.

With such an hectic life, Mother Teresa's health began to deteriorate. In 1990, she fell seriously ill and a search for a successor to her was made.She survived. On September 6, 1997, she died in the Mother's House at Calcutta."You feel smaller when your mother dies", because she was kind and compassionate, "carried you,loved you, taught you'. To the sisters, when she was gone, the room looked empty without her.The sisters kept vigil, their faces traced in low light by candles,murmuring 'don't leave us',as Nancy Gibbs would later say on the passing away of Pope John Paul.People all over the world mourned for her.

Mother Teresa had become a legend in her life time. Her cause was acknowledged everywhere. Some people wanted her to be declared a Saint. While alive, she wielded enormous power and unlimited resources, had access to presidents, prime ministers, financiers and multinational corporations that willingly extended her all support for her humane work. Her virtuosity was acknowledged and acclaimed all over the world.

Notwithstanding her virtuosity, there were some who were critical of her work. They protested her religious zeal and thought that in a subtle way she wanted to convert people to Christianity. Also, they said that wittingly or unwittingly, she prevented the growth of the spirit of protest against unjust, corrupt and offensive order of the society. Some thought she wanted to valorize submission to poverty. Pop singer Bole Geldof said, "She struck me as being the loving embodiment of moral good .There was nothing otherworldly or divine about her". The author of Is That It writes," She was a deft manipulator of media. She was outrageously brilliant. There was no false modesty about her and there was a certainty of purpose which left her little patience. But she was totally selfless, every moment her aim seemed to be, how can I use this or that situation to help others. In 1994, a journalist Christopher Hitchens fiercely attacked her in a TV program "Hell's Angel". He monstrously and mendaciously abused her that she was a hypocrite, consorted with dubious dictators, administered dubious medical treatment, and blindly objected to family planning. When asked for comments, Mother Teresa simply said "I will pray for those who made it".

Some critics pointed out that there was nothing unique about her work. Prior to her Arfon Roberts had worked among lepers and blinds. Leonard Cheshire and Dudley Gardiner, other well known persons worked for their welfare but they never sought any publicity for themselves. But Mother Teresa had excellent relations with media. A politician said,:"Media has created an impression that Indians are indifferent to suffering and it is the Westerners, symbolized by Mother Teresa who help the poor" But. India has tradition of charities. Not only Birla and Tata, even ordinary people have set charitable institutions. Mother Teresa received support from politicians, including B.C.Roy and Jyoti Basu, Chief Ministers of West Bengal. Is not it strange that she had support of Communists and Marxists? It is undeniable that perceptive people do not easily shed of the habit of ideological orthodoxy and see even in her dedicated service of homeless and lepers, some sort of class struggle and conspiracy of moneyed people. But they ignore such conditions in the case of Mother Missionaries' work. Why did the Calcutta Marxists not criticize Mother Teresa's efforts ending in preserving poverty, economic inequality, social injustice, ill health, child immortality et al? Journalist Sumanta Bannerjee questions: Who do the poor people need more? Mother Teresa or Mother Courage?"

One deficiency in the Charity's work is that it provides for home for the poor but not for their medical needs. Instead they provide for relief by Christian religious methods. Hindu suffers pain in the belief that it is a result of his past Karma and in suffering pain he is paying for his sin. Thus the poor out- castes lead a condemned life and become immune to material sensibilities because of their past Karma. What a way to attain Nirvana! In Mother Teresa's solution too one comes to the faith that subjection to poverty is what He wanted. The Bible also says," Blessed are the poor in spirit for them is the Kingdom of God." A critic says this is an excellent motivation for the poor to remain poor.

Another controversy about her was: Was her work religious or social? Mother Teresa had herself explained: We are first of all religious; we are not social workers. We serve Jesus in the poor. We preach Christ not by word but putting his and our love in serving dying poor.The world over the Sisters lead a regulated life They dress alike, have a rosary in the hand in the street and go in twos. They come back home for lunch at 2P.M. do house work half an hour's rest, an examination of conscience, say the divine office and the stations of the cross.Half an hour's reading, a cup of tea and at 3 they go out. Novices stay home. They have classes of theology and scriptures and other Constitution. Between 6.15 and 6.30 they are back home.Half an hour decoration with the Holy Sacrament. By 7.30 they have dinner, next day preparation and say night prayer. Mother Teresa said, "Today the biggest disease is the feeling of being unwanted, uncared for, deserted by everybody. The greater evil is the lack of love and charity, the terrible indifference towards one's neighbor living at the roadside, the victim of exploitation, corruption, poverty and disease."

Teresa'.s method of removing the suffering and poverty was non-violent, like Gandhi's, not merely by word of mouth but by actual physical conduct and moral support to the poor, handicapped, lepers, dying, uncared. World -wide attention was focused on the needy Remove the poverty and not the poor The nobility of the Missionaries cannot be doubted. Mother Teresa denied that she wanted to convert people to Christianity.Her supporters also pointed out that religions other than Christianity invest suffering and submission and God's will with moral sanctity so that individual may discover God's benediction. Karen Armstrong, the author of *History of God* says that Teresa had been useful to the Vatican. Her success shows that there is no need to break the barrier between the rich and the poor. She wants to help the poor but never questions why there is poverty and why the cycle of poverty? Mother Teresa, passed away on September 5, 1997.

# 16
# AMARTYA SEN
(B. 1930)

Courage of conviction is a virtue. Should a man or woman imbibe it and should he also possess originality of thought and capability of expression with frankness and boldness, that man is bound to attract people's attention.Should the core of his thought be relevant for the humanity, his talents may win him wide recognition. Such attributes of Amartya Sen were recognized, and these won him the coveted Noble Prize in Economics. He was the first Indian, in fact the first Asian, to obtain the Noble award in Economics.

Amongst the comity of academia for half a century ( to be precise since 1956), Amartya Sen is not just an economist, he is also one of those who are regarded as the world's great economic philosophers, that rare breed of thinkers who remind people that economics is about the real world, about choices and transactions which involve or assume values, institutions and patterns of behavior. Amartya Sen is the economist's economist. After recieving the award when he visited India,  the 'Indian establishment went ga-ga' and the Asian Recorder of New Delhi commented that the award was 'an honour for India.'

The scope of Amartya Sen's work is vast. He develops a social order which spans different fields, from hard core econometrics to the relationship between deprivation and social structure, from secularism to Indian culture, from understanding of social choices to promoting equality. Sen's work is a dual enterprize. To be candid, his work is a dual enterprize. In one, he opposes obscurantism and in the other he theorizes an enlightened , social order. He does not use too many high sounding technical terms or clitches and expresses his ideas in a lucid way.

Sen opposes obscurantism by theorizing on market fundamentalism , religious orthodoxy and social conservatism, political cynicism and nuclearism. He exposes market fundamentalism through investigation of market limitations relating to poverty and development. In his opinion market- led growth alone can not eradicate poverty. Public action and state intervention are also necessary. He concedes the role of market as an indicator or transmitter of signals. Even so he does not endorse neo liberal orientation favored by organizations like the World Bank, International Monetary Fund, US Treasury and right wing think tanks that stand for total deregulation, rampant privatization, unbridled globalisation, trade and exchange control liberalization.

Sen advocates State intervention in nutrition, health, education and social insurance which are intimately linked to the outcome of economic processes and empower people to becom economic agents. He belongs to the tradition of classical- political economy which deals with actual power relations among people and institutions.

The award of Noble Prize to Amartya Sen is an acknowledement that market dogmas have run out steam and a new approach has become necessary.

Sen is a defender of human rights. For him liberty is a basic entitlement. He regards a society without compassion as undesirable. While he wants equality of opportunities for all, he favors support of certain basic requirements e.g. nourishment, freedom from diseases, self respect and dignity. This capability - based perspective provides foundation for affirmative action, positive discrimination and empowers the powerless. This makes elitism repugnant as would be the diversion of resources away from the social priorities, such as nuclear weapons, high military budget. He rejects militarist notions of security as weapons of mass destruction. In Indian context, he says, bombs can not produce security and as such they would be incompatible with social priorities and with considerations of justice. Theories are all right but reality has to be faced. Is India not surrounded by neighbors who cannot be called friendly and she has to defend herself? India's prime minister Jawaharlal Nehru used to pontificate peace but when the country suffered humiliation in the 1962 War, it learnt the lesson that the country must be strong to face an invader.

Amartya Sen's work is holistic, it has analytical vigor and logical elegance and is humane. It is derived from multiple traditions, and is grounded in Indian culture as well as in refined Western radical thought.

Amartya Sen was influenced by the reformative resurgence of Raja Ram Mohun Roy and Rabindra Nath Tagore Tagore who gave impetus to the various modes of culture. He established the Shanti Niketan, a unique university, which attracted talents not only from India but from various parts of the world also. Amartya Sen was a student of Vishva Bharati.

Sen inherited Tagore's liberal, enlightened, modernist and extrovert traditions. Shanti Niketan is open , non-hierarchical, secular, plural, prosperous society where human beings can live with dignity and without fear.

The award of Noble Prize to Sen vindicated the humanist, radical, secular project. It reaffirmed modern rationality and importance of human agency in the making of the world, including its opaque, impervious economic progress, state structures and above all the structures of the mind.

Sen disapproves of Samuel Huntigton's theory of civilizational clashes. He says dividing the world into several civilizations distracts people's attention from prevailing politics and violence. He faults Huntinton's illusion of singular identity and also with his charaterisation of world civilizations as homogenous and insular than warranted by empirical analysis of their past and present

Sen is opposed to thinking of democracy as a quintessentially Western idea.. He denies the impact of Greek experience on modern day electoral government in Britain, France or Germany nor was there any semblance of democracy in contemporary cities in Iran, Bactria or India. Moreover democracy should not be equated with ballots and votes. It concerns with public deliberation and reasoning which flourished in Greece as much as in ancient civilizations. (In 6th century B.C.E. India, conventions were held to settle disputes between different views of Buddhism. Adherents of different points of view got together to argue out and settle their differences.)

Secularism is a pillar of democracy. Amartya Sen's engagement with secularism and India's identity are more intense.He has repeatedly called for State intervention in matters relating to communalism. He called demolition of the Babri Masjid as violation of Hindu tolerance and coexistence.

Sen is a celebrity and his statements, particularly about India wherefrom he came, are heard with respect and he should not keep on repeating statements that appear anti-indian, Hindus are fair in their approach and do not talk in terms of revenge but at the same time they donot want to suffer from further atrocities in the name of humanism and democracy.The events of 9/11 are an additional reminder for them. They do not forget that in the past they suffered huge atrocities at the hands of invaders.

Sen has been a consistent supporter of the pluralistic Indian society. It is heterogeneous, multi-religious, multi-lingual, syncretic and tolerant. Indian people have been by and large broad minded and liberal. The Western media have been derisively calling India 'Hindu India', orthodox and conservative.The Western media invariably prefixed India with Hindu—Hindu India—using Hindu in an undesirable sense in stead of appreciating India's pluralism.Indians had accepted the Partition of the country. In 1947 they had shown that they were reconciled to the creation of Pakistan. Then why should anyone denounce India and Indians as illiberal.

The fact is the West has been biased against India.Take the case of the unfortunate incident at Godhra railway station, in Gujarat. The West and even the Indian media kept quite and uttered not a word against the criminals who had torched the compartment. They uttered not a word in sympathies with the people burnt alive in the Railway compartment .Was it because they were Hindu pilgrims returning from Ayodhya; a place of pilgrimage for Hindus;and two, apprehensive that if they expressed sympathies with Hindus, they would be branded conservative and Hindu-sympathisers.That was so with majority leadership; it was not surprising that Muslim leadership kept quite. But when Hindu rightists retaliated the entire media criticised the gruesome atrocity.It was good the media did so. But even in focusing attention , they did not mention the Godhra tragedy.And for that fact which of the leftist and Congress leaders condemned the wrongs? (The majority community, appreciatively,

on the other hand, condemned the attacks on the minority in Gujarat.)
Most of Indians therfore fail to understand why Sen kept silent
about their hurt but keeps on talking only of Hindu fundamentalism
Those who died were human beings, matters little they were of
one or the other community. This shows fundamentalism of a
different hue.

Indian society is pluralistic in structure, so is Hinduism
pluralistic with its innumerable castes and schools of thought. Sen
supports its openness but opposes its anti-Western Swadeshi style
Xenophobia, which he says is a cloak for conservatism. He thinks
India is plastic enough to absorb changes. But this is no reason to
be silent.Silence is interpreted in various ways. However, Sen is
fair enough to criticize social Darwinism and militarism.

Sen is well versed in Indian art, literature, music, films, and
issues relating to food . In India peoples following different religions
for instance Hindus, Muslims, Sikhs, Christians, Jains and Parsees,
and atheists and agnostics have flourished for thousands of years.
Hinduism is tolerant and accommodates differing views and view
points. It is not right to say that only the West possesses tolerance
and liberty. Liberty is not an old historical feature of any country or
civilization. Plato and Aristotle were not less authoritarian in thinking
than was Confucius. Bruno was burnt at the stake in Rome in 1600.
Compare this with Asoka's tolerance, Or take Akbar who in 16th
century heard differing views on religions in his court at Fatehpur
Sikri, near Agra.

Amartya Sen is a witty person. He narrated a personal
experience in a meeting at Berkeley which is worth reproducing:
"Many years ago when I was a student at Cambridge, one of my
Economics professor , John Robinson, told me during a tutorial,
"Let me tell you about the Chinese, Japanese and Indians. The
Japanese are much too polite, you Indians are much too rude. The
Chinese are exactly right." I readily accepted the generalization
as the alternative would have been to give further evidence of
Indian propensity to argue." Sen questions, "What about apartheid
in South Africa?" Indeed the weaponry of hateful characterization
draws on perfectly ordinary features of human life and this makes
for them more difficult to overcome and eradicate the use of rabid
and calamitous.

Amartya Sen was born on 3 November,1933  son of Ashutosh and Amita Sen at Shantiniketan. He was educated at the Presidency College, Calcutta and Trinity College, Cambridge. He was Professor of Economics, Jadhavpur University (1956-58), Fellow, Trinity College, Cambridge (1957-63), University of Delhi (1963-71), Chair, Department of Economics (1966-68), Director of Agricultural Economics Research Center, Delhi (1966-71), Professor of Economics LSE (1971-71), Oxford University(1977-81), Drummond Professor of Political Economy (!980-88), Harvard University (1987-98),Professor Emeritus (1998-), Master, Trinity College, Cambridge (1998-), Sen was Fellow and visiting professor in several universities.He was recipient of docorate honoris causa from several institutions. He has a large number of publications to his credit and has contributed to various journals in economics, philosophy and political science.

Dr. Amartya Sen was born in a family of scholars. His father K.M. Sen was reputed as a great scholar.In 1960, Amartya married  Navneeta Devi.They divorced in 1975. He married Eva Colorni in 1978 and on her death in 1985, he married Emma Rothschild. He has two daughters from his first wife, and one son and one daughter from the second wife.

Expressing his candid views about the award to Sen, an economist friend said, " The award also signifies the discrediting of the neo-liberal economic paradigm."

# 17
# SURYAKANT TRIPATHI NIRALA
## (1899-1961)

Rainer Maria Rilke says in a poem that we should try to love the questions.In ancient india the seers posed questions with mystique import and offered replies in very subtle ways. In some of his poems, Nirala sounds mystic,especially when he expresses his feelings in a tortured frame of mind. Whereas the Western writers talked of existentialism and humanism, Nirala led a life that was like an open book of humanism. An episode in his life to that purport was:

Decades ago, we donot recall the exact year but guess it was late 1950s. New Delhi had grown into a great cultural center. Yet the Bombayites mocked at and called Delhi a big village. Nevertheless, no one challenged New Delhi's claim to being the hub of Hindi literary pursuits. Hindi writers, publishers and bulk distributors conducted their pursuits from this hub. The Shanivar Samaj (Saturday Club) held its meeings at Jainenra Kumar's place in Daryaganj which attracted top Hindi writers and journalists. They assembled on Saturday, as the name itself conveys. By turn, they presented their creative writings. The gathering assessed the literary merits and evaluated the works inn comparison to contemporary writings in English and Indian languages. At times prominent writers of other languages visiting Delhi also joined. It wes in one such meeting one winter that a Hindi critic who had just returned from Allahabad narrated an incident, relating to the Hindi Poet Surya Kant Tripathi Nirala, to which the critic himself had been a witness.

Nirala, escorted by two eminent citizens, emerged from a building after a reception held in his honor. He was decorated with a shawl and presented with a cash award and a replica of Saraswati, the goddess of learning. As they descended the steps, he saw an old woman with shrunken eyes, shivering from the cold wind. Almost instantaneously, Nirala took off the shawl and covered the old lady's shoulders with it. "Son, may you live long", blessed the woman. One of Nirala's escorting companions protested that Nirala himself was not properly covered and he had given the costly shawl to a beggar. The humanist did not take any note and tenderly said that the old woman's need was much more than his, adding that he would survive but the skeleton as the lady was, looked in a bad shape. Nirala was a self realized person which reflected profusely in his writings. One could call Nirala's act as whimsical or capricious but the fact remained that he was a very sensitive person and could not see others suffering. The occasion was misused by some people to spread a canard that Nirala was mentally unsound.

We were reminded of Valmiki, the great Sanskrit poet, who was moved by the shriek of a Kraunch bird whose companion was shot dead by a hunter's arrow. Touched by pathos, poetry burst out of his mouth and that was how one of the greatest epics, the *Ramayana* was written. Similar, was the story of Rabindranath Tagore's *Kabuliwallah*. Nirala is a wonderful character and someone from Allahabad can write even now a biography of the great poet. It will be a great service. Quite a few such incidents are associated with Nirala's name.

Nirala's life was full of extreme hardships. From childhood he saw nothing but adversity, suffering and sorrow which explains his recourse to Advaitavad to express his thoughts in his works that appeared through various media. He wrote poetry, prose, drama, essays, short stories, literary criticism on various themes and topics all in innovative styles.

Nirala means peculiar or rare. His family name was Suraj Kumar Tiwari but school and other records show his name as Surya Kant Tripathi. He was born on February 21, 1899. (According to some the year was 1896.) Long time back job opportunities had necessitated his ancestors to move from their native place, Garhkola in U.P. to Calcutta (Kolkata) in Bengal. Nirala's father was employed as a police official in Midnapur. From his father, Surya Kant inherited a strong physique and also a liking for wrestling.

Midnapur had beautiful surroundings (and so was Garhkola) which developed his aesthetic sense. That accounts for imagery in his writings, especially poetry. From his parents, he learnt legends of scriptures which he would remember as he matured. His mother died while he was young and the responsibility of bringing him up fell on father. Suraj went to school but because of family circumstances, he had to discontinue studies before he could complete his matriculation. Being intelligent and hard working, he acquired a good knowledge of languages-Hindi, Bengali, English and Sanskrit. Thinking that Surya Kant would feel greater responsibility , father arranged his marriage. The girl was accomplished. This did some good to him. She would motivate him to read and write for Hindi periodicals. Besides small money recieved as honoraria, publication of writings brought him recognition also. He was now invited to Kavi Sammelans (Poetic Symposia) which meant larger circle of acquaintances.

Unfortunately, by the age of 20, he lost all his dear ones, including father and wife. She left behind a son and a daughter. He had also to take care of four orphaned nephews and faced a very tragic life. For survival's sake, he moved from place to place .It was a sheer chance that he met a businessman who admired his poetry and asked him whether he could look after his accounting work. Nirala agreed to the proposal. The businessman started a journal and sought Nirala's help.He appointed Nirala as its Editor. This proved a God-sent opportunity. Nirala won applause for the overall production of the journal as also for his writings. But as time passed, the owner became jealous of Nirala and started interfering in his work. A situation arose when Nirala had to leave the job.

Bengal was those days dominated by the thoughts of Vivekananda and Rabindra Nath Tagore. The two were like icons and had influenced not only the media and life styles of people but also made them conscious of their social and economic conditions. In fact the two great Indians influenced the entire country. Nirala imbibed their thoughts and expressed them in his writings. A time came when he had to leave Bengal. For a short period he went to his native place to manage the property he had inherited. He carried on his writing work and roused nationalist feelings through his writings.

During the first quarter of the Twentieth Centuary, the themes of Hindi literary works were mostly devoted to nature, religion and nationalism. Young Hindi writers were borrowing from Engish, Bengali, Marathi and other Indian and European languages and literatures. Bankim Chandra Chatterjee's *Anandmath* and his historical novels had become popular among Hindi-speaking readers. Hindi writers did not hesitate to borrow vocabs from Sanskrit and English and thus both, language and literature, were being enriched. Nirala made significant contribution to the development of both .His multi-linguism came very handy. The usage of the terms in his writings appeared notmal.

Nirala was a prolific writer. He used various forms and media. And, in this respect he has been compared to Tagore and Jayashankar Prasad ,another prolific Hindi writer and Nirala is counted amongst outstanding writers of India .Other leading contemporary writers are Mahashweta Devi (Bengali) , Shivaram Karanth (Kannad), R.K.Narayan and Mulkaraj Anand (English). (The authors were helped in selection of Nirala and R.K.Narayan by Indian scholars including the Sahitya Akademi's Mr.Satchidananda and Ms. Padmanabhan.)

Nirala's works in brief are mentioned below:

Poetry: With two cotemporary Hindi poets, namely Jayashakar Prasad and Sumitranandan Pant, Nirala set a new trend of poetry which became famous as Chhayavad. Nirala's poetry was rich in practically each significant trait of Chhayavad viz love for nature, attraction for mystical and abstract, personal perspective, and freedom in use of form and content.

Nirala asserted freedom from bondage of traditional rhythmical meters and took to blank verse. Many opposed his usage and ridiculed him. He did not pay any heed to the critics and finally blank verse became acceptable and Nirala was recognized as its master craftsman. Nirala's cocept of beauty which was earthy and transcendental differed from the traditional concept. To this class, belong his poems-*Juhi ki Kali, Preyasi and Rekha*. To his another style of poetry-mystical- belong *Tum aur Main, Payal. Ram ki Pooja,* and *Tulasidas* are his well known mythological and historical poems.His treatment of the poems is full of grandeur. Nirala's poetry on nature is mostly thematic and is full of picture images.

Nirala's poems have appeared in collected works. These are titled *Anamika* and *Geetika* and of each several editions have appeared. The themes of poems in *Anamika* relate to various sources such as Puranas, history, religion, nature, and contemporary and social events. .All these poems have a flair for imagination. The main poems of *Geetika* are: *Aina(1943), Apara (1946), Archana (1950), Aradhana* (1953), and *Geet-Gaya* These poems relate to devotion and resignation. The former work had mostly philosophic contents.The change in themes and forms of poetry was due to the influence of Western thoughts and communism. The progressive themes can be noticed in *Bhikshuk, Bahu, Deen, Woh Todati Pattha*r which are nearer to Pragativad-poetry full of sympathy with the oppressed. The Pragativad school had followed Chhayavad. The sympathy for the poor came to fore in *Kukurmutta (1942)* and *Naye Patte* (1946). Mixed with a tinge of humor they make an impact on listener as as much as on reader. What makes them interesting is their attack on rich, progressives and smug intellectuals. Besides, the poet also introduced radical changes in style and language. Easily understood words have replaced uncommon Sanskrit words and language matches the exquisite ideas. This was possible because Nirala had command over language.

Nirala's poetry conveys human emotions appropriately.

Poet Nirala was familiar with the life of common man, his hope and despair, self confidence and doubt, victory and defeat, propensity and penury. His poetry is devoted to man's love, compassion, urge, beauty, doubt, despair, defeat, determination, sacrifice, poverty and faith. Man wants and makes efforts to enjoy full life. In one of his poems, Nirala confesses his love for humanity and asserts that he shared their sorrow.

Poets do not create philosophy; at best they propose a view of life, which originates from their faith and involvement. Generally, man accepts positive values but confronts time-consuming negative values. Perhaps, such was Nirala's experience that he said, " I have been expelled but my inside is full to the brim." Which explains why his love remains unsurpassed. He adds, "There is no obstacle in dedication, no doubt in devotion, no lack of determination, no despair in poverty." All that is is self sacrifice. It is natural for man to achieve self realization at different levels and in various positions.. Poetry is his constant companion. Treading the path of love and assimilation, he merges with nature. He is compassionate. His writings are "luminous, challenging, stimulating, revealing and sometime oracular."

Nirala's wirtings

Novels: *Apsara(1931), Alaka(1933), Nirupama (1936), Prabhavati !936), Choti ki Pakad (1947), Kale Karaname !950), Sarkar ki Ankheyn annd Chameli.*

*Short Stories: Five collections—Lili and Sakhi (1935), Sukul ki Beewi (1941), Chaturi Chamar (1945), Devi (1948), The stories* depict real life sketches.

Reminiscences : *Kullibhat and Billepur Bakariah*

Social-Pollitical Works : Four Collections

# 18
# R.K.NARAYAN
(1906-2001)

R.K Narayan (given name Rasipuram Krishnaswamiyer) is one
of the foremost writers of English fiction in India. The creation of
an imaginary place, Malgudi,that recurs in his novels brought him
fame not only in India but in the entire English-speaking world,
including England and the United States. Malgudi continues to sustain
readers' interest even now when Narayan is no more alive. But
how strange was it that for long many years, he was not known to
the people of his own town, Mysore until, P.G. Wodehouse and
other writers visited Mysore as Maharaja's guests and inquired
about one of the city's residents, Narayan, the novelist. It was
strange that even the elite of Mysore did not know about him. In
fact they had not even heard of such a novelist. Truly. 'darkness
pervades unded the lamp'.

Malgudi was a chance name- a product of imagination
and creative urge of the sensitive mind of R.K.Narayan.To be fair,
any other pleasant rhyming name would have served for the locale
for Narayan's fiction and would have attracted readers. No Freud
was required to make an analysis of the choice. In *Malgudi Days*,
Narayan tells the story of his childhood's funny companions. Much
before a pup, which is child's first preference for a pet, would enter
in Narayan's life, monkey, peacock, mynah and parrot were brought
for his entertainment by his grandmother, Parvati Amman, and a
pleader maternal uncle, with whom he lived. Incidentally, the pets
amused the neighborhood as also the passers by. The first pet to
enter was Roma, a monkey, followed by a peacock, and when the
two disappeared , others came in train, one by one since the uncle
did not like lo leave the nephew without a company. If it happened

to be an extraordinary company all the more good. Freedom-loving Roma, the monkey, could not be kept in its cage and it did not take it long to learn to free itself. And, once a creature becomes aware of the importance of freedom, it is impossible to keep it under detention. The monkey left, never to return. Came the turn of peacock that fed itself constantly on insects, including ants. With its tail spread, the peacock made a delightful sight, and when it produced a shrill sound, sure enough it gave clue to the direction and the distance of its presence, which could be easily guessed. How sad, it met its painful death at the hands of passersby. who craved for its meat. One day when it went out, unseen by family members, they twisted its neck and threw the remnants inside Narayan's compound.

The child Narayan was a good observer and he learned so many things about animal behavior-the monkey's antics and the peacock's dietary habits. Came in the mynah, the parrot, the kitten and the puppy to fill in the vacuum. Each creature that was brought whetted Narayan's curiosity.

Narayan's father Krishnaswamy, a highly Anglicized person, was the headmaster of a government high school at Chennapatna in the Mysore State. After his marriage with Gyana Amman, he severed all relations with his paternal family. When Narayan, the second child was born, maternal grandmother Parvatiammal reared him up. It was because Gyana Amman had a succession of deliveries. Of them, only three children survived and she found it difficult to look after the family. Narayan was the middle one.and she sent Narayan to her mother. The grandma affectionately called Narayan. Kunjappa, that is the Little Fellow. When Narayan started going to school, animals and birds made way to participatory activities like cycling, sports, scouting. Narayan's life was full of love, affection and curiosity. But he was not worldly wise. .

Narayan's observation was sharp. As he grew up and gained experiences which he stored in a corner of his mind and when he grew adult, he narrated these in the form of fiction. Obviously, the company of unusual pets made unusual stories. In school, Narayan did well in language. He was good in English, but not bright in other subjects. He wrote down the incidents mixing with them the flavor of his imagination. The childhood experiences made interesting stories. Narayan's stored up energy mixed with rich and varied information found its way in his creative works which entertained everybody.

The grandma was well versed in Karnatik music. She performed on Veena also. She introduced Narayan to the various ragas of Karnatic music, which would he his chief entertainment thoughout life. He learned playing Veena from her. He took interest in gardening and had a special gift for humor.

When Narayan was 16, his father was posted at Mysore. Narayan then went to live with his parents. He came across interesting persons, one of them was the leader of a caravan that was going to Hasan, known as poor man's hill station. With a staff in hand, the man menacingly called people to make way for the carts he was escorting and they would make way for him. This left an impression on his mind and he wrote about it.

At Mysore, he was under the direct supervision of his parents and the elder brother. The elder brother ensured that Narayan did not go astray. Once, when he found Narayan traveling without ticket, he admonished Narayan and brought the younger brother to the right path. This was his second formative stage when happy family relationships are founded. He joined the High School. but in the school life was uneventful. He passed the examinations, with poor grades. He failed in the Mysore University Entrance examination; first he failed in English, then in Tamil. Later, he failed in B.A.and only after one more year, in 1930, he passed B.A. with his younger brother R.K.Laxman. During his spare time, Narayan made in-depth study of English poets, particularly Word worth, Byron, Browning and Shakespeare. Novelist Merri Corrolie made deep impression on him. In 1924, he started writing. He saw the city and city life and relative impressions provided the vignettes for his penmanship which the readers found absorbing.

Narayan was a voracious reader. After B.A., he tried to secure employment but was not successful. With his father's influence, he got a teacher's job but he could not adjust to rowdy students. Moreover, the Headmaster also did not help him in disciplining the rowdies. Therefore he left two school jobs. And, then in 1930, he finally decided to take to writing as a profession-as a source of income for livelihood. He said that Mysore was an excellent place to live in, but it was Madras (Chennai) where he could market his products. With father's prodding, Narayan met some well placed persons who had been his father's students and whom his father had helped. Some of them- Railway officers and Bank executives-were in position to help but they did nothing.Not only that they derided his father which hurt him. Out of disgust, Narayan left Mysore for Bangalore where he did odd jobs. He wrote for *Justice*, an anti-Brahmin newspaper (Narayan was a Brahmin),and reviewed books for *The Hindu*, a reputed daily published from Madras. This was how Narayan's literary Career began, Malgudi took birth and writing of short stories started. In the morning he would walk, with an umbrella in hand to the park, sit there in calm atmosphere and write short stories and vignettes of 300 to 400 words each. Swami was the first character he developed. Once, his maternal uncle came to Banglore and stayed with him.He took the struggling author to publishers and editors but to no avail. However, a few short stories found place in *The Hindu* which fetched him small honoraria. Even the small amount that he earned came very handy.

While Narayan was determined to take to writing,as a career, his father was pessimist and frankly told him that it was futile to think of making a living from writings.

At the age of 29, Narayan completed his first novel – *Swami and Friends*— in the setting of Malgudi. Swami was anarchic, a unique mix of sadness and beauty. Graham Greene saw the story and spoke appreciatively of Narayan's efforts. Meantime, an article published in the *Punch* brought him a check of six Guinees, a fabulous amount those days.

An emotional development complicated Narayan's early professional life. One day, he saw a girl fetching water from a well which proved love at first sight. Incidentally, the girl was daughter of a Brahmin gentleman who was, like his father, headmaster of a high school.The impulsive involvement was a clear violation of customs and convention. Narayan approached the girl's father (something unusual). The girl's father was satisfied about the boy's caste, family etc. But when to the query about his employment, Narayan replied that he was a writer and lived on his income from writings published in newspapers and that the income would suffice for a family, the girl's father was not satisfied. Narayan then brought out the check of six guinees he had received from Punch that morning and showed it to his would be father-in-law, the gentleman was quite impressed The two families met. After crossing all the hurdles, Narayan and Rajam, 16, were married in 1934. Rajam was taller than Narayan. In 1936, the couple had a daughter and for sometime led a happy life.

With happiness came grief. Narayan's father passed away. This was followed by Rajam's death on June 6,1939 after a married life of only five years. Now Narayan had to live at home to look after his daughter and he devoted most of his time to her.While he had no stable income, he had to share family expenses. He was worried how to arrange the payment of rent for the house.The landlord asked him to vacate the house. On the advice of his elder brother, he paid rent at enhanced rates. But after sometime the landlord turned up again insisting that he vacate the house. But the landlord also asked him whether he could publish his article in the Journal he was editing, Narayan agreed to publish it but soon he felt that it was a sort of prostitution and returned the article. Narayan and his brother shifted to another house.

Rajam's death changed Narayan's values-spiritual,social and literary. After two years of psychic training, he experienced Rajam's presence. His family and relatives pressed him to go in for second marriage he declined. He was in his youth and knew 'sexual need would make life miserable.' But he found a doctrinal way. Whenever he saw a beatiful woman, he would say to himself, Oh mother,who sustains all creatures, I see in her a passing glimpse of your radiant form."Thus he would get over his temporary weakness. Narayan's fidelity to his late wife was unequivocal. Rajam's death tormented him. Then one day he met a couple, Mr and Mrs Rao who were interested in communicating with dead through stances. Narayan did not tell them about his desire to talk to his wife. But the Raos sensed and arranged Narayan's conversation with his wife.Narayan wrote about stances in his book *The English Teacher.*This proved an anti-dote to his grief.

Narayan's eldest brother worked with the Mysore government and he had a stable income. The younger brother R.K.

Laxman was an artist and did free lance till he got a job with the Times of India. Narayan took up a reporter's job with *The Hindu.* After great efforts, Narayan's first collection of short stories *Malgudi Days* was published in 1942 . But at the same time, some of his writings came back unpublished from newspapers. The novels too would have met the same fate but for the help of his friend Purna who was studying at Oxford. Narayan had sent him his novel, which Purna sent to Graham Greene. The famous author liked it and he helped publication of his books by reputed publishers in Britain. Publication was followed by recognition and fame. Narayan's three novels published by three different publishers were *Swami, Mr. Sampath : A Printer of Malgudi* (1949) and *The English Teacher.* The publications brought him royalties and he built a house of his own in Mysore. He had achieved success. By early 1960s, Narayan was driving down from Madras (renamed Chennai) in his own blue Mercedes to visit his daughter at Mysore where she lived with her husband.

It was something unique for a writer in India to live on writing. Once when Narayan was visiting Delhi, he was invited to speak to a group of writers and intellectuals. He spoke on 'Living by Writing'. He recalled that while his wife was alive, he could not buy her a sari and now he had a Mercedese and a house, all from his income from writing. Narayan had inherited a wry humor from his mother's side. He had little patience or tolerance for pretensions. When a reviewer criticized one of Narayan's books and a friend asked Narayan about the review and the reviewer. Narayan said the reviewer was a 'tenth rate' man. When the questioner protested, Narayan relented and promoted the reviewer to 'third-grade'.

Narayan's novels and short stories appeared one after the other all by different reputed publishers. Although he had income, he knew nothing about money management –keeping accounts of royalties and payments received from different sources at different times. Once he was asked by the Chief Minister of the Mysore State to write a book on Mysore. He was to be paid an honorarium of Rs.1200 by the State Government. He wrote the book. But when it came to payment, he faced many odds even though the Chief Minister had ordered immediate payment. His worse experience was about the scripting of *Guide*, his own novel, in which actors and writers were involved. On the pretext that 'Guide' failed to attract audiences, they tried to put Narayan off. The matter was taken to court. But Narayan's experience was nothing but sad.

After the Second World War, Narayan's income slumped as the sales of books in England had declined and in India also sales were no way better. Narayan's financial condition was not very happy. And, to top it, he unwisely spent much of his time and energy on the venture of publishing a magazine.

Narayan's other novels were. *A Tiger for Malgudi (1980), Talkative Man (1985), and World of Nagaraja (1990).*

Before India's independence, as a policy Narayan had never written about India's freedom struggle. He felt ambivalence about the mass movement against the British. But soon after Independence, he wrote a short story *'Lawley Road.'* It portrays some impulses about nationalism and describes how an administration dismantled bureaucrat Lawley's statue and then reinstated when it was found that he was the founder of Malgudi.

The ambivalence is franker in *Waiting for the Mahatma (1955)* which has two quaint characters. One of them is chairman of the Municipal Corporation who reveres Gandhi as Mahatma but remains indifferent to self-awareness. Before Gandhi's visit to Malgudi,he replaces the pictures of kings in his house with portraits of Congress leaders. Another character is a young man who joins the 1942 Quit India movement but is persuaded by an egotistical terrorist into becoming a saboteur. The novel also talks of socialism, secularism and non-alignment and discusses people and society led by the decayed customs and herd impulses.

Narayan's other writings of post-Independence period are : *My Dateless Diary (1964), the Vendor of Sweets (1967), and the Painter of Signs (1977).* Whereas the first two follow the pattern and style of earlier fiction of Narayan, the third one, i.e. *The Painter of Signs* written during Mrs. Gandhi's Emergency deals with Daisy, a girl who has the mission to control the country's population. Raman, a young drifter, attracted by her, joins her family planning campaign, and hopes to win over her. But she drops Raman after agreeing to marry him. Raman returns to his old life.

Narayana's fiction is divided into three parts: the early

novels with energetic young men (Swami, Chandran and Krishna), the middle novels with restless drifters (Srinivas, Swami) and the later novels with the wounded and exiled by the modern world (Jagan, Raman).This division is based on author's intellectual journey of the middle class in former colonial societies which make them conscious through education about individuality and nationality, anti-colonial assertion, and post-colonial inadequacy, unfulfilled private lives, distrust of modernity and individual assertion; and finally search for cultural authenticity, once great past is neglected.Narayan evolves his characters with sympathy and affection but their 'religious seeming acceptingness' gives his novels peculiar irony rooted in faith of Hindus. Their conflicts are minor disturbances in the life of cosmic order.

The *Guide* (1958) is Narayan's best novel. It won him the Sahitya Akademi award in 1961. Guide's Raju invents new historical past for tourists. He seduces a married woman, becomes a culture promoter, steals, is jailed; and is abandoned by everyone. On release, he becomes a holy man, lives at the bank of a river, a role that is imposed on him by villagers. Then there are no rains and the river dries up. The villagers look up to the holy man to intercede with the gods. Raju goes on a fast but eats furtively whatever little food he had saved. Then abruptly, out of a moment of self-disgust comes his resolution that he will do something with sincerity for others; if fasting can bring rains, he will fast. He stops eating and becomes weak. News of his efforts goes round, devotees and sight seers gather at the riverside, and create a religious occasion out of the fast. On the 11th day, when he stands on his legs, he staggers and dies, mumbling "It is raining in the hills. I can feel it is coming up under my feet, up my legs?"Characteristically Narayan does not say whether Raju's penance actually caused rains.

One significant event in Narayan's life was his visit to USA.Recognition as a writer had brought perks and travel grant and he was happy to see the country, lecture at places, and meet the intelligentsia in USA. The travel grant was offered by the Ford Foundation.

Unfair dealings by publishers and film producer in India and abroad involved Narayan in litigation, and writers being poor managers of such mundane matters, Narayan too had his share of bitter experiences.

With his wry humor, Narayan's fiction captures the foibles of ordinary people, mostly male and few female as in Malgudi. To name a few: Savitri of the *Dark Room* (1976), Daisy is a typical character. An emancipated woman, she runs away from home, disowns her caste, and also the very name her parents had given her. She works alone as a family planning counselor and lives alone, but leaves Malgudi in the pursuit of another job.

Narayan's themes and language go well together. Unlike other writers, he does not present India as an exotic place for aliens. He has written on various subjects – legends from *Mahabharata, God, Demons* and *others (1964). Ramayana Travelogue (Emerald Routes 1978), Autobiography (May Days 1974), My Dateless Dairy 1960).*Narayan has written essayas which are remarkable for their lucidity. Three of his best stories have appeared in a collection titled *A Horse and Two Gates.*

Prior to Narayan, three novelists in South India B. Rajam Iyer, A Madhaviah and K.S. Venkataramani had won recognition. Each of them had written in English and in another language in which he was proficient. Their works were enjoyed by the readers knowing two languages. .

How did Narayan become a successful writer? A critic said, "The secret of Narayan's success was his sanity and normality". Narayan sarcastically said, "The first step of self realization is good faith".

Narayan fell ill. In 1990 he moved to Madras to look after his grand daughter.In 2001, he passed away in peace.

# 19
# SATYAJIT RAY
## (1921-1992)

Satyajit Ray, the renowned film maker, was tall. Unusually tall for an Indian. One day, when he was sitting in a class in his college his height became a matter of amusement. A lecturer did not turn up to take the class. The students did not know what to do and became boisterous. A professor who was passing by entered the class to see what was going on. The students became silent. Ray stood out amongst the students and the professor's eyes fell on him. He asked Ray why he was standing on the bench. Satyajit was sitting on the bench. He stood up, 6 feet 3 inch tall. The professor laughed, so did the class. Satyajit was not only physically tall, he was later counted amongst the tallest filmmakers and designers. Many of the qualities that Ray possessed were hereditary, it appears. He had a powerful personality, high stature, booming voice. A man of versatility and culture, he belonged to a family of brilliant writers.

Satyajit, known as Manik in childhood, was born on May 2, 1921 son of Sukumar Ray (1887-1923) and Suprabha. The Grandpa, Upendra Kishore Ray (1863-1915) had a business of printing press and studio, named after him as U Ray & Sons and enjoyed a status in the society. He was a friend of Rabindra Nath Tagore. Sukumar Ray's niece ( daughter of younger brother Kulada Ranjan Ray (1878-1950) was married to Prafulla Mahalanobis. Prafulla had developed fondness for Manik and used to bring records of children's music for him.Once he gave him a little blue gramophone, with bright pictures on its body, called kiddy phone. At the age of 2, Manik was given proper name Satyajit. That very year, when father Sukumar died, mother Suprabha with Manik moved to live with her brother Prasant Kumar Das in Bhawanipore where Satyajit grew up with his cousins. He was educated in the Bollygunge Govt High School. Mother Suprabha,who was a well known artist, worked as a teacher in Vidyasagar Vani Bhavan. Once Manik was asked to what he intended to be in future. The child's response was , "I would like to be a film maker." Young Satyajit was given a camera as present and he used to take snap shots. He had a good sense of humor, knew music and made 'nonsense songs' for games. He graduated in Economics from the Presidency College, Calcutta.

Living together in the same house,Satyajit fell in love with his cousin Monku but since marriage between cousins was repugnant to and came under prohibitive category, they could not marry. Manik and Monku traveled to Bombay to get married. After their marriage, they returned to Calcutta, rented a house and started living together separate from their families. He did a short course in Art from Shanti Niketan which equipped him with proficiency in photography, artwork, composing and allied pursuits and made full use of his learning. Satyajit joined an advertising concern D.J. Keymer as an Assistant Visualiser. Within a few years, he rose to be an Art Director. When DJ Keymer with Mrs. Nilima Guha Thakurta set up the Signet Press, Satyajit Ray was appointed Book Designer. In designing a book, Ray gave importance to the looks of the book which he thought should draw the buyer's attention by outstanding in the crowd of books when displayed at a counter in the book shop (or in an exhibition.). Secondly, the format of the book should be determined in accordance with the book's character. Ray made significant changes in the book covers which were widely appreciated.

In 1950, DJ Keymer sent him to England for training. In London, as already decided in Calcutta, he designed Vibhuti Bhushan Vandopadhyay's books, and initiated action to make a film Pather Panchali based on one of his novels. In England, he saw many realistic films. which sharpened his film sense and gave him fresh ideas about forms and techniques of film production.

Back to Calcutta, Satyajit joined a group of like-minded film and art enthusiasts and formed the Calcutta Film Society. Its members were talented young men like Chidanand Dasgupta and Bansi Chandragupta. The group met at their *adda* in the Chowringhee Coffee House. (Calcutta is rightly proud of its *addas*.)

Ray had not forgotten his decision about the Pather Panchali. He prepared a script, acquired necessary knowledge of music, both Eastern and Western, and found a producer. The shooting of Pather Panchali started in right earnest in 1952.

Commenting on Ray's production, R.P. Gupta wrote that Ray mostly opted for outdoor shooting except for some interior scenes with sets specially built for the occasion, as required by the art director, without using the conventional props and sets of a studio. Ray did away with stage make-up, costume incongruities, anachronisms in period details, various clutches – visual and musical – that still enthralled Indian audiences. Working with such a spirit, it was essential to dispense with professional performers and technicians. Thus whims, expenses and unnecessary delays were cut short and production was expedited. But as far film production concerns- why production of film alone, in each effort of production – the producer shirks from investing money and ditches at one point or other. The Pather Panchali and Satyajit Ray were no exception. The producer of Pather Panchali vanished. But determined persons and/or group find their way. The production of Pather Panchali was not withheld. When it was over, to everybody's, delight, it was found, the film was like poetry and in the film even ordinary things and greasy domesticities looked differently. The product was comely.

Satyajit Ray emerged not only as a film-maker but also as a good writer. Satyajit Ray's Prof. Shanku was a lovable, absent-minded scientific inventor. The characters of Feluda and Jatayu were found exotic and interesting. Satyajit considered himself primarily a filmmaker, writer only secondarily.

He made two mystery films- Jai Baba Felunath and Sonar Kella. As a film maker, Ray never compromised with his artistic principles. He would strictly adhere to the schedule of time. We learnt of Ray's determination to adhere to his commitments to artists when he refused to break his commitment for the convenience of a VIP he did not bother who that VIP was.

Once Ray happened to be in Delhi when Indira Gandhi extended him an invitation for dinner . Ray expressed his inability. Another time, a similar invitation was received by Ray from Mrs. Gandhi. This time too the date clashed with the schedule of filming and he again expressed his inability to attend, explaining that the occasion clashed with his shooting schedules.

Media respected Satyajit Ray because he was never rough with them. Despite his name and fame, he extended courtesy even to ordinary men. In real life, he was self effacing, gentle, and witty. Like a child at times, he was full of wonder and never lost his creativity.

Ray did not want to depend for publicity on others. He himself did graphics – for posters, bill boards, ads, designs, covers, calligraphy, type faces, sketches for costumes, sets and film shots. This created sensation and set new trends. All outstanding. Everything got a new look, pages got new typography, legibility, illustrations wherever necessary. Aesthetics was stressed in everything that was taken up. In 1956, Ray designed publicity material for Pather Panchali.

Music critic, Adi Gazdar, considered an authority, wrote about Satyajit's music: Ray liked music from the Gregarian chants down to the era of Bach, Beethoven and Brahms.

Ray was an image-maker. For him, cinema was a means of expression. A humanist, he contributed human values to the world cinema.

Two anecdotes relating to Satyajit Ray's affairs with two actresses - Madhavi Mookherjee and Sumitra Sanyal— were mentioned by his son, Sandeep Ray in Ameder Koya. It was alleged that Bejoya felt that these forays were against propriety and in 1965-66 threatened to divorce him. Ray realized the gravity of his indulgence and apologized to his wife, assuring that he would never let such a thing happen again.

Satyajit Ray passed away on April 23, 1992.

One of the special features of Ray's films is that his films convey whole personality. Ray's films are antithesis of conventional Hollywood films, both in style and content.

Satyajit Ray's mystery books include: The Bandits of Bombay, Trouble in Gangtok, Ray and the Humanist. He recreated the story of film Charulata.

Pather Panchali: The production of film Pather Panchali

proclaimed that India is capable of producing films of quality. It is one of India's greatest works in the history of world cinema, say film critics. Pather Panchali was authored and is the master work of Bengali novelist Vibhutibhushan Bandyopadhaya. The skill of Satyajit Ray brought to bear on the script- writing as well as direction and shaped it in original form. Subrata Mitra was the cinematographer, and Bansi Chandragupta, the art director. They produced the film with patience, dedication and endurance. It is to be remembered that no commercial director was ready to invest money and help in making and completing the film. They said the film had no songs or dances or cheap funs and games to attract audiences. When BC Roy, the chief minister of West Bengal came to know about the difficulty of finances, his government came forward to help. A critic appreciatively says that there is not a single dispensable segment any where in the film, with such precision the film was made.

The story of the Pather Panchali evokes empathy in the audience. Its story in brief is : Harihar, an empoverished Brahmin supports his family consisting of wife Sarbajaya, daughter Durga, and an old cousin Indir Thakrun. Harihar takes out time to write for the Jatra and nurtures the hope that some day his plays will be a runaway success and they would not be poor any more. Under these circumstances Appu is born and Harihar also gets a job. Indir who had moved out comes back. Appu grows up and pampers about with Durga. Their aunt next door cannot stand them because they are poor. Appu joins the school. One day playing hide and seek with Durga, he goes beyond Kaash groves and is thrilled to see a train. Harihar again loses the job and the family again sees privation. His wages are blocked for months. Harihar goes to Vishnupur in search of job and does not return for four months. Thakrun comes but is not received with warmth and so she goes out hungry and thirsty and sits under a tree. Durga and Apu find her there. They touch her and she rolls over the ground. She is dead. The children are struck with awe. The monsoons drench the children which they enjoy. Durga has high fever. A kind neighbor calls a doctor but Durga dies. Harihar returns a few days later, with money and gifts. He hands over one Sari to Sarvajaya for whom he had brought it. Next, he hands over another sari he had brought for Durga. Sarbajaya breaks into a gush of tears held back for too long, as Durga was no more alive. Soon after Harihar decides to leave for Benares with his son. Neighbors come to know about Harihar's decision, and they turn up and ask him not to leave the place and go to Benares.

The story has no drama. But the way the film was designed by Ray, it stirred the viewers' emotions. He wanted to portray greater frankness in Ghare Baire in the characters of Sandip and Bimla. But the portrayal lacks realism because the two were never in a bedroom – they were always in a show room which had physical disadvantage to being intimate. In the World of Apu intimacy in honeymoon scene could be shown but the film maker had to keep in mind the writer's sensitivities. Bidhubhushan would not tolerate any such intimacy. Ray told a magazine editor : Love between man and woman is an elevating experience and on screen too it should be treated as such. West Bengal government wanted some change in the end but Ray won't. Finally, with Nehru's intervention, Pather Panchali. was finally produced and released.

Satyajit Ray conveys through his films a sense of whole personality. These are antithesis of conventional Hollywood films, both in style and content. He eschews glamour, gimmics and technical polish. His characters are of average ability and talents. Perversion does not appear in his films, except in Mahapurusha .

The film was entered in Cannes Festival in 1956 and won the coveted prize. The late Nargis Dutt had criticized the film for being too realistic and creating a wrong image of India abroad. Ray was accused of portraying India's poverty abroad – only to win a prize. Bombay film makers suggested that modern India should have also been projected. Satyajit Ray is against raising any wall of casteism around him. He considered himself a liberal humanist. Yet they accused him of being an Anglophile. (He was a Bramho).

One of the affects of Satyajit Ray on films was that they compelled filmmakers to examine their techniques of production. A new crop of experts like Shyam Benegal, Adoor Gopalakrishnan and G. Arvindam that emerged has produced films, which are called 'new' but are not commercial. Some critics have compared Ray with Ghatak and Kurosowa ( Japanese filmmaker). But each one had his specialty and life style. For instance, Ghatak, a communist, had his projections tilted.

Glamour and arbitrary power never excited Roy. He had no appetite for publicity. He remained open to new experiences. His wife Bijoya said: "Satyajit maintained till end simplicity, honesty, generosity and kindness." Till his end, Roy continued to experiment with his subject matter and style. Yet, he remained true to his original conviction that a film maker should "first use common, strong and simple themes embroidered with apparently irrelevant details which instead of obscuring the theme only help to intensify it by contrast and instead create an illusion of actually better."

Satyajit Ray's films:

1. Pather Panchali (Song of the Road)
2. Aparajito (Unvanquished)
3. Paras Pathar (Precious Stone)
4. Jalasaghar (Music house)
5. Apur Sansar (The World of Apu)
6. Devi (Goddess)
7. Teen Kanya (Three vergins) – Postmaster, Sampati and Manihar
8. Abhijan (The Expedition)
9. Mahanagar (City)
10. Charulata (Name)
11. Kapurusha –Mahapurusha (Coward, Brave)
12. Nayak (Leader)
13. Chidia Khana (Zoo)
14. Goop Gyne Baga Byne
15. AranyerDin-Ratri (Day and Night)
16. Pratidwandi (Competitor)
17. Seemabaddha (Forbidden)
18. Ashani Sanket
19. Sonar Kella (Golden Fort)
20. Jane Aronya (Middle Man)
21. Shataranj Ke Khiladi (Chess Players)
22. Jai Baba Felunath
23. Heerak Rajar Deshey (In the land of Heer & Ranza)

24.    Ghare Baire (In and Out of home)
25.    Ganashakti (People's Power)
26.    Shakha Prasakha (branch & sub-branch)
27.    Agantuk (Guest)

**Documentaries & Short Stories**

28.    Rabindranath Tagore
29.    Sikkim
30.    Bale, Piko, Sadgati

# 20
# RAVI SHANKAR
(B. 1920)

Ravi Shankar's 'divine music' transcends all boundaries,says one of his admirers. He popularised Indian music in the West, built bridges between the Eastern and Western music systems and led a colorful life which transcends all imagination. These are not wild or hypocritical statements about a musician and his achievements. The Raag Mala authored under the joint names of Ravi Shankar and George Harrison portrays.Ravi Shankar's romance in an uninhibited manner – it is free, frank and honest.

Shankar Brothers – among whom Uday Shankar known the world over as a dancer-choreographer and Ravi Shankar as a sitar player- are prominent.The two have been acclaimed as the greatest talents in their specialized spheres. To a spectator, Shankar family's achievements appear like a dream-world.They are legends of performing art and music.

Ravi Shankar was born on April 7, 1920 at Varanasi (or Benares), son of Shyam Shankar Chowdhary. The family had emigrated from Jessore in East Bengal, now Bangladesh to Calcutta and then moved on westward to Varanasi. There Shyam Shankar completed his post graduate studies in Sanskrit, and to his good luck he got an appointment as Dewan in the princely state of Jhalawar. An official work took him to London. There, he had plenty of spare time which he utilized in completing a research project which earned him a doctorate. He also did Bar-at-Law. While he was in London , he got an appointment with the League of Nations at Geneva. He resigned the State job and moved to Geneva. The League's work took him to London, New York and many other places.

Shyam Shankar dropped his surname Chowdhary and adopted the latter half Shankar for his end name. While at Benares, Shyam Shankar was married to Hemangini and had raised a family. The family had continued to live at Benares when he had left for London. In London, Shyam Shankar fell in love with one Ms. Myrll, a young English lady and married her. This embittered Shankar's relations with Hemangini who having no alternative continued to live with her children at Varanasi, sustaining the family from the savings they had made.

Ravi Shankar, at the age of 10, came to Paris with the cultural troupe his elder brother Uday Shankar a talented dancer had brought to give performances of Indian dance and music in Europe and America. Uday Shankar is rightly credited with popularizing Indian dance and music in the West. Sir William Roythenstevi of the Royal Art College, London was impressed by his talents and took him under his mentor-ship. A famous Russian lady dancer saw Uday Shankar and thought he could help her in producing two ballets on Indian themes : Hindu wedding, and Radha Krishna, as a part of her oriental impressions. In one of her productions ,Shankar acted as Krishna , while she acted as Radha. For a year they toured USA, Canada, Mexico and South American countries. For another five years, they stayed in London and Paris where Eastern artistry and climate of bonhomie proved very receptive to them. Uday Shankar was joined by two young and pretty women- Simkie, a pianist-dancer, and Alice Boner, a rich sculptress from Zurich. The wealthy woman helped Uday Shankar with money.

In 1929, Uday Shankar accompanied by Boner left for India for one year to assemble a group of dancers and musicians. They studied Bharat Natyam and Kathakali. In 1932, Ravi Shankar went to USA and saw many film shows. His Hollywood experience was intoxicating. He was growing in an extraordinary way-traveling the world, meeting celebrities and being acclaimed at a young age. This year (1932) ,the audiences saw him debut in both music and dance.

The troupe returned to Europe. Many women who had found ravi Shankar cute, came to meet the shankar brothers, they kissed and fondled Ravi. "Little did they know that I was very excited all the time", said Ravi Shankar. Ravi too used to visit the house of Uday's friends, Georges and Nudmillo who had five daughters of ages 12 to 18, and "he was in love with all of them".

Then the troupe returned to India. Ravi Shankar traveled to Shantiniketan and was thrilled to meet Rabindra Nath Tagore. He was thrilled to see the great poet and connoisseur of arts. He decided to learn music from Ustad Enayat Khan and a day was also fixed for the *ganda* - initiation) ceremony. But a day before the ceremony, the Ustad fell ill and Ravi had to find another guru. In 1934, he accidentally met Ustad Alauddin Khan, master of Sarod, and.pioneer of Hindustani instrumental music, who was attending the All-Bengal Music Conference at Calcutta. The Ustad, acceded to Ravi's request to accept him as his disciple. Alauddin was accompanied by his 12-yearold son, Akbar Ali Khan, who was of Ravi's age, and the two became friends. After sometime Ravi with another troupe proceeded to South East Asia.

Shyam Shankar, Ravi's father, died in 1935. Soon afterwards, his mother fell seriously ill and she also died. Before her death, she gave Ravi's hand to Ustad Alauddin Khan and asked him to treat Ravi as his own son. That year, the troupe traveled to London via Palestine and Egypt. During 1936-38, Ravi was again in Paris and saw most parts of the beautiful city. From Paris, he wrote a letter to Ustad Alauddin Khan at Maihar in India expressing his desire to be Baba's disciple. (In Bengal in music circles the Guru is respectfully called Baba.) Later, one of Ravi's elder brothers (Mejda) took him to Maihar and arranged for Ravi's lodging, near the place of Khan Sahib. Ravi already knew Akbar, and now he became friendly with his sister Annapoorna, a daughter of Ustad Allauddin Khan. Ravi Shankar fell in love with her and the marriage of Ravi Shankar and Annapoorna was properly organized after the consent of elders on both sides was taken..

Uday Shankar had established a large Cultural Center at Almorha, a pretty town in Kumaon Hills in U.P.(now in Uttaranchal). The Center had four great gurus – Ustad Alauddin Khan (expert in instrumental music), Shankar Namboodari (Kathakali), Amobi Sinha (Manipuri) and Kandappan Pillai (Bharat Natyam).The gurus were eminent in their respective arts and the Center earned a country wide fame.It was a heavenly abode.

In 1941, Mejda married Lakshmi , a talented young artist. She had a younger sister Kamala, a very pretty girl and at the very first sight Ravi left in love with her. (He called her Saraswati). The center used to get financial aid from Europe and USA, but when the Second World War began, the source of aid to the Center dried up. The center had to be closed in 1944. Uday Shankar diverted his attention to film making and  went to Madras to make the film 'Kalpana'.

Annaporna gave birth to a son whom they named Shubhendra. Sometime later, Annaporna fell ill,. Ravi Shankar took her to Delhi for a medical check-up. Doctors identified an intestinal problem and after treatment she came back to normal. In Delhi, they stayed with the industrialist Lala Shree Ram. Lala Sree Ram's son Bharat Ram was keenly interested in learning Sitar. Shankar gave him lessons in Sitar. Bharat Ram is now a reputed Sitar player.

In June, the couple returned to Maihar. But unfortunately Shankar developed a rheumatic fever and for 2-3 days he was running 106° temperature which would not come down.. He was in a state of delirium and when Baba , as the Ustad was affectionately called, came to see him, in that state, Ravi Shakar shouted at Baba. After Shankar recovered, he was full of remorse for his behaviour. In the wake of critical illness, it came to his mind that he  had learned music from Baba for seven years and it was time for him to be on his own and move out of Maihar. Shankar with his family left for Bombay.

At Bombay, Ravi rented a house near Mejda's house. To maintain the family, Ravi resumed  giving programs  on the All India Radio and took up a job with His Master's Voice (HMV). But after working for sometime, he found  the work in HMV was not creative and gave him no satisfaction, He therefore left  HMV and joined IPTA (Indian People's Theatre Assuciation).

That very time Kamala (Saraswati) came to stay with her sister (Ravi's sister-in-law). Ravi had been friendly with her and resumed his relations with her (Saraswati). This could not remain secret from Annapoorna and her relations with Annapoorna became embittered .Even so, Ravi Shankar's relations with Ustad Alauddin Khan - of guru and Shishya—remained normal and until 1955 he continued visiting  Maihar for 3-4 months each year.

Ravi Shankar had joined IPTA as its Music Director. He composed a ballet, India Immortal,that portrayed the cultural political history of India. IPTA provided him opportunity for creature work and gave him satisfaction. The work was different from the cinema which featured fighting and violence, but prohibited kissing and exposure on screen. Also,in cinema the dialogues and lyrics tended to be full of double entenders and vulgarity. But for the entertainment of public, obscene dances were performed and costume was designed in a way that allowed provocative exposures of body.

For films,Ravi Shankar developed a new style of music which laid emphasis on incidental music and went well with scenes that were appropriate for plain and exploitative portrayals..He wrote,"I was attracted (to IPTA) because of creative involvement but now I found pressure of communist propaganda and felt suffocated." He reminisced, so far his sound track career and writing had involved in all the score of two realistic films – Dharati Ke Lal (of Khwaja Ahmad Abbas) and Neecha Nagar (of Chetan Anand). . They dealt with exploitation of poor. Produced in 1944-46, these were the first films with real people. Formerly, films concocted story and dialogues and dance sequences. In 1945, he created a new Rag Nat Bhavai.

In early 1946, Shankar left IPTA and joined the Indian National Theater (INT). An artistic group which Ravi Shankar and friends formed became its part. Annapoorna played Sitar for the group. Ravi Shankar was asked to write the tune of the song Sare Jahan Se Achcha, which was written by Iqual in 1904. Ravi's new melody was catchy and gave the song a bright mood. It became a national song.

In the Indian National Theater, Shankar created a two and half an hour film on Discovery of India of Jawahar Lal Nehru. It was shown at the Asian Conference in March 1947 at Delhi. The audience included 'Gandhiji, Nehru, Rajaji, Radhakrishnan' and other prominent personalities.. It was a grand success. But soon thereafter INT stopped its support to Ravi Shankar's group.

Ravi and friends formed another troupe – India Renaissance Artists (IRA). For survival's sake, Ravi gave Sitar recitals at meetings and in private houses. Ravi Shankar writes in Raag Mala that he was that time under great stress and thought of even committing suicide. Hee clarified that he refrained from doing so under the influence of Tat Baba. The sage reprimanded Shankar to keep off from such foolish ideas.

At the end of 1948, All India Radio appointed Ravi Shankar as the Director of Music for the External Services Division. With the role of Composer-Director, he organized a new instrumental ensemble. After three years he switched over to the Home Services of All India Radio where Shankar became a star attraction for tourists, he writes.

In 1954, Ravi went to the Soviet Russia with a cultural troupe. There, he met Ulanova and Maya Plisetzkaya. Ravi gave performances. Accompanied by Krishna Maharaj on Tabla, he played Dhamar (14 beats), Pancham Sawar (15 beats), and Shikhar (17 beats). From Russia Shankar went to Prague, Warsa, and Poznan.

Ravi stuck friendship with Yehudi Menuhin when he came to India. In 1956 Ravi visited the West. He was the first Indian artist who bridged the cultural gap between East and West and entouraged appreciation of Indian music in Europe and USA. He was established as the International Musician who combined charm, candor, dignity and humility of deep spiritualism and impish fun. He combined time in India with frequent trips abroad for concerts, recordings and festivals..

Ravi visited Japan in April. He was fascinated by love of Japanese for nature.

In 1958, Ravi participated in the concert for UNESCO. When he returned to India, he found Annapoorna had returned to him in Delhi. But by this time, he had established relationship with his old flame Saraswati (Kamala) who had become widow. In February 1967, he left Annapoorna for good.

Shankar has done quite some work for films e.g. Anuradha which won President's award. He provided music to Godan, a Hindi film based on the Hindi novel of Munshi Premchand. In this Lata Mangeshkar and Asha , Geeta Dutt, Rafi, Manna De and Mukesh were playback singers.

Uday Shankar and Ravi Shankar produced a ballet titled Samanya Kshat (Minor Loss) for the Tagore Centenary.

Ravi Shankar appeared at the Edinburgh Festival in 1961. The same year he toured US. coast to coast. Ravi was Visiting Professor of Music in the City College of New York. His brother-in-law and friend Ali Akbar Khan taught music in Sanfrancisco. When questioned, why he was making so much effort in West, Ravi said he felt he had a mission to complete. In 1968, Ravi Shankar wrote *My Music, My Life.*

In 1966, he met Harrison. Ravi Shankar and Harrison's collaboration gave birth to Raag Mala, which 'featured a stunning collection'. Shankar's circle of friendship was wide and included Yehudi Menuhin, Zubin Mehta, Philip Glan. His success story is full of super stardom of 60s, Montereyand Woodstock and covers Bangladesh. Where a great human tragedy had occured.

Harrison says: "Music is his (Ravi's) life. He is the music and Music is him. Music drives him on."

Sometime later Ravi went to London on an invitation from an impressario John Coast. He gave performances in which he was accompanied on Tabla by Chaturlal and on Tanpura by Node Mullick. John Coast presented Ravi to the Royal Festival Hall. He played concerts in London, Germany, Netherlands and US. He had a long playing album of his which featured many Ragas : Jover, Simhendra, Madhyamam, etc. The LP was released under the title Ravi Shankar. It plays three classical ragas. His show at New York was considered 'splendid'. Later, he participated in a concert for UNESCO

In Delhi at the Triveni Kala Sangam, Ravi staged his first Magnum Opus "Melody and Rhythm". in which he wanted to present a complete musical without any dance. It featured the combination of a choral group and a medium size orchestra – in all of 60-70 boys and girls. The program consisted of a variety of items on one theme which concerned the entire history of Hindustani Music, starting from Dhrupad- Dhamar singly through contemporary forms, including Khayal, Tappa, Tarana, and Thumri, followed by folk songs and modern compositions with some orchestra pieces in between

In 1971, Ravi Shankar founded a Ravi Shankar Music Center in Los Angels. In India too, he had set up a center in Bombay.

It was named Kinnar. He made a film titled Rag and made an EP for Bangladesh for Apple Records.

He set up Chandalika, a ballet in which he incorporated Western instruments along with Indian instruments. An artist, Penny by name, also came in his life. In fact too many men and women have come in his life.

In 1979 he produced a Hindi film titled Meera.

In 1980 Ravi Shankar and Zubin Mehta came closer. Ravi supplied music for the film 'Gandhi'.

In 1981Ravi, contributed the musical and artistic direction for the ASIAD (Ninth Asian Olympics.) (In 1981,Sukanya, a married lady,gave birth to a girl,who she said ,was ravi Shankar's daughter. Shankar owned her as his daughter.The shankar-sukanya affair had started in 1979.)

In 1982 Annapoorna asked for a divorce to which he gave his consent..

In 1991 he provided music to the film 'Tiger'.

In 1992 his son Shubhendraa died. He felt his life was full of grief.

Ravi Shankar's life has been eventful. At the age of 12, in 1932 ,he first performed at Berlin. He became a superstar in the 1960s when he played at the legendary Pop music events such as Woodstock and the Monterey Pop festival. He formed a life long friendship with Beatle George Harrison. He first toured Europe in 1930s with a troupe of Indian classical music on Sitar for the 1950s. This has been played with Violinist Yehudi Menhuin and Composer Philip Glas.

The Queen of England bestowed on Shankar an honorary Knighthood. President of India bestowed on Ravi Shankar Bharat Ratna, the highest award.that India offers.

"I have always been attracted to women. They have been source of information, spurring on me to do creative work in the field of music as well as providing general motivation and keeping me so active. At different times different women have given me so much and in return I have also given myself completely to whomsoever I have been without the time however long or short.

## INDIAN ART MOVEMENT

The advent of European powers influenced Indian art.The European painters focused on the picturesque (landscapes and ruined monuments). But traditional Indian paintings also received attention e.g.Kalighat paintings devoted to mythological subjects. Introduction of photography in 19th century displaed portrait painting.Nationalist feelings encouraged folk art and at the same time modern art also developed.Raja Ravi Varma was the first modern artist of India to achieve international fame.He painted mostly deities.As interest in art grew,there came up schools of art: Chennai in 1850 , Kolkata in 1854 and Mumbai in 1854. Excavations carried out in different parts of the country also gave rich art works, most of which were taken away by museums and private collections in Western countries.The intelligentsia emulated the West to reach the modern surface effects of the European oil paintings and to develop their ability to paint in the tradition of Italian renaissance.

After Independence, artists faced a dilemma whether to revive traditional painting, establsh links with rural life and village craftsmen and visualize objects and motifs ingrained in their conscience.Nandalal Bose and M.F.Hussain represent the traditionalists and progressives , respectively.

The Bengal School of Art produced a number of artists among whom Abanindranath Tagore (1871-1951) and Rabindranath Tagore ( !851-1941) are prominent.Abanindranath integrated the New, Japanese and Indian arts to create a new aesthetic medium. The Shantiniketan artists blended modern and folk art motifs. Amrita Shergil and Jamini Roy belonged to this movement. Nandalal Bose carried forward the traditional stream.

**K. L. Verma**

# 21
# NANDALAL BOSE
[1882- 1966]

Nandalal Bose's life, it is said, was wedded to art. Early in life, he had imbibed both the traditional and the classical arts of India. Besides, he had also imbibed the spirit of of nationalism when the British were authoritatively ruling over India.He regarded the *sadhana* of art akin to Yoga and believed that "Artist strives to achieve a totality of rhythm, movement, form, color and other attributes."

Nandalal was son of Purnachandra Bose and Kshetramani Devi born on December 3, 1882 at Kharagpur in Monghyr District of Bihar.The Bose family originally hailed from Banupur, a picturesque place on the bank of Hooghly, near Calcutta. One time they had seen better days but as their fortunes declined, they moved out of Banupur and Purnachandra joined service as the manager of the Kharagpur tehsil in the princely state of Darbhanga. As a child, Nandalal, was not bright in academics but was a keen observer. Kharagpur also was a beautiful spot and the river, the paddy fields, forest, birds and animals impressed young Nandalal's mind and those early impressions are discernible in his art works. He inherited qualities and virtues from both of his parents. From father he learned discipline and from mother Bangla language and crafts and line drawing He received initial education in his village school. But more than reading and writing in school, he evinced more interest in art and creative work.

When Nandalal was 15, he went to Calcutta for his Entrance Examination studies in the Khudiram Bose's Central Collegiate School. After passing Entrance, he joined the General Assembly College but failed in F.A. He moved to the Metropolitan

College but the results were no way better.The reason was that he devoted all the time to art activities and none to academic work. He learned to paint, draw and model, and copied works of European masters (e.g. Raphael' s Madonna), and amongst Indian masters Raja Ravi Verma (Mahashveta) and Abanindranath Tagore (Buddha, Sujata, and Bajra Mukut). When he was 20, he married Sudhira Devi .About this time, his father died. His father-in-law, to enable Nandalal continue his studies supported him till Abanindranath Tagore came forward to take Nandalal under his wings.

How Nandalal came in contact with Abanindranath is an interesting story. Nandalal wanted to show his paitings to the great master but was timid to go alone. With a few of his paintings and a friend, he went to Abanindranath Tagore's house at Jorasankho. He showed his works to Tagore and Havel and Lala Ishwari Prasad, two prominent artists who were already present there.They were impressed by his work and in 1905, Nandalal joined the College of Art, Calcutta. Abanindranath was its vice-pricipal. He was fired by the stories of Ramayana, Mahabharat, and Jatakas ,as also by the episodes of Kali, Shiva, Krishna, and Betal. Bose studied for five years and developed his own style which was appreciated by Gagnendranath , Kumaraswamy and O.C. Ganguli.

Abanindranath and his associates and disciples-. Asitkumar Halder, Surendranath Ganguli, Samarendranath Gupta, Kshitindranath Majumdar, Surendranath Kar, K. Venkatappa, Hakim Mohammad Khan, Shailendranath Dey, Nandalal Bose and Durga Simha brought in renaissance of art in Bengal.

The school gave Nandalal a scholarship of Rs 12 per month. Once Sister Nivedita saw his art works.and was impressed by his talent. For his outstanding work ,Sati Mounting the Pyre, exhibited in the annual exhibition of the Indian Suciety of oriental Art , he was awarded a prize of Rs. 500.In 1910-11, he with the team of Lady Herrington made copies of Ajanta paintings which gave him an opportunity to understand nuances and subtleties of traditions of ancient art of India.When he finished his education, he joined Abanindranath's team.He came in contact with Ananda Coomarswami, Sister Nivedita, Okakura (a Japanese painter), and Rabindranath Tagore.

When Rabindranath Tagore founded the Kala Bhavan, in 1930, Nandalal joined it.He was given a free hand with the institution. Nandalal approached the task in " a home spun way." He conversed in Hindi and his medium of instruction was Hindi and ordinarily, he liked to talk in Hindi though his mother tongue was Bangali.This may sound odd but the fact was that he was born in Bihar and the childhood influence did not wear off. He preferred the oriental trends to Western trends of art, both conceptual and visual manifestations.Although he coceded that artists should have knowledge of anatomy,form and proportions but not in European academic way. He believed that the mind and not the eye is the artist. He emphasized that in a painting life movement should consist in that line which pulsates with utmost life and renders unity, completeness, truth and character to the work.He considered the technique a means to an end.

Bose believed that even common people's houses should give artistic appearance.They should have paintings in their homes. Once, during a visit to Banupur, he drew a number of pictures. He sold them to the village people for four Annas a piece i.e. 25 Paise or one-fourth of a rupee. Whosoever heard of this eccentricity of his was amused. but not Abanindranath who went over to Banupur and bought the whole lot.

On Sister Nivedita's advice, Bose went to Ajanta and made copies of the frescos. Later, he made copies of the Bagh caves also. He came in contact with Arai Campo, a Japanese artist of Okakura School. From him, Nandalal learned the Japanese style of using the brush and ink technique.

From time to time Bose used to accompany Rabindranath Tagore on foreign travels. In 1924, he visited China, Japan, Malaya and Burma. Later in 1934, he visited Sri Lanka. In Shantiniketan he painted some murals. At Maharaja of Baroda's invitation, he painted murals in Baroda city.. He did many paintings of Gandhiji and on his saying posters for the Haripur and Faizpur sessions of Congress. For the Haripura Session alone, he did as many as 83 paintings. Nandalal Bose's name is associated with traditions. Tradition means different things to different people. For Ravi Verma, it meant colonial style; to an orientalist it meant Mughal style; to contemporary artists it was the life of rural India, cross fertilized by a myriad of influences as widely scattered as Japanese screen painting, German expressionism, cubism, Gupta sculpture and Pahari miniatures. Bengal masters like Gagnendranath, Rabindranath, Nandalal Bose and Ramkinkar were traditionalists. It was left to artists like Jaimini Roy, M.F. Hussain, K.H. Ara, S.H. Raza, F.N. Desouza, V.S. Gaitunde and a host of others to fill in the space.

Nandalal Bose received many honors. In 1955, he was awarded Padma Vibhushan, a gold medal in Lucknow, and prizes by the Academy of Fine Arts and the Asiatic Society of Bengal. He was a prolific artist and worked in numerous media such as water color,wash, tempera,wood cut, lithograph, dry point, pencil sketch,pastel work, batik on cloth and frescoes. It is difficult to tell the number of his creations and paintings. Some of these have been lost. Amongst his illustrious students can be named-Mukul Dey, Protima , Binod Bihari, Ramakinkar and Shabita Thakur.

On April 16, 1966, at the age of 83 Nandalal Bose,the great artist, passed away. The Lalit Kala Akademi and Vishva Bharati published a commemorative Centenary Volume. Nandalal's important works are on Hindu religious and mythological themes in which he employed Shilpa  Shastra through rhythmic lines, fine stripping, sensitive colors and multiperspectives. Nandalal's greatness lies on his absorption  of the spirit of oriental art. He derived the style from the Kalighat Pat paintings and extension of folk style. After meeting  Nandalal, Gandhiji had  felt that Bose's art reflected the spirit of rural people. His posters on themes done in the wash technique were epitomes of Gandhian.

Nandalal Bose's art work is huge.The National Gallery of Modern Arts purchased his collection from his family' This consists of 6744 items, including 9 wash paintings, 118 tempora, 1947 water colors, 4568 drawings, sketching including scrolls and tracings, 52 linocuts, 7 lithographs,and 43 drypoints. Initially he painted mythological subjects e.g. Kama worshipping the Sun, Gandhari,vow of Bhishma, savitri and Yam, Sati, Ekalavya,Ahilya, Drona, Uma, Shiva, Arjuna, Durga. As time passed, the coverage became wider. He painted birds, insects, animals, plants, flowers, clouds, rains, landscapes, mountains etc. Some of his paintings were criticized for their social contents e.g. revivalist paintings of Krishna and Buddha and Sati on Pyre.

# M.F. HUSSAIN
## (B.1915)

Artists maintain a sort of 'mystic' about themselves and their works are generally shrouded in mystery. Strangely even art critics imbibe this trait and review art works in mystical language not understood by the common man. He gets confused at the appearance of the artist with a goatee, unkempt hair,and his carelessness about the dress. But what is unusual can be attractive and may generate interest and curiosity. Some time these features make him controversal. M.F. Hussain, a member of Mumbai's Progreesive Group, is such an artist. The great painter has been involved in several controversies.

M.F. Hussain (full name, Maqbool Fida Hussain, Maqbool is his proper name (Fida his father's) was born on 15, September 1915, at Pandharpur (M.P.), according to Prof. Bagchee who recently reviewed the artist's works in an exhibition. There appears a flaw some where This Pandharpur in M.P.should be different from Pandharpur,the place of pilgrimage in Maharashtra. When Maqbool was only 3, he lost his mother. Fida Hussain remarried and moved to Indore which is in M.P. May be, there are two Pandharpurs. At Indore, Fida might have given son Maqbool some education but there is no mention anywhere.of his going to the art school at Indore which was very much there.Indore Indore had an art school. When Maqbool was 20, he moved to Bombay (now Mumbai). Confusion again.According to information from one source, at Mumbai, Maqbool joined the well known J.J. School of Art. But another source isays that he had no formal training in fine arts. Neither at Indore nor at Bombay. The confusion remains. Whatever that be, his eminence as as artist is beyond any shacow of doubt, Maqbool, according to a reviewer of his works, married a girl whom, the artist acknowleges, and says she influenced his life in a big way. The couple had three children of whom two sons-Shamshad and Usman-are artists. They acknowlege their father's influence in their career.

Maqbool faced a hard life at Bombay. He made his living by painting cinema hoardings and sometime did odd jobs. Why should anyone ridicule him for doing odd jobs like painting the hoardings. He was working and earning, which is a respectable way of life. Once he made 'firework toys' for a factory for children. May be it was out of piety or it was to associate himself with poor or feeling comfortable that he used to go places barefoot. But some derisively called him 'barefoot artist' Once his barefoot caused him an embarrassement when he tried to enter a club in Calcutta.

In 1947, M. F. Hussain participated in the annual exhibition of the Bombay Art School. His painting "Sunhera Sansar" which was displayed in the exhibition caught the eyes of connoisseures. Art critics commented that that the artist's work was influenced by Emile Nold and Oskar Kokoschka. In 1951, Maqbool visited China. The next year he held a solo exhibition at Zurich.In the coming years, his paintings were shown in Europe and USA.In 1967, he was awarded the Padmashri.Also, the same year he made his first film'Through the Eyes of a Painter' which won him a Golden Bear at the Berlin Festival. Hussain decided to paint works of art in series. In 1978, he exhibited his Sufi series at the Pandole Galleries.During 1980s, he held the Shwetambara Exhibition of his works in the Jehangir Gallery of Art at Bombay. Next he gave a performance of his art at the Tata Center of Art at Calcutta. He painted six goddesses which attracted huge crowds to see the artist engaged in the creative work. But something affected him. On the last day of the exhibition of his performance, he splashed white paint on the paintings of gods and goddesses..This was not to the liking of people who thought Hussain was crazy and his behavior abnormal. Was it a frustration of the artist that he indulged in destroying his own work?

At Calcutta occured another unseemly incident involving Hussain which was widely noticed in the Press. It transpired that Hussain was denied admission in the Calcutta Club on the ground that he was not properly dressed- he was not putting on shoes.The Calcutta Club was a club of high brows The Club Rules required.that members and visitors to the Club must be properly dressed. In the past it was a race conscious club and that is how its rules had come to be strictly applied especially to Indians.

In 1987, Hussain was nominated to the Rajya Sabha (Upper House of Parliament).During the course of next six years, Hussain produced a Sansad Portfolio of paintings. In early 1990s, his paintings were put up for permanent display at Ahmedabad in the Hussain Doshi Gufa. The paintings were put up in galleries in other cities also.

Hussain was fond of horses. He saw in the horse a form of Ardhanareeshwar, that is half male-half female.He visualized the front part of the horse as a male, who is very aggressive. And, he saw the back part of the horse as a female. The horse is a metaphor and Hussain does not treat it as an animal He painted a series of paintings of horses.

Other series that Hussain painted related to Mahabharata. This was followed by the Ramayana series.

A series of major cities covered Calcutta, Benares, Rome, Beijing etc.

The British Raj series consisted of paintings done in either Portraits or Pictures. Two of the paintings in the series referred to Indore, the city where Hussain had grown up as an adolescent. One of the paintings was titled 'Lord and Lady recieved by H.H. Maharaja Holkar' Another painting carried in a corner the epithet in artist's hand, My Childhood Railway Station, Indore"

One portrait of 20th century, 40 ft high depicted personalities of arts,science,dance, literature, politics.

Hussain says the art of the coming centuries will be more dynamic because in future people would have come to know forms of arts and artistic expressions.

Hussain was impressed by mother Teressa and he did a series on her. But People from Kalkata object to her being called 'Mother Teresa of Kalkata', because it gives a wrong impression that Teresa is the saint- patron of Calcutta and it belonge to her and therefore the missionaries adopted it. It also gives the impression that she has brought a ray of hope into an entirely hopeless city .It can not be forgotten that the legendary Rani Rasmoni's name was linked with the charitable work of the city much before mother Teresa's coming to the city.

Hussain recognized' through his nomadic eye India's ancient cultures which, he found, were multi layered,multi-faceted, unsettled, iconic, absurd but palpably vital. Hussain's film paintings have wide repertoire-from stright representation to metaphysical suggestion -in clear and vivid to evocative and obscure patterns of color and shade, snapshots to movie.

In 1990s, Hussain started work on a film on the well known actress Madhuri Dixit .He said Madhuri looked like Mona lisa, but is Mme D' Avignon .This was Hussain's first feature film after 12 short films.For a painter of film artists, this was a dream come true. This was Gajagamini,meaning a lady with the graceful gait of an elephant.An experimental film, it celebrates womanhood. The Gajagamini is a woman's journey through mythology and history. Hussain deals with the aesthetic,philosophic and literary aspects of the film in an artistic style.It has no story , no hero , no heroine, no plot.Gajagamini is the story of a woman-all that she has been to man through time-mother, beauty,the oppressed, the muse. The film portrays all these in a frame of timelessness. These are the faces of truth through knowledge (Gyan-symbolizeed by Kalidas) and Vigyan (science symbolize by Einstein).

Gajagamini is a series of miniature tablets of life that keep intersecting and interconnecting at all stages of life. The ladies are represented by Monalisa, Shakuntala,Sangeeta, Nirmala , Monika etc. Hussain has painted them all on canvas. Madhuri dances in every avatar.She essays four characters. Hussain says, " The film is a combination of realism and illusion. The story and dialogues are told in dance form.It is colorful and full of folk music.It is told in traditional style of Barakatha and Yakshagana. Hussain in a painting treated Saraswati in a secular way.The prayer said to her is a beautiful piece of poery. Beautifully worded,.before the eyes of the person invoking her appears a figure of a damsel of grace,beauty and intellect that evokes nothing but reverence .The painting of Hussain was reverentially done by him but the men and women who saw her, saw it differently.

## NOTE IN FABRICS

Indian business has developed under adverse circumstances. Formerly, the business thrived when it was conducted through novel modes of production and trade was managed at long distances. For long time Indian economy suffered at the hands of colonialists and Western capitalists. In the past the European capitalist enterprise tapped India which could meet their demands for supplies as their production fell short due to paucity of capital. This stunted the growth of Indian enterprises, even though they were familiar with market orientation and possessed rich experience in commerce and trade, and were well versed about cash crops, agricultural processing. In addition to these there was no dearth of specialised artisans and business communities like Marwaris, Chettiars, Khojas and Parsis. Ambani's success and eminence should be assessed in the perspective of upward trends in Indian economy in relation to world trade and domestic wealth.

After 1850, Indian business could not progress because of regulations, domination and interference by British rulers and alien businessmen which crippled many developing Indian businesses (for instance, Car, Tagore & Co, with rich experience in steam navigation, salt, tea and coal, suffered when the Union Bank crashed in 1848 and lead to crash in indigo price and foreign exchange dealings). For sometime exclusive European enterprises like Andrew Yule and Jardine Matherson thrived on export trade in commodities like cotton, indigo, opium. Dealings in new commodities started with the introduction of tea in Assam in 1839; coal in Raniganj (Bengal) by Alexander & Co; founding of a cotton mill each in Broach by James London and in Bombay by Cowasjee in 1854; and first jute mill near Calcutta by George Aclan in 1855. However, some English historians are of the view that the Indian economy was transformed by import by European manufacturers and exports of Indian agricultural produce. (In the opinion of authors this is a partisan view. It is not recognized that a secondary revolution was ushered in by Indian factories). The following figures of imports will subtantiate this:

1828-1829: cotton yarn worth Rs 4 million and

1829: cotton goods of Rs 12 million

1867-8 textile 858 million yards

1886-7 textile 2156 million yards

1910-11 textile 2309 million yards

The number of mills, looms and spindles added :

1875'6 47 mills; 9000 looms ; 9million spindles

1913'4 217mills, 104000 looms ; 6.7 spindles

Indian exports as below subtantiate

1882-3 : 156 million yards

1940'1 390 million yards

At the end of the 19th century, imports accounted for 635 per cent of cloth consumed in India,of which Indian mills accounted for12% and handicrafts for 255%. Between 1909-10 and 1913-14 corresponding figures were 56%, 23%, and 20%. The pattern of textile business changed during and after the First World War. More importance is now given to variety and fashion than to utility.

**Deepika Mehra**

# 23
# DHIRUBHAI AMBANI
## (1932—2002)

During the British rule Indian business faced paucity of finances. Though the problem eased somewhat after Independence it did not totally disappear.Dhirubhai proved it to the world that Indian businesses could manage to raise funds, that Indians are not afraid of competition,and that India is a nation of achievers. And, Dhirubhai proved that he could achieve his goal by earnestly working for it.

Dhirubhai Ambanie was when he died the richest man of India and one of the richest in the world. How he rose from rags to riches is a story worth telling. But let it be clearly understood that it is a unique and true story and not a fiction. Unique, bacause it was that an Indian with a poor background from rural area carved out a niche at the top which was crowded with business Moguls. But that is Ambani's uniqueness that by his his diligence, intelligence and luck he made such a meteoric rise. It is fiction- like that he owned riches worth Rs.80000 crores.at the time of his death in 2002. To him, of course, is correctly applicable the Hindu epithet that he came to the world empty handed and left it empty handed. But is it not fantastic that working untiringly with his hands and utilizing his talents, in three decades he coaxed lady luck to smile on him and to help build single handed the gigantic conglemorate Reliance Corporation , the only private company of India, to enter the Fortune 500 List of the world's largest corporations. Ambani was listed by *Forbes* as the year's 138th richest person of the world, superseding the Tata and Birla who had enjoyed pre-eminent positions for several decades in the country. Ambani's hands appear to have had Midas's touch in that, as some of majority of those who had business dealings with him also became millionaire. The

Ambani empire spanned over vast resources. The story of india's rise after 1990s is primarily the story of an enterprizing private sector.

Dhirajlal Hirachand Ambani (a.k.a. Dhirubhai) was born on December 28,1932 in Chorwad village in Gujarat in a poor businessman's family. To improve the prospects of his family, Dhirubhai, at the age of 14, left for Aden where he would join a few prosperous Gujarati business families. The first job he landed in was that of an attendant at a petrol station. After a little while he got a clerk's job with a sole petrol distributor. This job brought him in direct contact with businessmen. He was a keen observer and noticed some discrepancy between the sterling exchange rate and the intrinsic worth of silver content in coinage. He made use of this knowledge and by exploiting the opportunity he earned $3000. With what he had learned about investments and savings, he planned to make the best use of the time that the clerical job spared , and the money he had saved. In the spare time he manufactured soap and pedalled down to sell the product to his prospective customers. By dint of his hard work, observing caution in supplying quality product, and using his persuasive power, he created a market for his products. Success brought him self-confidence which is so necessary for a businessman. Also, he learned that honest dealings can win customer's confidence not only in the product but also in the salesman as well as in the manufacturer.In short, he had learnt the practical business management.

In 1958, Dhirubhai wound up his business and returned to India to start a business with his savings. He set up a modest trading enterprise under the banner of Reliance Commercial Corporation, later to be famous as Reliance. The spirit of adventure that he had developed in Aden proved him helpful in his new business. Who says what is there in a name? 'Reliance' proved a magic name. It aroused curosity in the prospective customers. Was Reliance really reliable to have dealings with? Would the businessman abide by what he promises or in talking tall, his object was to make money like other businessmen? To test the Reliance's reliability,they negotiated with Ambani and found business dealings with Dhirubhai Ambani were fair and beneficial. Dhirubhai would work with patience, and make a thorough study of the market before launching a product .His close watch on the market showed him that if he wanted his business to succeed, he would have to manage (or manipulate?) the license-permit- quota Raj. Only businessmen with political connections could corner export, import, and manufacturing licenses and thus they could accumulate fortunes, leaving others behind.

The study also showed that business related to import of polyester yarn and export of spices would prove very beneficial. He therefore took to import and export business in a big way.

Dhirubhai studied the needs and purchasing capacity (power) of people in India. This gave him the clue that people in higher income brackets could afford to buy better and expensive clothes and that the textile industry provided ample opportunity to earn with a large margin of profit. He sought and managed to receive clearance from the government to manufacture cloth from polyester fiber. In 1966, he established his first textile mill in Naroda, near Ahemadabad. He gave his product the brand name *Vimal*, that is pure. He concentrated on creating and building his business market and cornered the import of polyester market by circumventing bureaucratic regulations. The textile business proved quite profitable. He was convinced that there was scope for expansion of the business but required capital. Where to get the capital from? Would the banks advance the loan? Rather than approaching the banks for capital, he decided to tap the Bombay Stock Exchange. He succeded and pioneered an equity system that transformed the corporate financing system in the country. In 1977, in response to Reliance initial public offering, 58,000 investors bought its shares. Eventually, the number of share holders climbed to three million!

Next, Dhirubhai began manufacturing cloth strong for suits, and fabric that was attractive for its glitter.Both proved popular with customers and demand for Vimal products increased by leaps and bounds. Millions of people invested in Reliance Industries, a sprawling conglomerate, raising its annual sale to $12.3 billion. What Ambani achieved was unique.He showed his countrymen that if there is will,even without education and family capital, one can build an ultra modern, profitable global enterprise in India and that the possibility of growth is boundless. Public faith in him had grown so much that he had enlisted as many as four million Indians in his adventure. He had convinced them that they can without any apprehension load up Reliance stock.

Ambani held out promise of good share value and those who had dealings with him in early years earned huge profits and became rich. In 1982, he began the process of backward integration and set up a plant to manufacture polyester filament yarn. Later, he diversified his business to chemicals, gas, petrochemicals, plastics, power and telecommunications services. How could he be so successful? What led to his unique success? One of the steps he took was to cultivate friendship with politicians who proved helpful. Those jealous of his success derided that the growth of Reliance could be possible because Ambani had managed to circumvent official rules and regulations, and had even got introduced, amended or scrapped import tariff to undercut his rivals and thus push his own business interests. His methods earned him many bitter enemies. But he managed the media so well that critical stories about Ambani's unconventional business methods seldom made it into the press. The final phase of Reliance's diversification occurred in 1990s when the company turned towards petrochemicals and telecommunications. But in this, he met a bitter rival, Nusli Wadia of Bombay Dyeing.

Ambani took keen interest in Information technology also. He arranged computer training for students and told them, "Be daring. Think big. If you think, where you will be the best, you will be the best." Reliance successfully bid for Indo Petro-Chemicals. Two months after this, on July 22, 2002, Dhirubhai passed away, leaving behind wife Kokilaben, two sons Mukesh and Anil, and two daughters, and their families. When he left the world, Ambani's was India's first business family and Reliance was the largest private sector company of India. On Dhirubhai Ambani's 70th Birth Day , the Government of India issued a commemorative postage stamp on December 28, 2004.

Ambanis have big dreams to make their company one-stop company which would provide every thing the customer needs-from piped gas in house, net connection to the world entertainment via the optic fiber links, schools and hospitals for the family and whatever be the family's need. It is a fantastic idea.

Business jealousies give rise to rumors of various types. Ambani's indulgence in politics exacerbated rumors. It was said that Dhirubhai Ambani helped Mrs Gandhi.This proved them mutually beneficial. The latest anecdote we heard was from Mr Saru Rangnekar In an interesting talk that he delivered to the seniors at the India Community Center, Sunnyvale, he recounted which in brief was: After Mrs Indira Gandhi's death, Dhirubhai Ambani sought an appointment with her son, Rajiv Gandhi. Being in mourning, Rajiv did not meet visitors and he said, 'No." But when Ambani pressed that it was an urgent business that he would take just one minute, Rajiv acceded to see him. All that Ambani did on entering Rajiv's room was to ask him," What should I do with the huge amount of money your mother has left with me?" With this Rangnekar closed his talk.and did not enlighten the audience what happened thereafter.

The publishers of *India Today* (published from New Delh) in their *The High and Mighty Power List 2004* placed the Ambanis at the top of 50 Indians who ride on high horse. The arbiter of hierarchy in that power list, as they make clear, is the mantle of wealth, and not wisdom. The number of tycoons is pretty large

It appears the big business families are losing their cohesiveness and close- knit ties. During the year 2004, there wss bitter acrimony among the members of several business houses, including the Ambanis and the Birlas, who were determined to take their disputes for settlement to the court of law. Mrs. Kokilabehn Ambani settled the matter between her two sons, Mukesh and Anil, amicably.

As in the case of other big business houses, much remains hidden from public eye. Author's left their Ambani research at a title *PolyesterFabrics* and Stocks. He was in a way a pioneer and eminent achiever.

## THE JUDICIARY IN INDIA

Fifty-seven years is a significant milestone in the history of India which for several hundred years had been under foreign rule. The merger and integration of 561 princely states with the British ruled provinces and establishment of a fair judicial system for the entire country are not mean achievements.The credit for this goes to the founding fathers, some of whom were well versed in law and jurisprudence and were guided by established practices.Having realized that only a strong and independent judiciary could provide a good base for good governance, they codified the law of the land which emphasized a perfect judicial pattern for the Constitution of India.It augurs well that over the years, the judges have interpreted it and have laid down juridical principles on a solid and firm foundation. But for the judiciary's vigilant watch, the fundamental rights that guarantee certain basic rights to the citizens would have been encroached by the Executive and Legislature and rendered illusory.

The Supreme Court and High Courts have in their pronouncements repeatedly cautioned against the arbitrariness, caprice and highhanded assumption of powers by the Executive Their landmark judgements have set out in clearer terms the fundamental rights. If an individual's rights, enumerated in Articles 25, 32, 136, 142, 226, and 227, are in jeopardy at the hands of the Executive or Legislature, he should feel assured that his grievances will be redressed by the court of law. Apprehensive of the Court's strictures, and wide publicity given by the media, the executive is hesitant to deviate from the right path. Yet it should ever be kept in mind thatpower has a corrupting influence.

The judiciary's significant contribution to the democratic experiment proves that India is on a firm footing and it is capable, impartial and sound. However, the country's political frame-work remains unstable and the vote bank misleading and the assumption of absolute power by the executive, and its actions come under judicial perview. No amount of coloring in the name of public good will succeed.

Judiciary itself needs to improve its ways of working.in several areas e.g.delay in disposal of cases,duration of trial,long wait for justice, and call for immediate and positive action. Procedural requirements,special attention to cantankerous litigants (who take advantage of loopholes), and provision for a number of appeals cause frustrations. To top it, whenever a move is made to change the law, protests and agitations by interested parties bring the entire machinery to a sandstill. Proliferation of public interest litigations and the tendency to formulate social and economic problems as matters of right are indicators of this.

The Supreme Court has helped the nation in many ticklish situations created by matters like Golaknath; Bank Nationalization; Abolition of Privy Purses;Keshavananda Bharati; Minerva Mills; Judges Transfer. The Hon'ble Court asserted their discretion to reject any constitutional amendment seeking to change the basic structure of the Constitution.They identified Art.142 and inherent powers as unlimited source of authority to meet the ends of justice. Judicial reform has shifted fast. Art.21 has opened a fresh air of liberty relating to right to property and life.The judiciary should,however,remember that the probity,dignity and rectitude associated with them are due to the authority they enjoy as compared to its counterparts.

—M. Santhanam, Former Judge & Retired Member, CEGAT

# 24
# MOTILAL C. SETALVAD
(1884-1974)

"The profession of a lawyer is known to be a gamble. So it was in my case," says Motilal C. Setalvad in his autobiography, *My Life*. The facts and events, described in the work , are drawn from a diary that Motilal maintained. The book also offers India's legal history during the years 1930 to 1974, but very little of his personal life or social-economic-cultural developments in the country or world. A reviewer comments," *My ife* spotlights author's success but omits his failures." Fali S. Nariman, one time Junior to M.C. Setalvad who contributed Introduction to *My Life*, says, "The important thing in the Olympic Games is not winning but taking part, the important thing in life is not conquering but fighting well." May be, but in practice at the bar, what matters for a lawyer's present and future is lucrative practice, which depends on arguing and presenting each case well, though winning every case may not be probable.

Motilal was born on November 12, 1884, son of Chimanlal Setalvad, a reputed pleader of Ahmedabad and Bombay. Motilal received his early education in a Gujarat School at Girgaum, and Wilson School, and later in Elphinstone College, Bombay, and in the end in Gujarat College, Ahmedabad passing his B.A. in 1904 and LL.B. in 1906. In 1911, he passed the Bar examination and was enrolled a member of the Bar at Bombay on 8 August 1911. Initially, he attended the Chamber of Bhulabhai Desai and there he learnt drafting. But like most of the new entrants to the profession, he too was brief- less. Since his father worked as a pleader on the appellate side of the High Court, he could not expect to get cases from him.This state of affairs was not for long. Hard work and intelligent and systematic way of working paid him and gradually work started trickling in. He developed a style of his own. His arguments were brief, cogent and logical. "There were no cobwebs in his well-stocked and well ordered mind."

From 1918, he started getting cases on his own. The first case he won was in the court of Justice Beaumont. After this, the work started coming in in plenty and with that his income also increased. He could afford to go on holidays to places in the country and outside also. In 1924, he visited England and some European countries. After 1927, his practice made rapid progress and he came to the front rank of lawyers and "mid-way in the front rank of seniors". The secret of Motilal's success, according to himself, lay in the excellent notes that he prepared and these gave him added advantage over his adversary. His advocacy was smooth and without flashes of wit or flight of fancy. Motilal's Junior Mulgaonkar accounted his senior's success to his suavity to the Bench, opposite counsel, and the client. In the court, he never used provocative or jeering language. "He might have been dull but the effect of his advocacy on the trained mind was deadly." He appeared mostly in cases on miscellaneous side against M. A. Jinnah and had as many as 25 to 28 applications out of a total of 33 to35 in the list.

Though Motilal was deeply absorbed in his legal work, he kept himself abreast of current events and literary trends. Though he lacked the varied and veritable quality, and friendly, amiable treatment of his father, he was free from bigotry, bitterness and self-conceit. For long, he enjoyed the combination of prestige, prosperity and respect. At the age of 44, he was offered the High Court's judgeship. He declined the offer, as he saw better prospects at the Bar.

In 1933-34, Motilal appeared in an important case against three advocates who were tried and convicted for professional misconduct. (Involvement in civil disobedience and Satyagrah Cases by advocates were called misconduct.) The High Court set aside conviction. Motilal's name and fame spread.

In 1937, in pursuance of Government of India Act, 1935, elections were held in provinces. The Congress won majority of seats and came to power. In Bombay, K.M. Munshi, one time a colleague of Motilal at bar, became the Home Minister of the State in the new government ,suggested Motilal's name for the post of Advocate General. Motilal's name was approved and he was appointed AG of the Bombay Province. As Advocate. General, Motilal appeared in several important cases, including cases relating to Prohibition, Property Tax Legislation, Raja of Darbhanga (in the Patna High Court), a dispute between the State of Kutch and the State of Morvi.

In 1942, cases came up against the participants of the Quit India movement. Motilal Setalvad did not like the Government attitude towards the agitation. Therefore, he decided to dissociate himself from the government and relinquished the charge of AG.

Motilal and his family had kept aloof from politics. However, at a later stage he entered politics and became a staunch Gandhian. Yet he publicity pointed out and pilloried follies, foibles, obduracy and obsession of the Congress Government, that was formed, as also of the Congress High Command.

After hectic time that practice required, Motilal used to plan and would go on holidays in India and abroad. Ooty was his favorite resort. For several years he went there and then bought a house there to which he would go alone or with friends. Relatives would also visit.In Bombay he purchased a plot in Juhu and built a house for his residence. Nearby lived his relatives which made socialization feasty.

In 1944, Motilal presided over the Bombay Civil Liberties Conference. On the retirement of Mr. Mitter as A.G. Motilal accepted the post of Advocate General.

In 1945, the Allies won the War against the Axes. In England, Churchill exited from power, and leading Labor Party men - Attlee, Stafford Cripps, Pathic Lawrence and others -formed the government. They soon realized that they could not hold India, especially after INA trial. Britain decided to relinquish power but the Congress and Muslim League could not reach an agreement about the formation of a government after the British left. Partition appeared to be the only solution. To see India free, Nehru, Patel and other leaders accepted the Partition of the country and planned the means to accept the reins of government. Motilal Setalvad played an important part in the relevant legal and constitutional matters of free India.

Between 1947 and 1950, Motilal Setalvad represented India at important forums He appeared before the Radcliffe Commission in Lahore. He made friends with many prominent persons of Lahore.

After India became free on 15 August 1947, and a Constitution was adopted in 1950, Setalvad was appointed the Attorney General of India. He appeared in important Government cases before the Supreme Court. He also advised the Government on law in important cases.

In 1954, Motilal C Setalvad became the Chairman of the India Law Commission and served it in that capacity for many years. It examined most of the laws of the land and in its report made numerous recommendations. Law had to work as an instrument of engineering but he observed that the government machinery worked very slowly.

The Government made Setalvad a member of Rajya Sabha and awarded him Padma Vibhushana.

In 1970, Motilal planned to write his antobiography which he titled *My Life*. It describes Setalvad's progress in professional and public life, which in his view was neither vain nor conceit or boast. The biography describes proceedings before the Radchiffe Commission, the Mundhra Scandal which brought about the resignation of Finance Minister T.T. Krishnamachari, Portugal's complaint about Dadra Nagar Haveli before the International Court of Justice, account of Emergency legislation, Parliamentary privileges, defections, and the Statesman controversy:

Setalvad asserts in *My Life* that he was not vain. But some friends in the Press don't' agree with this self-assessment of his. When we asked for comments of a senior journalist retired from the Statesman, he said he did not have pleasant memories of the Trustee of the Statesman and added that Motilal Setalvad was a big snob. Friends and our colleagues at the Bar in the Supreme Court told us that Sitalvad was meticulous in his work and always in possession of facts of the cases on fingertips and was well versed in relevant law. He was always well prepared to present the matter before the court. The members of the Bar Association of India which he founded remember his punctuality and foresight.

Motilal was popular among organizations like Congress

because he would not charge them any fees for taking up their cases or for appearing in court on their behalf. He made it clear that it would be wrong to accept fees from the Congress because it was a public organization. The fact was that such an attitude helped in building an image of Setalvad and made him popular. For instance, when he went to Lahore, the Hindus and Sikhs of that city gave him a grand reception and he declined to accept any fee from them. A prominent citizen, Dr. Gokuldas Narang appreciatively said, "He (Motilal) was a worthy son of a worthy father who had rendered great services to the Punjab after the atrocities of martial law days."

On his way back from Lahore to Bombay, Setalvad broke his journey at Delhi. He met the Prime Minister. Jawahar Lal Nehru who enquired of him whether he could go to USA as an Indian delegate to the United Nations General Assembly. Setalvad agreed. When the matter of butchery on India-Pakistan border came up, he said the responsibility for the butchery rested on those who did not want the British to leave India.

Setalvad's views on Kashmir and Sheikh Abdullah as they appear in *My Life* do not generally conform to those held by the Indian citizens. He says, "Sheikh Abdullah made determined efforts to obtain self government for the people of the state. On release, Sheikh defined his attitude, which was that the wishes of the people should be obtained to decide whether they wish to accede to India or Pakistan." Abdullah is reported to have said, "Our first demand is complete transfer of power to the people of Kashmir. Representation of people in a democratic Kashmir will then decide whether the state should join India or Pakistan." Setalvad says India acceded to the request of Maharaja and Sheikh Abdullah, and accordingly Kashmir acceded to India.

Look at the British attitude towards the accession of Kashmir. The British suffered from prejudices. The question is why did the British and Americans adopt anti-Indian attitude in UNO? The reasons are many. One, the Englishmen at the head of affairs have never forgotten that it was 'Hindu India' which robbed England of the brightest Jewel of the British Crown. Two, USA had interest in Pakistan as it had allowed it to create a powerful air base against the Soviet Union in its territory. Three, they held that Kashmir being a Muslim majority state should go to Pakistan, which would balance Hyderabad's accession to India. The British ignored the fact that India had as large a Muslim population as the West Pakistan. Also to put it in a different perspective, West Pakistan had cleansed itself of the Hindus and Sikhs; some had escaped to neighboring places in India and some were put to eternal peace. Four, India's policy in respect of Kashmir has been weak and vacillating. Nehru was no doubt a great democrat and a unique leader of men but he was weak and idealistic. India did not select men capable of carrying on administration of Kashmir. The Kashmir administration has been corrupt and inefficient.

India did not take any definite measures to conciliate Kashmir or make it truly an integral part of India. Sheikh Abdullah was released but without any assurance from him, in the hope that he would accept status quo. Abdullah was bitter about his incarceration and fake charges, leveled against him. In spite of not too good experiences from Sheikh Abdullah, he was released from the second detention as an experiment, which greatly damaged India's image in foreign countries and encouraged some people to think that Pakistan's interest in Kashmir was legitimate. At the same time Abdullah had asked for plebiscite in Kashmir to determine its future. The Westerners exceeded the limit of their interest when they talked of an independent Kashmir guaranteed by India, Pakistan, China and USSR. Setalvad says that Sheikh should have realized that Kashmir had a future only in India, and that Kashmir and Kashmiris can never be happy in Pakistan which is both theocratic and autocratic; nor can it be independent as it is too small and poor to exist by itself, and Pakistan would try to devour it by force. as it has been trying since 1947.

It is interesting to know from *My Life* that at the time of inauguration of the Supreme Court on 28 January, 1950, it had only six Indges - CJ Kania, and Puisne Judges Fazl Ali, Patanjali Shastri, Meharchand Mahajan, Bejan Kumar Mookeyea, and SR Das.In 1951, two more Judges, Chandrashekhar Aiyar and Biman Bose were later added.. (Today the Supreme Court has more than 20 Judges.)

Motilal Setalvad found some weaknesses in the Constitution. To point out just one in the Chapter on Fundamental Rights, which has no article and is headed "Protection against arrest and detention in certain cases". It provides for Parliament to make a law for preventive detention with certain safeguards under Article 22. This was noted in Gopalan's case.

On legal matters, the Government at times asked for legal advice from the Attorney General of India and the President also, though such occasions were rare, asked for his opinion. Setalvad tendered advice howsoever pleasant or unpleasant it was. His advice on Hindu Code Bill and President's powers, was not to the liking of President Dr. Rajendra Prasad.

Besides, the Attorney General was approached to inaugurate conferences and seminars or to preside over or be chief guest at functions. In December 1950, he read a paper on a regular war between Executive and Judiciary' in the UP Lawyers' Conference, at Meerut, which he had inaugurated. The Executive stressed that an executive action was not open to judicial review. Setalvad corrected the wrong view of the Executive.

Motilal was a person of independent nature. In 1952, CM Bombay, Morarji Desai, and Shantilal Shah met Setalvad and asked him to resign from the post of AG so that his name could be proposed for the office of Law Minister. Setalvad declined.

When Kania died and Shastri became the Chief Justice, the Law Secretary in 1962 invited Setalvad's attention, at prime minister's instance, to Setalvad's critical references to India Government's "errors and omissions" of China policy, to "Nehru's trusting the glib protestations of friendship and and powering action of the Chinese failed to preserve the dangers in spite of weighty warnings from his colleagues in the Government" and to President Dr. Rajendra Prasad's observation that the India Government had been "negligent and credulous".( This was a reference to Sardar Patel's letter of 1950 to Nehru in which he had drawn the latter's attention to the danger of having a powerful nation on the northern borders of India and asking for caution in dealings with China.) as "unforgivable flounder", Setalvad boldly said that the Chinese action had shattered "Nehru's ideals" and "his assumptions and conclusions had been shown to be wholly wrong.".

Setalvad retired from the post of Attorney General of India. Gajendragadkar's efforts at formulation of an extensive labor jurisprudence by the Supreme Court were appreciated by Setalvad.

On Justice Sinha's retirement as Chief Justice of Supreme Court, Justice Gajendragadkar became the Chief Justice. He accepted public felicitations. Public felicitations of Judges/Chief Justice was criticized by Setalvad.

Motilal C. Setalvad after more than half a century's service to Judiciary and law passed away in 1974. It was indeed a long innings - fruitful too.

# NANI PALKHIVALA
(1920-2002)

Nani Palkhivala was a legendary lawyer. In matters relating to constitution, his opinion was treated with utmost respect not only by the Government but by the legislators, legal fraternity and the intelligentsia also.

Palkhivala had deep respect for the Constitution because he had realized its cardinal value and basic and essential features. He reminded people what the great American jurist, Joseph Storey said, "The constitution has been reared for immortality. It may nevertheless, perish in an hour of folly or corruption or negligence by its keepers." Palkhivala believed that the Constitution provides for the exigencies of the moment also and the Constitutional provisions endure over ages. He urged that the constitution should impact a momentum to the living spirit of the rule of law so that democracy and civil liberty survive beyond our life time. The original constitution provided for stability without stagnation and growth without destruction of human values, but the amendments introduced of late have brought stagnation without stability and destruction of human values without growth. All the same, Palkhivala believed that a constitution can be amended or changed because laws as an institution must go hand in hand with the progress of humankind. Also, it should be inferred that a constitution which is unchanging and static has past its use. A constitution to be living must be growing, adaptable, flexible, changeable as society changes; as conditions change, we amend it in the proper way.

Nanaboy, which was how his parents had christened their

child, was born on January 16, 1920 in a middle-class Parsi family of Bombay. Later, he came to be known as Nani, may be out of affection. The family had been in the profession of Palkhis (i.e. palanquins which were fitted to horse carriages) and was, therefore, known as Palkhivala. Nanaboy received his early education in the Master Tutorial High School, Bombay. After matriculation, he joined the St. Xavier's College, and did his M.A. in English Literature. He was a brilliant student and was interested in teaching. He applied for a lecturer's job in the Bombay University but was not selected. He won't regret the loss. He joined the Government Law College of Bombay, and received a law degree (LL.B). In 1944, he joined the bar and the chambers of Sir Jamshedji Kanga, He did extremely well at the bar. Unlike many others, he had not to wait long, soon he started getting important cases in the High Court and had a meteoric rise.

The first important constitutional case in which Palkhivala's appearance (as the junior most counsel) made a mark was Fram Nusserwanji Balsara V State of Bombay [reported in AIR Bombay 1951 p. 210 (FB)]. In this, he had challenged various provisions of the Bombay Prohibition Act. The decision in the case caught public eye because of social norms and stress on prohibition. Not long thereafter, Nani Palkhivala started arguing cases independently. After Partition of the country, many Muslim families left for Pakistan but a larger number of families came to India. Consequently, there was too much litigation relating to evacuee properties and Palkhivala made the best use of the opportunity. He was in the forefront to challenge the validity of the administration of Evacuee Property Act and the Land Requisition Act. These Acts were repealed by the Bombay High Court. In 1950 -51, Nani Palkhivala distinguished himself in two important cases – Abdul Majid Vs PR Nayak, and State of Bombay Vs Hemant Santlal Alreja. This increased his clientele.

Besides his legal practice, Nani Palkhivala taught law to students in the Govt. Law College, Bombay. As a young man, Nani used to stammer but by giving it due heed, proper care and attention, he overcame the deficiency. Moreover, by his wit and humor, he embellished his presentation and arguments so much so that no one could notice the drawback in his speech. In 1954, he won an important case concerning the interpretation of Articles – 29(2) and 30 of the Constitution in the Bombay High Court. The matter concened the right of students to admission to an Anglo-Indian school which provided for teaching through English medium. A Division Bench of the Bombay High Court struck down the circular of the Bombay State. The Bombay State took the matter to the Supreme Court. Palkhivala appeared as a counsel in the appeal and argued the case. The Hon'ble Supreme Court upheld the High Court judgment and ruled that the impugned circular violated Article 29(2) of the Fundamental Rights that protects educational rights of minorities.

In 1970, Palkhivala made a signal contribution to the development of Indian Constitution. According to Senior Advocate Soli Sorabjee, in the Bank Nationalization case Palkhivala succeeded in persuading the Supreme Court to decide that the Articles 19 (1) (f) and 31 (2) were not mutually exclusive. In the case of Privy Purses, Palkhivala argued that the Government action was unconstitutional and also caused a breach of constitutional morality. He said, he believed that the survival of Indian democracy and the unity and integrity of the nation depended upon the realization that constitutional morality is no way less essential than constitutional legality.

In democracy, freedom of information and media play important role. Any restriction on them affects people's right of freedom of speech. When the Government imposed restrictions on the import of newsprint, the newspapers protested that the restriction affected their right. It stifled Press freedom. Bennet Coleman and some other companies owning newspapers challenged the import control policy. Palkhivala argued the case in the Supreme Court on behalf of Bennet Coleman. He pleaded that newsprint did not stand on the same footing as steel. Newsprint would manifest whatever is thought of by man. The Court struck down the restrictions.

Palkhiwala wrote his magnum opus titled *The Law and Practice of Income Tax*. "Lawyers, judges, income tax practitioners regarded the book as their Bible," opined one of Palkhivala's juniors on the publication's popularity. Its first edition appeared in 1950. Another subject that he expounded in simple language was the *Annual Budget*. He explained its intricacies through his speeches which   proved very popular amongst the audiences. Listeners enjoyed the fun that there were two budgets , one by the Finance Minister and the other by Palkhivala.

Palkhivala was against the tinkering of the Constitution by politicians who make hasty and ill conceived changes and fail to preserve its integrity. He firmly believed that Parliament's right to effecting changes is not absolute, the amending power is subject to inherent and implied limitations which do not permit Parliament to destroy its essential features and damage its basic structure.

Palkhivala's success lay in persuading the Supreme Court to accept the Doctrine of Basic Structure in the Keshavanad Bharati case. This is Nani Palkhivala's greatest contribution to the constitutional jurisprudence. Keshavananda's case is a check on Parliament's tendency to ride roughshod over fundamental rights and its insatiable appetite to encroach upon fundamental rights. His arguments in the case before the Bench were at the height of eloquence to which Palkhivala had risen and had "never been surpassed in the history of the Supreme Court", observed Justice H.R. Khanna, who was one of the judges on the Bench.

Another important case of Palkhivala related to the Minerva Mills. In this matter, his advocacy prevented defacement and defilement of the Constitution, remarks Soli S. Sorabjee. This led the Supreme Court to declare the clause (4) of Article 368, which excluded judicial review of constitutional amendment as unconstitutional.

Palkhivala's deep knowledge of industrial law, labor legislation and economics came to be discerned in the Premier Automobile case that dealt with fixation of price of automobile, and in the Jalan Trading case in which the constitutionality of the Payment of Bonus Act was assailed.

The freedom of religion guaranteed by Articles 25 and 26 was well expounded by Palkhivala in the case of Seshammal Vs State of TN. (AIR 1967 SC 691)

Palkhivala was knowledgeable and well versed in International Law also. He represented India at Geneva in the Special Tribunal appointed by UN to adjudicate upon Pakistan's claim to an Enclave in Kutch. In another case, he appeared before the International Civil Aviation Organization (ICAO) at Montreal. He represented India before the World Court at the Hague when Pakistan claimed right to fly over India.

Palkhivala's erudition, legal knowledge and advocacy had no match. He possessed clarity of thought, precision, elegant expression, impassioned plea, court craft and extraordinary ability to think while on legs before the court. Several universities conferred on him the Honorary Doctorate of Law.

Naniboy wanted to practice at law and avoided to take up a government job. He declined the offer of the post of Attorney General of India and later, according to his juniors, the office of Judge of the Supreme Court of India. But it was surprising that he accepted Directorship in the House of Tatas.. He was appointed Ambassador of India to USA under the prime ministership of Morarji Desai.

Palkhivala was ever helpful to the needy and gave monetary help to needy organizations.

Palkhivala did not like the way the Parliament functioned which he thought was because of the poor caliber of many of the members in the Parliament. He was of the view that some minimum qualifications should be prescribed for those who seek election to the Parliament. He said that an attendant to a boiler needs years of training, an engineer needs training and so does a doctor. It was strange that there is no requirement of any education or equipment in case of an MP who steers the lives and destinies of millions of his fellow men. It was strange that he did not comment on the qualifications of Members of Assembalies or other public organizations. Is it not a fact that quite a few M.L.As. or M.L.Cs. become M.P.s?

Nani was a thorough gentleman. He was upset to see that corruption had not spared even judiciary. This showed decline of values in our social life.

Nani Palkhivala breathed his last on December 11, 2002.

## ACKNOWLEDGEMENTS

The Authors benefited from information on the 25 eminent persons available in published literature viz books, periodicals and visual media and they sincerely thank their authors, editors and publishers.

The authors thank Ms Padmanabh of Sahitya Akademi and Jaya Prakash Benegeri of Sangeet-Natak Akademi in New Delhi, Librarians of the Bar Library of Supreme Court and Sunnyvale Public Library.

Authors benefited from discussions on the drafts of write-ups on the 25 Eminent and more persolalities with politicians, scientists, literatures, artists, industrialists, and connoisseures of art, journalists and lawyers.They are too many to be named individually. Besides, some did not want to be identified. Authors however thank for varied types of help MB. Lal, Dr L.C.Gupta, Lt. Gen. S.D.Gupta (retd.). Swaminathan Aiyer, Dr Anjali Masodkar, Onkar Mehra, Ravi Vyas, Shelly Singh, Rajeev Ojha, Dr. R. Meera (Coimbatore), Dr. Jagdeesh Rustagi, G.L.Sanghi, Anis Ahmad Khan, Manisha, Ranapati Ghosh, Dr. Rajendralal Mehra, Ms Kamal Kumar, Sankar Sivadas, Ram Sevak Srivastava, and Shaju Mangalam. Thanks also to Drs.Wong and Mary Ann Lloyd but for whose timely help this publication might not have been completed.

. The authors thank M. Santhanam, Deepika Mehra and K. L. Verma for their prefatory notes to write ups on judiciary business and arts.

The authors appreciate the assistance of their grand children, Malvika and Rishab in computer work. Thanks also to Gautam and Mukta for everything.

## BIBLIOGRAPHY

**GENERAL READING**

Dictionary Of National Biography ( 20 volumes )
Disraeli : Robert Blake
Eminent Victorians : Lytton Strachey
History of India : Peter Robb
India- A History : John Keay
Infidels: Andrew Wheatcraft
Intellectuals : Paul Johnson
Jinnah, Pakistan and Islamic Identity: Akbar S. Ahmad
Kashmir in the Shadow of War ; Robert J. Wirsing
Marx Revenge :Meghnath Desai
Nehru Tryst with Destiny: Stanley Wolpert
Pakistan Eye of The Storm : Owen Bennet Jones
The Muslims Of India :A.G. Noorani
The Siege Within : Akbar M.J.
Wings Of Fire : A.P.J. Abdul Kalam
Zulfi Bhutto of Pakistan : Stanley Wolpert

Journals : India Today, Outlook,Economist, Foreign Affairs, Time,
          Newsweek

Chapter 1 : Rajaji: Raja Mohan Gandhi
Chapter 2 : Rajendra Prasad : Publications Division
            An Autobiography: Rajendra Prasad
            Presidents Of India : Janakraj Jai
Chapter 3 : Sardar : A Film
            History of Congress : Sitaramayya
            Indian Muslims A Political Diary : Ramgopal
            Vallabhbhai Patel : Saggi
Chapter 4 : Eight Lives : Raja Mohan Gandhi
            Islamic Seal on India's Independence : Saiyidain
            Abul Kalam Azad : Douglas Iian Henderson
            The Muslims Of India: A.G.Noorani

245

Chapter  5  :  Ambedkar  Publications  Maharashtra Govt
                Riddles in Hinduism : Baba Saheb Ambedkar
Chapter  6  :  Jaya Prakash Narayana: Ajit Bhattacharya
Chapter  7  :  Lal Bahadur Shastri : C.R.Srivastava
Chapter  8  :  Indira Gandhi : Inder Malhotra
Indira Gandhi : Nayan Pranay Gupte
Dear To Behold An Intimate Portrait of Indira      Gandhi (Mc
Millon)
The Nehru Gandhi Dynasty T.V. Book : Jane Adams & P.
Whitehead
Chapter  9  :  The Nobel Prize in Physics : Presentation Speech
Chapter  10 :  Journal of Obstetrics and Gynecology of India
Feb.1971
Medical Dictionary ; Dr. L.C. Gupta
Chapter  12 :  Biography of Chandrashekhar : K Wali
                Chandrasekhar (autobiography)
Chapter  13 :  Radhakrishnan : S. Gopal
Chapter  14 :  The Autobiography of a Yogi : Yogananda
Chapter  15 :  Mother Teresa : Navin Chawla
                Mother Teresa:BeyondThe Image :Anne Sebba
                My Life For The Poor : Mother Teresa Of Calcutta
                Mother Teresa ; Candice F. Ranson
                The Life And Times Of Mother Teresa : Tanya Rice
Chapter  16 :  Development and Freedom: Amartya Sen
Chapter  17 :  Nirala Kavya and Vyaktitva ; D. Verma
                Nirala ki Sahitya Sadhanaa : R.S.Sharma
                Nirala smriti Grantha : Onkar Sharad
Chapter  18 :  An Illustrated History of English Literature
Chapter  19 :  Nandalal Bose ed. By R.L.Bartholomew
                Nandlal Basu Centenary Volume
Chapter  22 :
Chapter  23 :  Odyester Fabrics:
Chapter  24 :  Autobiography
Chapter  25 :  Supreme Court Cases (2003)4: Soli Sorabjee